Regionalism and Realism

A Century Foundation Book

Regionalism and Realism

A Study of Governments in the New York Metropolitan Area

Gerald Benjamin
Richard P. Nathan

BROOKINGS INSTITUTION PRESS
Washington, D.C.

ABOUT BROOKINGS

The Brookings Institution is a private nonprofit organization devoted to research, education, and publication on important issues of domestic and foreign policy. Its principal purpose is to bring knowledge to bear on current and emerging policy problems. The Institution maintains a position of neutrality on issues of public policy. Interpretations or conclusions in Brookings publications should be understood to be solely those of the authors.

Library of Congress Cataloging-in-Publication data

Benjamin, Gerald.
Regionalism and realism : a study of governments in the New York metropolitan area / Gerald Benjamin and Richard P. Nathan.
p. cm. — (A Century Foundation book)
Includes bibliographical references and index.
ISBN 0-8157-0088-1 (cloth : alk. paper) — ISBN 0-8157-0087-3 (pbk. : alk. paper)
1. Local government—New York Metropolitan Area. 2. Regionalism—New York Metropolitan Area. 3. Intergovernmental cooperation—New York Metropolitan Area. I. Nathan, Richard P. II. Title. III. Series.
JS1230 .B46 2001
320.8'09747'1—dc21 2001001376

9 8 7 6 5 4 3 2 1

The paper used in this publication meets minimum requirements of the American National Standard for Information Sciences—Permanence of Paper for Printed Library Materials: ANSI Z39.48-1992.

Typeset in Sabon

Composition by Northeastern Graphic Services, Inc.
Hackensack, N.J.

Printed by R. R. Donnelley and Sons
Harrisonburg, Virginia

THE CENTURY FOUNDATION

The Century Foundation, formerly the Twentieth Century Fund, sponsors and supervises timely analyses of economic policy, foreign affairs, and domestic political issues. Not-for-profit and nonpartisan, it was founded in 1919 and endowed by Edward A. Filene.

Foreword

Over the past decade, in a variety of contexts, social scientists—especially those interested in economic and political development—have started to reemphasize the importance of the special characteristics of individual nations. These "peculiarities," which often seem irrational to outsiders, sometimes turn out to be critical elements in the determination of which policies work and which are doomed to failure. Indeed, it may well be that the more unusual a "custom of the country," the more likely that it reflects fundamental values—values that only revolution or very long periods of evolution can alter. However, while history may complicate the transition to economic modernization, it would be a mistake to conclude that there only is one way to modernize. Nations such as Indonesia, Malaysia, China, Poland, and Hungary have found ways to achieve economic success within the constraints of their very diverse "national characters."

Americans have, for some time, thought of themselves as providing the best model for just about everything that composes both democracy and capitalism. Maybe that is one of our national characteristics, or maybe it is an inevitable result of the success our nation has enjoyed. Whatever the reason, we are not reluctant to hold up our system as the model that others should emulate. But the United States is not without its own peculiarities—particularly in the way it structures government at all levels—that seem quite impractical to outside observers.

For a modern state, the United States has an unusually decentralized federal system. And while a great deal of attention is focused on the relationship between states and the national government, the delegation of authority goes considerably deeper, including the remarkable array of local governments, school districts, and special jurisdictions. The latter category encompasses such diverse functions as water supply, mosquito control, and transportation.

The resulting crazy quilt of local governments has been the subject of study by political scientists for generations. For the New York metropolitan region, perhaps the most complex quilt of all, the most important book examining this phenomenon was the classic *1400 Governments,* by Robert C. Wood. Other scholars, notably Michael Danielson and Jameson Doig at Princeton University, added critical works enhancing our understanding of how this uniquely complicated pattern of governments manages to function. Studies such as these have noted the difficulty that divided government causes and most emphasize the need for more regionalization. To be sure, the metropolis does have a number of regional institutions, including the Port Authority of New York and New Jersey and the Metropolitan Transportation Authority. But, even these powerful agencies are good examples of divided politics, often nearly immobilized by frictions in the region. Indeed few, if any, observers at the beginning of the twenty-first century would assert that the transportation agencies or any other regional agencies will gain additional authority in the future. At present their hands are full fighting to retain what they already have.

In this environment, with the interdependency of the tri-state area continuing to grow, there is critical need for a fresh look at how the region functions, as well as for new prescriptions about how it might deal more effectively with its problems. The authors of this work, Gerald Benjamin, dean of the College of Liberal Arts and Sciences and professor of political science at the State University College at New Paltz, and Richard Nathan, director of the Nelson A. Rockefeller Institute of Government of the State University of New York, are in many ways perfectly suited to fill this important task. They are students of government with a deep understanding of both politics and administrative issues, and they have a long-term perspective on the region. The result is a book that is both comprehensive and realistic.

The authors recognize that cumbersome decisionmaking by many local jurisdictions often undermines efforts to control urban sprawl, to deal with economic segregation in the schools, or even simply to dispose of garbage. They also make clear that in a region as densely populated, heavily developed, and much traversed as the New York metropolitan area, the need for additional transportation is patently obvious. But they explain that for more than a generation, most significant efforts to achieve breakthroughs on these issues have been stymied.

Benjamin and Nathan provide a detailed and insightful history of the region. Had they done nothing else, their contributions in this area would greatly enhance our understanding and ability to seek solutions to common problems. But they go a good deal further. They have analyzed the reasons why regionalism succeeds and the conditions under which it fails. They have found lessons not only for policymakers in the New York metropolitan region, but for others across the country.

American exceptionalism, a much-noted phenomenon on the global scene, also exists at the state and local levels. We are a people who are rather proud of our parochialism, our regionalism, and—as an outsider might put it—our idiosyncrasies. Our politics remain intensely local, and the state governments, despite their constitutional authority to intervene, are considerably constrained by such political realities.

It is no surprise then that Benjamin and Nathan conclude that broad visions of new regional authorities are simply not in the political cards for the foreseeable future. They do, however, offer a constructive view of possible improvements in the way regional problems are dealt with by government. They believe that there are ways to achieve economies of scale and to share burdens in a more sensible manner. In some cases, they argue for even more decentralization. They conclude that in New York City, for example, the boroughs are too large and should be broken down and decentralized into smaller towns and villages that enjoy considerable autonomy. In other words, they offer not simple, one-size-fits-all solutions, but rather ways of thinking about the problems and remedies that meet the challenge of ensuring better governance in this unusual region.

The Century Foundation has been producing work on the nexus of state and local authority for a good many years, books and reports such as Jean Gottman's *Megalopolis,* David Rusk's *Inside Game/Outside Game,* and a series of reports on the effects of devolution. We are currently supporting an examination of community-based organization and action by Richard Briffault, an analysis of the evolution of metropolitan America by Paul Jargowsky, and a look at urban futures in an era of globalization and devolution by Norman Glickman, Michael Lahr, and Elvin Wyly.

On behalf of the Trustees of The Century Foundation, I want to express our gratitude to Gerald Benjamin and Richard Nathan for their careful analysis and thoughtful insights.

Richard C. Leone, President
The Century Foundation
February 2001

Preface

In the fall of 1994, Claude Shostal and Robert Yaro of the Regional Plan Association (RPA) sought the help of the Rockefeller Institute of Government for the governance portion of the Third Regional Plan for the New York–New Jersey–Connecticut (tri-state) region. Though we were busy at the time, we were intrigued. The project has a strong intellectual pedigree. The First Regional Plan, completed in 1929, was a seminal document. Robert C. Wood's book *1400 Governments,* on local government in the New York–New Jersey–Connecticut region—written in connection with the Second Regional Plan—helped define the study of urban government in the United States in the 1960s. The project that was proposed to us raised the possibility of taking a special look at the governance of New York City, at the region's core, guided by the landmark work of Wallace Sayre and Herbert Kaufman, also published in the early 1960s.

Under the aegis of the Rockefeller Institute, we worked on what such a study of governance in the tri-state region might cover and look like. The challenge was to conceive a study that was specific enough, using case material, and smart enough in its interpretation to be valuable within the region, while at the same time contributing thoughtfully to the renewed national interest in regionalism. With help and support from the Twentieth Century Fund (now The Century Foundation) in July 1995, we proceeded with the project. Then, assisted by the RPA, we obtained additional financial backing from the Fund for New Jersey in New Jersey and from the Fairfield County Foundation in Connecticut. We are grateful to these foundations for their support—and their patience.

Time in residence as Serbelloni Fellows at the Rockefeller Foundation's beautiful facility in Bellagio, Italy, in the summer of 1996 allowed us the opportunity for collaborative thinking and writing. However, Gerald Benjamin's work on constitutional revision for New York State and his return to SUNY, New Paltz as dean slowed the project. The Third Regional Plan was published in February 1996, without our report. Although we had a first draft of our book in hand and presented some of our findings at the RPA annual meeting in 1997, we were not yet ready to publish.

In the summer of 1997 we participated in a national meeting on regionalism held at the Chautauqua Institution, organized by Kevin P. Gaughan, founder of the Chautauqua Regionalism Conferences, and chaired by Stan Lundine, former lieutenant governor of New York State. In an effort to develop and build upon the interest in regionalism in western New York, this four-day gathering included many of the leading thinkers on metropolitan regionalism in the United States. Our participation at Chatauqua convinced us that the work of many leading advocates in this field is characterized by unexamined internal tensions and relies too heavily on unsuccessful proposals from an earlier time. As a result, while retaining our focus on the tri-state region, we decided to organize this book around what we identified as the four values of metropolitan regionalism in the United States: equity, efficiency, competitiveness, and community. We proceeded to look for lessons in the tri-state area by focusing on the interplay of these values, not only at the regional level but also in subregional settings and in the relationships between state governments and localities.

This book takes the long view in seeking to understand local government in the tri-state region and elsewhere in the country. Local governmental structures are the expression of previous generations' solutions to problems of governance; they can be understood best in a historical context. This approach of learning from history is evident in many chapters of our book, especially those on the governance of New York City, the nation's first, and arguably still the most ambitious, experiment in metropolitan regionalism. The importance of understanding the historical evolution of local governmental arrangements can also be seen in our examination of the webs of suburban governments in the three states in the tri-state metropolitan area.

This book has gone through a number of revisions and was more challenging to write than either of us had anticipated. Lyndee Kemmet prepared background material for its early stages. Also early in the process, Susan Wallerstein assisted us by studying regionalism in education in Connecticut. In the middle stage, Robert Cohen provided very helpful editorial assistance. Later on, David Rusk's comments provided valuable correctives. At Brookings, excellent editorial assistance was provided by Starr Belsky, Carlotta Ribar proofread the pages, and Shirley Kessel provided the index.

We thank Barbara Fanti of SUNY, New Paltz, for her secretarial assistance to Gerald Benjamin on this project. Also at New Paltz, Jonathan Curran, a Geography Department graduate, helped with maps. At the Rockefeller Institute, we extend thanks to Michael Cooper for monitoring this project; and thanks are also due to Irene Pavone and Carol Kuhl. Irene Pavone assisted with this project from its earliest days. This book could not have been brought to completion without her research support. Carol Kuhl worked hard and effectively to produce the final manuscript.

We dedicate this book to our fathers, Rubin Benjamin, a great New Yorker (from Brooklyn) and a source of inspiration and guidance to his son, and Sidney R. Nathan, a dedicated New York upstater and also a source of inspiration and guidance to his son.

Gerald Benjamin
SUNY–New Paltz
New Paltz, N.Y.

Richard P. Nathan
Rockefeller Institute
Albany, N.Y.

Contents

PART TWO
REGIONALISM AND THE NEW YORK CITY EXPERIENCE

PART THREE
FUNCTIONAL REGIONALISM

PART SIX
CONCLUSION

PART ONE

Understanding Regionalism

CHAPTER ONE

The New York Region: 2,179 Governments

Forty years ago Robert C. Wood opened *1400 Governments,* his classic study of governments in the New York–New Jersey–Connecticut (tri-state) metropolitan area, by calling the region's system of governance "one of the great unnatural wonders of the world . . . more complicated than any other that mankind has yet contrived or allowed to happen."[1] Wood's study was one of nine on the region's governments and political economy prepared by the Harvard Graduate School of Public Administration for the Regional Plan Association (RPA). The first and best-known nongovernmental regional planning agency in the United States, the RPA was then developing its second regional plan. Wood's rich descriptions of the region's crazy quilt of local governments—the actual number was 1,467—captured a large audience, especially among students and government reformers.

There was more than a little irony in Wood's expansive characterization. While it is true that the New York metropolitan region has a high density of local governments, numerous and layered local jurisdictions have been and are a relatively widespread phenomenon in large U.S. metropolitan areas, particularly in older parts of the Northeast and the Midwest.

As Wood did forty years ago, we began our study of local governments in the tri-state New York metropolitan region by counting and describing local governments in the region. It is apparent that governmental proliferation has not stopped. The total number of local governments in the counties Robert Wood studied in 1960 has now grown from 1,467 to 1,583. Moreover, for this book we accept the RPA's current, more extensive definition of the tri-state region, developed in connection with the Third Regional Plan.[2] This region includes thirty-one counties: five in New York City; nine others in New York State (on Long Island and extending up the Hudson River); fourteen counties in New Jersey; and three in Connecticut, where counties are geographical entities and not government units. According to the U.S. Bureau of the Census there were 2,179 governments in the region thus defined in 1997. We view the tri-state metropolitan region as having an urban core, comprising New York City and Hudson County, New Jersey, surrounded by three concentric rings (figure 1-1). This image reflects the stages of development and expansion that still continue as advances in transportation and communication allow people to live farther from the center while continuing to participate in regional life, as workers and in many other ways.

This governmental proliferation and complexity has spawned many efforts to rationalize and otherwise reform the structure of local government in U.S. metropolitan regions. We examine the New York region's experience to explain how and why local governments in large American metropolitan areas are organized the way they are and to consider strategies that have been and can be used to change their organizational structure. Although the New York region is unique in many ways, it still provides broad lessons about metropolitan regionalism in the United States.

New York City and the Region

The New York City we know today, "one great and glorious city," was created over a century ago as a result of an unprecedented governmental consolidation (described in chapter 3). In 2000 the city covered 321.8 square miles and was home to 8 million people, about 37 percent of the region's population. Except for Indianapolis, which was consolidated much more recently, New York City has the largest territory of the nation's central cities east of the Mississippi River, and it is by far the most populous American city. (Los Angeles, second in population, had less than half as many people—3.6 million—in 1999.) Because other older metropolitan regions in the United States today have much smaller central cities, the overall structure of local government is less fragmented and complex in the New York metropolitan region than it is elsewhere.

Figure 1-1. *Tri-State Region, 1996*

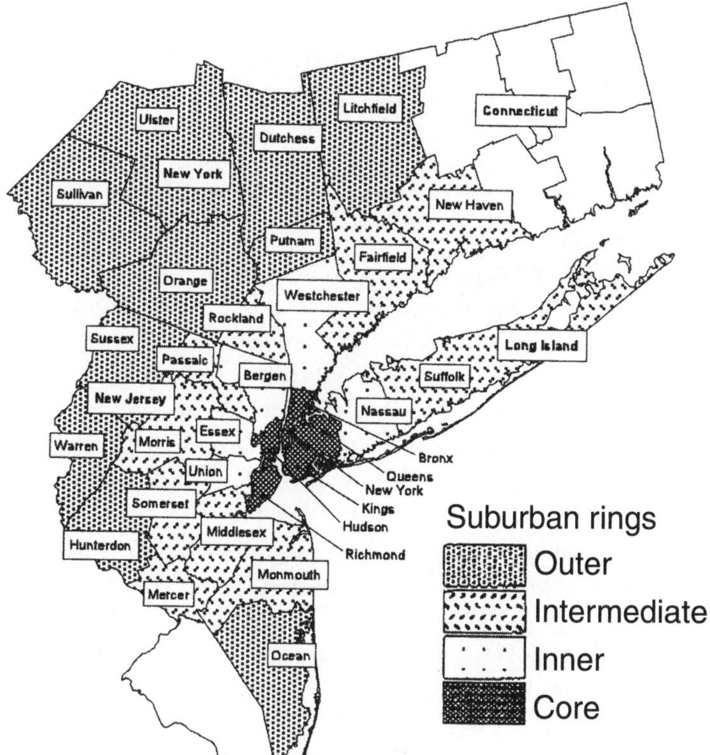

Source: Based on data from the U.S. Geological Survey and the Bureau of the Census in *ESRI Data and Maps 1998*, CD-ROM no. 1 (Redlands, Calif.: Environmental Systems Research Institute, 1998).

However, despite the early consolidation of New York, it is like most other central cities in large metropolitan areas in the U.S. in that it is surrounded by multiple suburban governments and overlaid by different special governments created over time for various public purposes.

There has been increased recognition over more than a century that metropolitan regions should be seen as an integrated whole. The advocates for creation of Greater New York in the post–Civil War period reflected this view. In 1886, twelve years before the city's consolidation, the U.S. Census Bureau stated that "the vast population occupying the cities of New York, Brooklyn, Jersey City, Newark and Hoboken . . . [constituted] . . . one great metropolitan community."[3] A quarter of a century later, the Census Bureau's first official reports on metropolitan areas included Hudson County, New Jersey, in the New York metropolitan region.

The region, as defined with the creation of the Port of New York Authority in 1921, included all or part of seventeen New York and New Jersey counties within a twenty-five-mile radius of the Statue of Liberty in New York harbor. (See chapter 6 for details.) Eight years later the first plan was prepared and issued by the Committee on the Regional Plan.[4] It defined the region as New York City and sixteen surrounding counties: one in Connecticut, six in New York, and nine in New Jersey. The Census Bureau defined the expanding New York–northeastern New Jersey area as one large standard metropolitan statistical area (SMSA) until 1950. Although the region was divided beginning with the 1960 census for what one authority said were "local political reasons" (it contained nine SMSAs by 1980), a brand-new category called "the standard consolidated area" or SCA (later the standard consolidated statistical area or SCSA) was created so that reporting on the three-state region, including part of Connecticut, continued.[5] Currently the term "consolidated metropolitan statistical area" (CMSA) is used to describe the New York metropolitan region, which includes nine primary metropolitan statistical areas (PMSAs).

Recent research by scholars based in Los Angeles stresses the dispersed character of American urban settlement. This school of thought contrasts the development of the Los Angeles region—a fragmented and decentralized metropolis supported by a diverse economy—with the development of northeastern industrial metropolises—centered on large growth poles focused on mass production industries.[6] As the evolution of federal definitions demonstrates, the tri-state New York–New Jersey–Connecticut metropolitan region has long been understood to contain numerous linked subregions. Jonathan Barnett, professor of city and regional planning at the University of Pennsylvania, has described the New York tri-state region as containing five cities: the City of New York plus urban concentrations to the north, west, and east.[7] But along with most analysts, we remain accustomed to consolidated reporting on economic and social conditions for the entire tri-state region.

In 1990 the tri-state region covered 12,688 square miles and was home to 19.8 million people. If it were a nation, the region would have one of the ten largest economies in the world. Because counties are the region's basic units, much of its territory (especially in the northern and western reaches of Dutchess, Ulster, and Sullivan counties) is rural. Nevertheless, the amount of developed land has increased 60 percent over the last thirty years. (Actually much of Greater New York City, even Manhattan Island, consisted of farms and woodlands when the modern city was created a hundred years ago.)[8]

Urban planners define a region as the heavily populated core area plus adjacent suburban communities that have a high degree of social and economic interconnectedness with the core and each other.[9] They count population size, measure density of settlement, and enumerate the commutes of workers who cross from one place to another, barely noticing the "Welcome to" or "Thanks for Visiting" signs along the way. In numerous ways everyday life tells us that the real region is one place in three states. The tri-state region is where you can buy the *New York Times* for seventy-five cents (or $3.00 on Sunday, with special sections for Long Island, Connecticut, New Jersey, Westchester, or New York City, depending upon where you live). Banks, utilities, retailers, and other businesses think regionally and ignore, or try to ignore, local and state boundaries in their activities. The region is where a career-threatening injury to a member of the New York Knicks basketball team is a cause for worry, where the football Giants or Jets winning a championship is cause for celebration, and where people root for the Yankees as their home team and hate the Mets, or vice versa.

The region is also the "Greater New York market" for media news and advertising. The Arbitron Company's designated market area (DMA) for the tri-state region in 1997 conformed almost exactly to the RPA definition of the region; this was also mostly true for the Nielsen DMA, which defines television markets.[10] On the power of the electronic media to define the region, one NBC researcher wrote: "There is no longer a New Jersey, New York or Connecticut, only a series of roughly circular areas with transmission towers at the center. In the electronic age it is the TV signal . . . more than arbitrary lines on a map, that gives both economic and political coherence to an area."[11]

Not insignificantly, in a federal system in which states define and control local government boundaries and structures, localities in this region operate within three distinct state systems of law and regulation and have been shaped by quite different historical experiences. This complicates collaborative regional action at the local level. Connecticut's New England heritage has resulted in the virtual abolition of counties and made towns the most important local government structures in its portion of the region. Meanwhile, New York's and New Jersey's tri-state-area counties have grown to be large, vital subregional governments.

The tri-state region includes more than two-thirds of all the localities in New Jersey, almost half of those in Connecticut, and more than a fourth of those of New York State. One of these, New York City, is the largest local government in population and budget size in the United States and the most far-reaching in its range of municipal functions. In 1998 the consolidated city celebrated its centennial as the nation's first great metropolitan government. The presence of this great metropolis, itself a regional government functioning within century-old boundaries, also complicates efforts to balance regionalism's values—efficiency, competitiveness, equity, and sense of community (see chapter 2)—within the larger region.

Other local jurisdictions in the tri-state region are suburban counties with billion-dollar budgets (Westchester and Nassau); suburban towns bigger than some states' biggest cities (Hempstead on Long Island); major cities such as Jersey City, Newark, and Bridgeport; and regional school districts that spend hundreds of millions of dollars annually. Also included in this number are many hundreds of small cities, towns, townships, villages, school districts, and single-function special districts. Regionalists claim that the diversity and number of local governments and their layered and overlapping jurisdictions cause the inefficiency, diminished competitiveness, and inequities in service delivery that they seek to correct.

Web of Local Governments: Origins and Consequences

The present configurations of local government in the tri-state region were not created as a system. Rather they are the result of incremental adjustment and change, a historical process driven by two forces: state needs and local demands. That is to say, the motivation for their creation has been either top down or bottom up.

Top-Down Origin

State governments have divided their territory and created localities to meet important governance needs. Often such top-down initiatives were aimed at rural or largely unsettled territory, which was carved into counties or towns (often square or otherwise symmetrically shaped) to make sure that taxes were collected, records kept, state laws obeyed, roads built and maintained, and other local functions performed.

Bottom-Up Origin

Impelled by the growing density of settlement, leaders in populated places asked state governments to create local governments (cities, towns, villages, boroughs) to meet their perceived needs. As urbanization advanced and people lived and worked in increasing proximity to one another, more local authority was needed to regulate daily interactions by taxing and spending for functions such as public safety (policing and fire protection), education, water, sewers, street cleaning and lighting, and care of the poor. In response to local petitions, the state granted charters or passed general laws that set out conditions for incorporation.

Urbanizing Rural Areas

The story of the industrialization and urbanization of the United States in the last century is well known. Massive inflows of immigrants from abroad and internal migration from the country to the city and from less developed to more developed parts of the country swelled cities and added to the demands upon their governments. Technological breakthroughs in transportation and communications allowed people to live closer together and farther from where they worked, driving both urbanization and suburbanization. National policy, by supporting highway construction and providing home mortgage assistance, encouraged people to move into sprawling suburban areas in even greater numbers. Rural areas became settled; former city dwellers in new suburbs demanded services to which they had been accustomed in the city. The response of many state governments, particularly in older regions of the country, was not to create new governmental entities devised for suburban areas, but to add powers to already existing local governments, which had been created in an earlier time for rural governance. Thus different types of local governments, originally devised for different purposes with different sets of powers, came to have similar powers and functions.

Social, economic, and technological change had two additional effects: it created the need for new services (often social services) and for delivery of services in larger territories. Because local power is a political ideal highly valued by many citizens, the response to such needs was often the creation of new entities in recently settled areas, augmenting the web of local government. These new entities, which typically were special districts overlying the general-purpose units, added to the web of local governments.

This description, while a simplification, allows us to make two important points. First, local governments in the tri-state region are not part of a system; rather they interconnect through a set of arrangements, a web resulting from years of adaptation and change. Second, this process evolved differently in each of the three states due to their unique histories and laws concerning local government.

Here is another important point: because localism has significant political value, changes typically are made by adding on, not replacing, existing local governments. There have been exceptions, such as the abolition of county governments in Connecticut in 1960 and the creation of Greater New York City in 1898, but generally speaking, attempts to eliminate local units are just too costly politically. Adding on is easier and politically safer.

Power of the Status Quo

Americans tend to maintain the status quo in local government for reasons that differ from those for which local governments were created in the first place. Local boundaries are important when people choose where to live and work. Their decisions are not based just on housing; they also consider the quality of the schools, who their neighbors will be, the amenities and reputation of the community, their commute to work—all of which are central to daily life. Change in the fundamentals (size, structure, powers) of local governance introduces uncertainties into these areas and others and is therefore likely to upset people.

Careers are also at stake when changes in governing structures are proposed; both elected officials and public employees are affected. If consolidation for political efficiency means fewer positions, office- and jobholders are likely to be unhappy. Their relationships with state elected officials tend to be strong and close, and they make their views known. State leaders with the formal power to make change have enough issues to deal with; understandably, they prefer to avoid controversies over issues of this nature.

Variations in Local Government

Because the region's web of governments evolved gradually, it includes many *types* of political units—counties, cities, villages, towns, townships, and boroughs—as well as special districts such as school districts. As noted earlier, this diversity arises in part because the New York metro-

Table 1-1. *General-Purpose Local Governments by Population Size and Type, Tri-State Region, 1990*

	Type of government						
Population	*County*[a]	*City*	*Borough*	*Town*	*Township*	*Village*	*Total*
Over 1,000,000	2	1					3
500,000 to 1,000,000	6			1			7
500,000 to 250,000	8	1		2			11
250,000 to 100,000	4	8		6			18
50,000 to 100,000	3	12		9	9		33
25,000 to 50,000		13	6	23	29	4	75
10,000 to 25,000		12	47	52	54	18	183
5,000 to 10,000		2	57	34	30	40	163
Under 5,000		1	88	44	40	115	288
Totals	23	50	198	171	162	177	781

Source: Compiled by the authors from the Bureau of the Census, *Census of Population, 1990.*

a. Counties in New York City and Connecticut are not counted as governments for the purposes of this table because there are special considerations that make them different from other county governments in the tri-state region.

politan region spreads into three states, each of which imposes different names and structures for various types and functions of local government. Moreover, the size of each type of governmental unit can vary greatly. For example, table 1-1 shows that ten local governments in the tri-state region had populations greater than half a million in 1990: eight counties outside New York City, one city (New York), and one town (Hempstead on Long Island). It also indicates that more than 80 percent of the region's governments (cities, boroughs, towns, townships, and villages) had populations below 25,000.

Similar Revenue Sources

Differences in type notwithstanding, localities are similar in terms of where they get the money to pay their bills. In the tri-state metropolitan region, local governments rely heavily on property taxes for "own source" revenue: they constitute 83.7 percent of local government revenue in Connecticut, 76.8 percent in New Jersey, and 45.1 percent in New York.[12] Partial exceptions are counties and cities in New York that levy a sales tax.[13] Suburban school districts, performing the most expensive local function, rely most heavily on the property tax. For the biggest cities in the region, states have allowed more diversified tax bases. New York City, for example, has both personal and corporate income taxes. Yonkers also has a local personal income tax, and Newark, New Jersey, has a payroll tax.

Similar Functions

Given the diversity of types, it is also remarkable how similar the functions of general-purpose local governments are. True, the existence of three state legal systems introduces differences, as does the fact that New York City is in a class by itself. Furthermore, counties in New York and New Jersey have a somewhat greater range of functions than other localities in those states. Nevertheless, as table 1-2 shows, local units of general-purpose government do not differ much in *what* they do. For those interested in promoting regional cooperation, the key point is that as things have evolved, nearby localities do not have to become cities or join them to gain the power to provide a broader array of services. All the different types of governments have more or less the same powers.

Special Burdens on Cities

City governments were created to be distinctive, to offer more governmental services to richer, busier, more densely populated centers of commerce, industry, and culture. However, over time other local governments in the region (counties, villages, towns, townships, and boroughs) acquired more power and expanded their services, competing with what the cities had to offer. When Robert Wood published *1400 Governments*, cities were coming to the end of their moment as centers of wealth, employment, and power. The RPA's Third Regional Plan, published in 1996, demonstrated how profoundly the economy of the region's cities had weakened in recent decades.[14] Now many of the cities are poorer; they are more likely to be populated by members of racial and ethnic minority groups, recent immigrants, and older citizens; and they are likely, therefore, to have very different governmental demands made upon them.

Dwindling Tax Base

In the tri-state region outside New York City, thirty cities had a higher proportion of their population living in poverty in 1990 than did the county that contained them. In addition, the gap in this measure often was enormous. For example, the average per capita income in Westchester County was more than twice that of two of its cities, Mt. Vernon and Peekskill. Only nine of the region's cities (16.1 percent) had higher per capita incomes than the county in which they were located: Rye in New

York; Norwalk, Stamford, and Milford in Connecticut; and Summit, Englewood, Bayonne, Hoboken, and Clifton in New Jersey.

This pattern indicates both a reduced fiscal capacity to provide governmental services coupled with an increased demand for those services. A study by the Connecticut Advisory Commission on Intergovernmental Relations found that cities in that state provided a greater range of services than other localities but had less resources to do so. Effective tax rates are far higher than in surrounding suburbs, yet they are arguably more burdensome to city residents because of their lower incomes. "Thus, the residents who can least afford taxation are asked to pay over twice the percentage of their lower incomes for local services than those who could afford it more easily."[15]

These problems have wide repercussions for local public finance in the region. A look at twenty-five cities in New York State by Moody's Credit Perspectives in 1996 showed that half experienced declines in their bond ratings since 1991, four of these to junk bond status. Manufacturing jobs were leaving and residents were not far behind, diminishing the property tax base, Moody's report noted.[16] What is most unsettling is that studies show that much of this lost property tax base results from abandonment and demolition. These properties will not be returned to the rolls, and cities have not yet found ways to compete with their suburbs for new development on these sites.

While industrial and residential growth and development have moved outside city boundaries, long-established, tax-exempt educational, cultural, and religious institutions remain. In the case of New York City, currently about 31 percent of the full value of property is tax exempt. For the rest of the cities in the state the ratio is even higher: about four dollars in every ten of property value is off the rolls.[17] This is another source of fiscal pressure.

Certain cities in the region have been dramatic examples of urban fiscal distress in recent years. Connecticut created a financial review board for Bridgeport in 1988. (To avoid its strictures Mayor Mary C. Moran unsuccessfully sought bankruptcy for the city in federal court in 1991.)[18] New York State created financial control boards for New York City in 1975 and for Yonkers in 1984.[19]

High Proportion of Minorities and Immigrants

Although many members of minority groups in the tri-state area do not live in stereotypical high-distress areas of danger and decay, they are still

Table 1-2. *Similarity of Functions among Types of Local Governments*

Function	*New York*				*New Jersey*						*Connecticut*		
	County	*City*	*Town*	*Village*	*County*	*City*	*Town*	*Township*	*Village*	*Borough*	*Town*	*City*	*Borough*
Education													
Community college	X				X								
Vocational education	X	X			X						X	X	X
Libraries	X	X	X	X	X	X	X	X	X	X	X	X	X
Health													
Health care services	X				X	X	X	X	X	X	X	X	X
Substance abuse	X												
Insect control	X	X	X		X	X	X	X	X	X	X	X	X
Hospitals													
Hospitals, clinics	X				X						X	X	X
Mental health	X	X	X		X								
Nursing homes	X	X			X								
Public welfare													
Financial assistance	X				X	X	X	X	X	X	X	X	X
Child welfare	X				X								
Support (day care, meals, other)	X	X	X	X		X	X	X	X	X	X	X	X
Veterans services	X	X			X						X	X	X
Services for the disabled	X										X	X	X
Transportation													
Highways	X	X	X	X	X	X	X	X	X	X	X	X	X
Mass transportation	X	X	X	X							X	X	X
Other transportation											X	X	X
Corrections, jails													
Jail	X	X			X								
Lockup			X	X		X	X	X	X	X	X	X	X
Juvenile detention	X				X								

Courts	X	X	X	X	X	X	X	X	X	X			
Fire													
Fire department	X	X	a	X		X	X	X	X	X	X	X	X
Fire advisory board	X												
Inspection, regulation	X	X	X	X	X	X	X	X	X	X	X	X	X
Police	X	X	X	X	X	X	X	X	X	X	X	X	X
Sanitation													
Disposal sites	X	X	X	X							X	X	X
Collection		X	X	X		X	X	X	X	X	X	X	X
Sewage													
Disposal, treatment	X	X	X	X	X	X	X	X	X	X	X	X	X
Local system, lines	b	X	X	X		X	X	X	X	X	X	X	X
Utilities, water													
Water systems	b	X	X	X		X	X	X	X	X	X	X	X
Gas, electric, other	X	X	X	X		X	X	X	X	X	X	X	X
Housing, urban renewal		X	X	X	X	X	X	X	X	X	X	X	X
Natural resources													
Flood control	X	X	X	X	X	X	X	X	X	X			
Soil conservation	X				X	X	X	X	X	X			
Forest, game management	X												
Parks and recreation	X	X	X	X	X	X	X	X	X	X	X	X	X
Planning and zoning													
Planning	X	X	X	X	X	X	X	X	X	X	X	X	X
Zoning		X	X	X		X	X	X	X	X	X	X	X

Source: Compiled by the authors from statutory sources.

a. Provided through fire districts covering all or parts of towns, or crossing town boundaries.

b. Provided through special districts in parts of counties.

likely to concentrate in the region's cities.[20] About 60 percent of the blacks and Hispanics in the region in 1990 lived in New York City; of the 1.36 million who lived outside New York City, more than half (56.4 percent) were in other cities. Three-fourths lived in just ten places: Bridgeport and New Haven in Connecticut; East Orange, Newark, Jersey City, Trenton, Paterson, and Plainfield in New Jersey; and Mount Vernon and Yonkers in New York. Virtually all blacks living in the counties of Hudson and Passaic in New Jersey and Fairfield in Connecticut were city dwellers.[21] When blacks and Hispanics are counted together, twelve of the region's cities with populations of 25,000—nine in New Jersey, one in Connecticut, and two in New York—have minority group populations that are local majorities.[22]

The region had 3.67 million foreign-born residents in 1990. Of these, well over half (56.7 percent) lived in New York City. Outside New York City, the non-Hispanic foreign-born population was less concentrated in cities than were blacks and Hispanics. Still, about half a million were urban dwellers. The result was "a wider-than-ever divide between an international urban core and suburbs that continue to be mostly white and native-born."[23]

Different Governmental Demands

Suburbs need money to build new infrastructure; cities seek money to replace the old and keep it working. Even when the services that both provide are similar, cities face higher costs. A good example in the area of public safety is fire-fighting services: many suburban areas still are served by volunteer fire departments whereas members of city fire departments are almost always paid.

City residents need more services but have less ability to pay, and education is the local service that places the greatest demand on the property tax base. Although education is not usually delivered by general-purpose local governments, school district boundaries are coterminous with those for localities in New Jersey and Connecticut. In New York State, New York City and Yonkers are directly responsible for education, and more than half of the remaining New York cities in the region have coterminous school districts. Seventeen of the region's cities had school-age population percentages above their county's average in 1990, yet per capita income for this group of cities averaged $6,885, more than 40 percent less than that for the counties in which they are located.

At the other end of the spectrum, the retirement age population is larger and growing faster in the tri-state region than in the nation as a whole and resides disproportionately in the region's cities. In some cities —Bridgeport, Jersey City, Perth Amboy, Newburgh, and Mount Vernon —populations are *both younger and older* than those of surrounding jurisdictions. Furthermore, a larger proportion of the older group are white, adding a racial dimension to fiscal and political tensions about spending levels for schools and other local services for families and children.

Myron Orfield described the process of decline in cities and in working- and middle-class inner-ring suburbs in the Twin Cities region of Minnesota (Minneapolis and St. Paul): "Poverty begins to concentrate around the inner cores. Middle class families begin to leave neighborhoods. Stores begin to suffer. The resources that support local government begin to decrease. At the same time that social needs are beginning to increase around the urban core, the tax base begins to erode. It's a wicked cycle."[24] This applies perfectly to most of the tri-state region's cities—and unlike the great metropolitan centers, these smaller places lack the resources and resiliency to resist decline.

Costs of Fragmentation and Layering

Until now we have discussed the size of local governments in the tri-state region in terms of the number of people who live within their borders. However, local governments are organized largely on the basis of territory, not population, and it is in this territory, this *place*, that they serve people—not only those who are residents, but workers, visitors, and people just passing through. Local government density is a measure of the number of local governments in a given place; it is useful because it tells about fragmentation—the sheer number of governments—and about layering—the number of governments serving a single place in the local government web (and, indirectly, about the diversity of governmental types as well).

Overall, New Jersey has the highest number of local governments per square mile in the nation (table 1-3). In fact, local government density in New Jersey is 8.5 times the national average. Using this same measure, Connecticut has about half the local government density of New Jersey yet still ranks seventh among all states. New York ranks eleventh. Despite the almost complete consolidation of local government within New York City, local government density in the current tri-state region (17.2 governments per 100 square miles) is higher than in any state in the union except New Jersey and Illinois.

Table 1-3. *Local Government Density, 1992*

Place	*Area*[a]	*Number of governments*	*Density*[b]
New Jersey	7,419	1,512	20.4
Connecticut	4,845	563	11.6
New York	47,224	3,298	7.0
Tri-state region	12,688	2,179	17.2
United States	3,536,342	84,955	2.4

Source: Authors' calculations from Bureau of the Census, *Census of Population, 1990,* and *Census of Local Governments, 1992.*

a. Square miles.

b. Governments per square mile.

In each of the region's three states, the reason for the high ratio of governments to territorial expanse differs. Connecticut has an unusually simple local government system: there are no functioning counties. Each person in the state is served by only one general-purpose government—a town or a city—and a coterminous school district. But towns are numerous, and the state is the third smallest geographically in the nation, factors that tend to produce high local government density. In addition, the use of special districts is greater in Connecticut, perhaps in part because of the absence of a second level of general-purpose local government.

New Jersey is also quite small in territorial expanse (it is the fourth smallest state in the nation), and its numerous local governments are more layered than those in Connecticut. (See figure 1-2.) All Jerseyans are served by both a county government and by a city, township, or borough. As in Connecticut, school districts in New Jersey share boundaries with general-purpose governments. This pattern of two layers of general-purpose government plus a coterminous school district is the one most common in the United States.

It is in New York State that layering and governmental density are most extensive (figures 1-2 and 1-3). Except for New York City, county governments are universal in the state. Within them, towns or cities are the next organizational level. But then there is a big difference: villages may be organized within towns or even across town and county lines, giving some New Yorkers three layers of general-purpose local government. Additionally, all of New York is divided into school districts; but unlike in Connecticut and New Jersey, New York's school districts do not necessarily share boundaries with general-purpose governments. Rather, as with New York villages, school districts may (and

Figure 1-2. *Local Government Layering, Tri-State Region*[a]

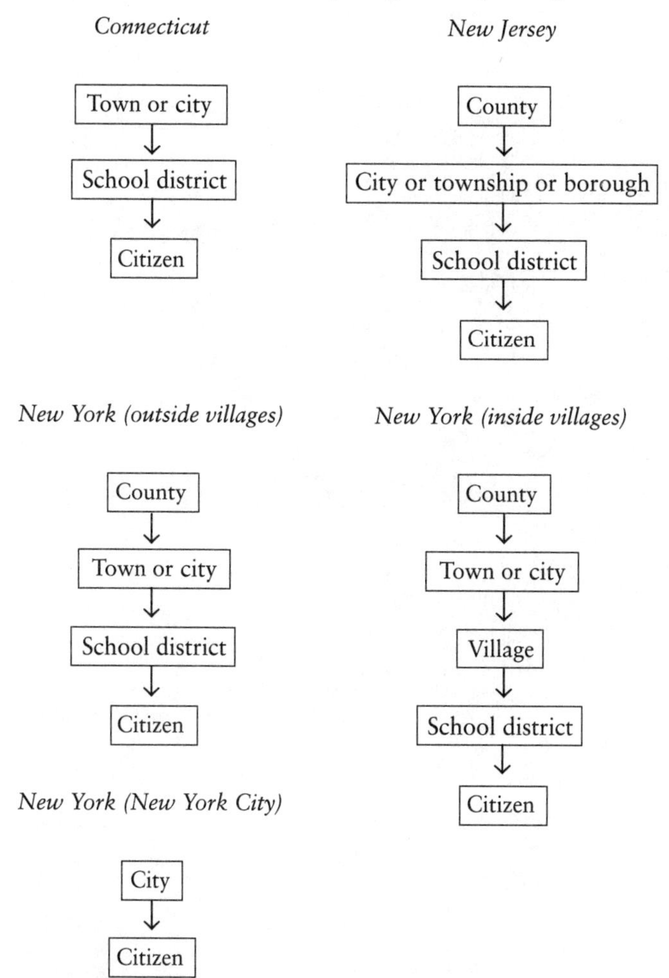

a. Represented are property tax levying entities only. Special districts, which may be organized at every level and without regard to general-purpose local government boundaries, are exluded. In Connecticut elected school boards decide on the school tax levy but do not collect it; therefore they are not counted as independent governments by the U.S. Census. But because these boards are elected and because schools are supported by property tax, we include them here.

often do) cut across county and town lines. Thus a New York school district may include all or parts of several towns or even several counties. This creates administrative problems and equity issues, not to mention added costs and puzzlement for citizens trying to keep things straight.

Figure 1-3. *Local Government Density in the Tri-State Region, 1992*[a]

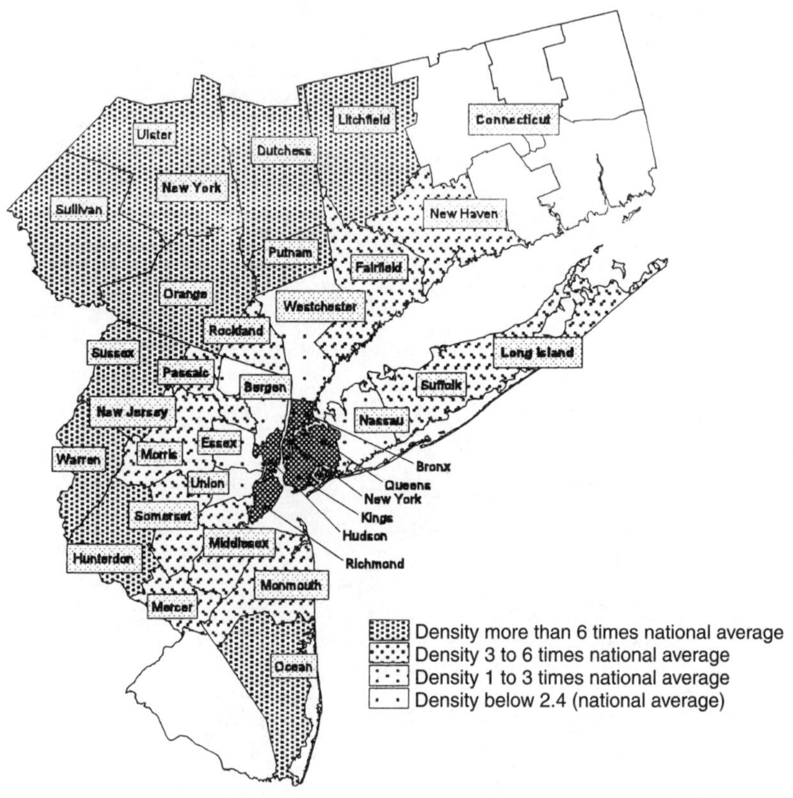

Source: Based on data from *ESRI Data and Maps 1998*, CD-ROM no. 1 (Redlands, Calif.: Environmental Systems Research Institute, 1998).

a. Expressed in number of local governments per 100 square miles versus the national average (2.4). Local government density is greatest in counties closest to the metropolitan core.

Figure 1-3 shows that local government density is greatest in counties that bound New York City. In New York and New Jersey, this happened because of their tendency to create additional general-purpose governments and school districts to serve the new concentrations of people leaving New York City and other urban centers in the region. For example, in Nassau County on Long Island, more than three-fourths of the villages were established between 1920 and the mid-1930s. Subsequently, growth was accommodated by giving new powers to governments already in place. In Connecticut, where there was major structural reform of local government in the 1950s, higher government densities close to Manhattan arose from extensive use of special districts.

Table 1-4. *Location, Administrative Costs, and Local Government Density*

Proximity to center[a]	Per capita administrative costs[b]	Local government density[c]: School districts	Local government density[c]: General-purpose governments
Core and inner ring			
New Jersey	156.81	26.1	23.4
New York	142.67	15.4	17.2
Intermediate ring			
New Jersey	149.53	7.5	6.8
New York	121.32	6.8	8.6
Outer ring			
New Jersey	134.20	6.1	5.6
New York	138.52	1.8	3.5
Connecticut counties	91.37	3.4	3.9

Source: Authors' calculations based on data from the *Census of Local Governments, 1992.*

a. See figure 1-1.

b. Per capita administrative costs are the total administrative costs for all local governments in the county (as reported in the *Census of Local Governments, 1992*) divided by population.

c. School district density is the number of school districts in the county per 100 square miles. General-purpose government density is the number of general-purpose governments in the county per 100 square miles.

As table 1-4 illustrates, a high density of local government is expensive as well as confusing. In Connecticut suburban counties, where the local government system is simplest and least layered, average aggregate per capita costs for local government administration are far lower than those in New York and New Jersey. Although detailed county-by-county data are not shown in table 1-4, and some exceptional cases skew averages, in general local government density decreases with distance from New York City, and lower density is accompanied by lower administrative costs. The comparison is particularly straightforward on Long Island: Suffolk County, adjacent to Nassau County but further east, was suburbanized later and has far fewer villages. Compared to Nassau its per capita costs for local government administration in 1992 were 15.7 percent lower.

One-third of the population in Nassau County, New York, is served by three layers of general-purpose local government: county, town, and village. The situation in Rockland County is similar. In Westchester County one quarter of the population is served by three layers of general-purpose local government. And these examples do not include school districts and special districts, which also collect taxes or fees from these citizens. According to Bruce Nyman, a Democratic Nassau County legislator from Long Beach, there are properties in his county that receive seventeen different tax bills.[25]

This evidence shows that governmental layering drives up the cost of local government, increasing the amounts that must be raised from property taxes. What may be less evident is that this complexity in governmental structure also extracts a price in democracy because it makes it harder for citizens to hold local officials accountable.

Special-Purpose Governments

Special districts are a principal manifestation of the increased complexity of local government in the tri-state region. These districts, which are used for a combination of fiscal, service delivery, managerial, and political purposes, link service to payment in a way that general-purpose governments cannot. They are created without disturbing the general-purpose local government web already in place, sometimes covering part of the territory of a local government, sometimes all of it. Frequently, they are organized to serve an area governed for other purposes by several local governments; this allows functioning at different scales for different purposes.

According to the U.S. Census Bureau, there were 742 special districts in the tri-state region in 1992: 186 in Connecticut, 333 in New York, and 223 in New Jersey. These constituted about two-fifths (43.1 percent) of the special districts in the three states. Almost half the special districts in Connecticut and New York and a third of those in New Jersey have been created with boundaries that are not coterminous with those of existing local governments.[26] This fact is important: it demonstrates that they were designed to respond to the need for different scales of service delivery while retaining existing general-purpose governing arrangements, thus accommodating the desire for local control.

Despite public perception, most of these special districts were small-scale operations meeting very localized community needs. In 1992 most reported outstanding debt of under $2 million. A good number of these had no debt at all.[27]

The Census Bureau uses "special district" as an umbrella term (inclusive, for example, of "public authority"). It counts as special districts only agencies that it regards as *independent*, that is, those that are not subject to administrative or financial control by a state or local government. But the situation is not clear cut: formal legal and financial independence may not mean political independence; formal dependence in law may not mean actual dependence in decisionmaking. According to Donald Axelrod, a leading expert in the field, the Census Bureau's criteria "excluded thousands of public authorities on the grounds of dependency, including some of the largest multi-billion-dollar authorities in the United States."[28] For example, two water authorities in Nassau County are included in the count, but neither the New York City Municipal Water Finance Authority nor the City Water Board, responsible for the world's largest regional water system, are counted as special districts by the Census Bureau. Enumeration practices seem inconsistent in other respects as well. A multitown solid waste authority in Suffolk County, New York, is counted but not county solid waste authorities elsewhere, even though all were created by special legislative acts and have similar functions.

It seems clear, then, that although the Census Bureau numbers are reasonably accurate for general-purpose governments and school districts in the tri-state region, they are significantly understated for special districts.[29] The net result, according to Axelrod, is that "no one knows what the exact figure is, not the federal government and not the states. No agreement even exists as to what a public authority, a special district, and a government corporation is."[30]

Private Governments

The census undercount of local governments has been exacerbated by the emergence of myriad quasi-governmental organizations; these deliver services like those publicly provided and collect fees or assess charges similar to taxes from the persons served. Private condominium and co-op associations often perform jobs formerly done by local governments in the cities and suburbs of the region. So do business improvement districts (BIDs) in New York City. (See chapter 4.) There is no good count of these "private governments," which actually seem to be developing more slowly in the Northeast than elsewhere. But according to one estimate, over 50 million Americans live within these kinds of communal, but not governmental, jurisdictions.[31]

Fairfield County, Connecticut, in the region's intermediate ring, offers an intriguing glimpse of what might happen to the overall statistics if all these quasi-governmental entities were counted.[32] The number of special districts that the census identified in the county almost tripled between 1967 and 1992, from thirty-five to ninety-eight. People who lived in the condominiums that were springing up were increasingly unhappy that their common charges that paid for municipal-like services were not counted as property taxes for federal income tax purposes and were therefore not deductible. Responding to pressure from condominium associations, the state passed a law that, with local government consent and review, allowed associations to organize into special service districts and count a portion of their common charges as property taxes.[33] As a result dozens of condominium associations were brought into the Census Bureau's count of special districts.

Regional Multistate Agencies

There are governmental structures organized for service delivery across state lines in the tri-state region, but these are state, not local, agencies. They must be approved by the U.S. Congress, and they serve goals defined in the state capitols of Albany, Hartford, and Trenton, all located outside or on the periphery of the region. The most important and powerful such agency, discussed in detail in chapter 6, is the Port Authority of New York and New Jersey, set up by interstate compact in 1921 to cure "destructive competition" among railroads serving the New York harbor and to create and implement a plan for orderly development of the greatest commercial port in the United States. At its creation the authority's jurisdiction in two states was defined by distance from the Statue of Liberty at the port's center. Its twenty-five-mile jurisdictional radius included all of consolidated New York City, Newark and Jersey City, parts of Westchester and Nassau Counties, a small piece of Rockland, and all or parts of eleven counties in New Jersey. Because the federal government authorized a *bi-state,* not tri-state, compact, territory in Connecticut was quite explicitly excluded; the region's boundaries came up to and ran along the New York–Connecticut line

A second agency in the region established by interstate compact between New York and New Jersey is the Palisades Interstate Park Commission. Joint action by the states to preserve and maintain the Palisades area overlooking the Hudson River dates to 1900. The modern commission, with five members appointed by the governor of New York and five by the governor of New Jersey, was created by legislation in each state and approved by Congress in 1937. It oversees, develops, and maintains the park and recreational facilities within the Palisades area, the largest proportion of which are within New York State.[34]

A smaller joint New York–New Jersey activity is the Waterfront Commission for New York Harbor, established in 1953 to eliminate criminal activity in the port area and later in regional airports. The little-known Interstate Sanitation Commission is the only officially designated tri-state organization currently operating in the region.[35] Largely dependent upon state appropriations, it was established by interstate compact between New York and New Jersey in 1935 with regulatory authority to combat "pollution of the harbor, coastal and tidal waters in [the harbor of New York] . . . and the tributary waters therein."[36] Connecticut joined in 1941. Responsibility for study, research, and policy recommendations concerning air pollution—but no regulatory authority—was added for New York and New Jersey in 1961 and for Connecticut in 1969. Because of its small size and especially its diminished state financial support, the agency's activities are very limited.

Two massive, single-state transit agencies—New York's Metropolitan Transportation Authority and New Jersey Transit—operate across state lines to some small degree. (See chapter 7.) However, as a general rule, official region-wide efforts to transcend state boundaries have foundered or limped along. During the 1960s, attempts to gain formal status for a metropolitan regional council through interlocal agreement failed because, as Joan Aaron wrote, "each state is subject to different environmental pressures, is committed to different philosophies of expenditures and revenues, and pursues varying policies with respect to local governments within its borders."[37]

Over decades a series of state-initiated or federally required structures for multistate transportation planning have had little region-wide impact. A tri-state regional planning commission, set up under federal pressure to foster collaborative planning in 1971, was ineffectual. It died ten years later when President Ronald Reagan drastically cut back national support for regional planning.[38] Federal legislation passed in 1973 mandating metropolitan planning organizations (MPOs) did remain on the books during the Reagan era, but these agencies provided little real regional coordination for transportation planning. The federal Intermodal Surface Transportation Efficiency Act (ISTEA) doubled funding for MPO operations and required the agencies to evaluate a variety of multimodal solutions to road congestion and other transportation problems. MPOs were also required to broaden public participation in the planning process and see that investment decisions contributed to meeting the air quality standards of the Clean Air Act amendments.[39] This federal support continued under reauthorization legislation passed in 1998.

As a consequence MPOs in some metropolitan areas have become important forces for coordinating transportation efforts, but not in the tristate region. The region has six MPOs, all organized within states. The two largest are the New York Metropolitan Transportation Council and the New Jersey Transportation Planning Authority. Robert Yaro of the Regional Plan Association of New York has observed that these agencies have had difficulty in coordinating regional transportation planning across state and even municipal lines and were only just beginning to do so at the turn of the century.[40]

Confirming their state rather than local government character, most of the larger public authorities in the tri-state region are not listed in the Census Bureau enumerations of special districts. The bureau does count as a special district the Port Authority of New York and New Jersey, but not the Metropolitan Transportation Authority or New Jersey Transit, both of which it regards as state agencies. According to Robert W. Bailey, "before the 1960's there were only three major public authorities in the New York region . . . by the 1990's there were almost forty. All together, these agencies accounted for more than 70 percent of regional debt issuance."[41] The boards of these agencies are controlled by governors, not by the region's mayors and county executives; yet they make crucial decisions concerning the region's physical development. Mayor Edward Koch provided the perspective of local elected officials when he observed, "What you always have with these independent authorities is they want to do it their own way."[42]

Details and the Big Picture

At about the same time that Robert Wood's book on the metropolitan region was published, Wallace S. Sayre and Herbert Kaufman released their famous study *Governing New York City*. It began with this observation by the Greek philosopher Heraclitus from the fifth century B.C.: "You cannot step twice in the same stream." As the authors explained, this is "because the water that washed against you and flowed around you the first time will the second time be far downstream." Sayre and Kaufman's point is that the details of governance, like a river, are always changing.[43] Still, we feel it is appropriate to begin this book with immersion in such details. It is true that the nature and interrelationships of the myriad and varied types of local governments within the tri-state region can be overwhelming. So be it; this information is not suited to easy generalization, and the terrain inevitably changes. However, these details illuminate certain broad patterns and themes that have been constant over time. Their presentation here provides the foundation for our next step:

the examination of values that underlie strategies for reforming local governance in metropolitan regions.

The four values of urban regionalism are equity, efficiency, competitiveness, and community. Often they are not congruent and sometimes they conflict, but they must be recognized and accounted for whenever attempting to change the structure of local government in metropolitan regions of the United States. This is especially true in older regions, where boundaries were set before the automobile was invented and where the size of local jurisdictions was determined by the distance people could travel on horseback or by carriage in a reasonable amount of time. Proposals to change the boundaries and functions of local governments provoke some of the strongest emotions, engage basic values, and require the command of some of the most detailed and intricate facts of American government and politics. Moreover, change is a subtle process; it rarely happens swiftly. It is more likely to occur in increments, after delicate political maneuvering to assemble a coalition of leaders and groups in support of a particular popular measure. This last point, which is about how to blend regionalism and realism (that is, political realism), is central to our analysis of potential strategies and processes for reforming the structure and power of local governments in metropolitan areas.

Approaches to Regionalism in the Tri-State Region

This chapter describes "the tri-state region divided" with its 2,179 governments and briefly examined its arrangements for local governance and their origins. We emphasized the importance of the region's multistate character for understanding the prospects and limits of regionalism and noted that it is not unique in this respect. The thirty-eight multistate regions in the United States contain more than a fourth of the nation's population. In the chapters that follow, we examine approaches to regionalism operative in or proposed for the New York–New Jersey–Connecticut tri-state region and describe and assess how they balance regionalism's values.

Any treatment of governance in the tri-state region must deal first with the city government that serves two of five regional residents and millions more people who come to New York daily to work or for other purposes. Part 2 considers New York City historically. The year 1998 marked the centennial of the consolidation of the Greater City, the nation's first great metropolitan experiment. We examine what the experience of the last

100 years tells us about regionalism, discuss how regionalists' core values were reflected in the course of the city's first century, and consider how they might be rebalanced in the future.

Part 2 comprises three chapters. The first clarifies the limits of the metropolitan, single-government approach. Any metropolitan structure is limited by state boundaries, and all local governments function in accordance with state laws. This is an absolute limit: there is no way in America for a general-purpose local government to exist across state lines. The challenge this presents for the efficiency and competitiveness (economic development) goals of regionalism becomes greater as economic regions expand over time, reflecting technological advances in transportation and communication.

Moreover, local governments are not sovereign; they are necessarily limited in their resources and their functions. They can get into trouble when they try to be redistributive, acting to increase equity between races and classes. Created as a great metropolis with great ambitions in a period of massive immigration and social change, New York City faced expectations that it act as an engine of equity. The tuition-free colleges it provided for the city's best and brightest high school graduates were for decades the symbol of its commitment to provide opportunity for all. Free tuition ended, however, in the midst of the mid-1970s fiscal crisis. New York in its recent history has been forced to change its expectations, reflecting the need to transform itself from the great metropolis as envisioned at the time of the 1898 consolidation to a mere city, with all the limits that entails.

The next two chapters in part 2 describe the century-long struggle between centralizers and decentralizers in structuring the city government. Here the efficiency value—the centralizers' priority—confronts the community value. In general, the centralizers have won within the boundaries of the greater city. This is the story of the eclipse of the boroughs and of the indifferent success (at best) of community school boards and community boards in responding to the need for "local government" in the consolidated city of New York.

There is a paradox here. As noted earlier, New York City is a local government in law, but it is not really local in the experience of New Yorkers who live and function in *neighborhoods*. In fact, none of the structures developed over the history of the city to respond to the need for community have been created at the human scale in which people live and work. The recent development of Business Improvement Districts (BIDs), as we see it, is a response to the desire for more genuine local government within the boundaries of New York City. BIDs have been created from the bottom up and respond to commercial needs at the neighborhood level. However, they are not democratic, and their operation raises serious equity issues. Building upon models drawn from suburban and rural towns and villages in the larger tri-state region, chapter 4 offers possible responses to the need for more vital community-level government in New York City. We propose that city leaders and citizens consider substituting towns and villages within the city for the current, largely ineffectual local structures now operating—boroughs, community boards, and community school boards.

Part 3 examines the experience with regionalism in the larger tri-state area, using examples that dig deep into the often abstract subject of regionalism to bring it to life. Our examples, focused on transportation and economic development, concern agencies serving large portions of the region: the Port Authority of New York and New Jersey (PANYNJ), the Metropolitan Transportation Authority (MTA), and New Jersey Transit (NJT). In effect, they demonstrate the value of large-scale functional regionalism. Most people interested in regionalism agree that transportation is one of the primary functions, if not *the* primary function, for which efficiency is achieved when it is organized on a multijurisdictional scale. Yet the New York tri-state region has failed to create an integrated mass transit system because the approach has not been overarching but rather incremental and situational, as a response to a series of transportation and related financial crises.

Mass transportation was "deprivatized" because of what in essence were a series of market failures: excessive competition between railroads in the port; the failure of private subway development and subsequently of commuter railroads and private commuter bus lines. These failures led to the formation of three large-scale mass transportation agencies, one organized under an interstate compact (PANYNJ), the others as state agencies operating to some degree across state lines (MTA and NJT). A further complication was the preexisting, very large scale general-purpose local government—New York City—with overlapping territorial jurisdiction. One result of such overlap was conflict over control of the region's major airports, a topic discussed in chapter 6.

Regional transportation agencies in the tri-state area operate according to state, not local, priorities. They are preoccupied with distributive equity—apportioning fair shares between states and between places within states—rather than with optimizing efficiency in the tri-state region to support its economic development.[44] In chapter 7 we suggest changes that would aid development of an integrated regional mass transit system, one that would support regional priorities.

In parts 4 and 5 we examine successes and failures of regionalism when dealing with localism in three arenas: subregional, statewide, and national. Chapter 8 shows that public elementary and secondary education is the most persistently local of functions. It is here that the community value is strongest, even within New York City.

Redistributive regionalists often call for abolition of certain local governments or even whole classes of governments in an attempt to rationalize local political structures. This, for example, is the theme of a report issued in the mid-1990s by the planning organization "Westchester 2000" in Westchester County, New York (population 893,412), located just north of New York City. There is experience in the tri-state region with eliminating an entire class of governments: counties in Connecticut. However, the unusual political circumstances under which this occurred, and the widespread failure of local government restructuring efforts elsewhere in the region in recent decades, demonstrate why such a strategy is not generally viable: it challenges the value of community head-on and threatens the political base of elected officials.

The real-life successes and failures discussed in parts 4 and 5 are useful for understanding policy areas where people and governments have indicated a willingness to collaborate. Such examples also show us under what conditions people and governments have acted and what methods they have used. Then we can try to generalize from these experiences about the potential for success and the pitfalls to avoid. Chapter 9 offers two approaches to regional reform—top down and bottom up—that focus on alternatives for shifting the scale of service delivery. Poll data from New Jersey show that public willingness to support intergovernmental collaboration is generally greatest when it affects functions in which the community value is less central, such as senior activities, libraries, and road maintenance; all of these involve less intense, one-to-one interaction of citizens with each other or service providers. This trend is confirmed by a review of reports on the collaborative experience. The evidence also shows that suburban communities avoid cities as partners in intergovernmental collaboration and that equity arguments to promote collaboration—urging fairness between races and classes—rarely work. Conversely, economy and efficiency arguments—promoting economic growth and constraining property tax burdens—do have force in selected functional areas. Thus the practical lesson is that equity is most likely to be achieved indirectly, not when it is the primary regionalist goal.

We also consider policy areas in which localism, or commitment to community, is most persistent: education, emergency services, housing, and land-use regulation. For housing, land use, and education, equity proposals that directly confront the value of localism—through measures such as regional or statewide land-use planning and school consolidation—almost always fail. What has worked regarding land use is bringing localities into broad-scale planning or housing programs early or shrewdly harnessing some local interests to create local advocates for regional goals. For education we examine another effective strategy: the creation of regional service delivery mechanisms (the BOCES system in New York State), using quasi-market mechanisms for service sharing and other techniques to extend the range of available services.[45] And in emergency services, we show how New York State deftly manipulated resources and political incentives to induce, but not mandate, countywide collaboration among local governments in implementing crucial changes in communication systems. Problems aside, and there were some in virtually every case, such approaches hold promise as models for state and local leaders who wish to extend regional collaboration.

The penultimate chapter on regionalism concerns a great but still not fully understood change of scale: from local to national. Here the story is about an attempt through planning to regionalize solid waste disposal, traditionally a local function. The initial impulse was provided by the environmental movement; to address environmental concerns efficiently, solid waste disposal, it seemed, could no longer be dealt with locally. With backing from state government, regionalization was encouraged, even required. Then, in midstream, privatization took hold. It often proved less costly to ship waste out of a region than to dispose of it, for example, at the county or regional level. Moreover, there was little desire for local control in this functional area.

However, the privatization of solid waste disposal led almost inexorably to nationalization. Disposal companies and markets operate nationally. Furthermore, the Supreme Court confirmed that solid waste disposal was part of interstate commerce; it found restrictions designed to assure the fiscal viability of regional approaches unconstitutional. Nationalization rushed forward, as did industry consolidation. Questions remain about meeting the obligations incurred (massive debt on the part of counties and newly created public authorities) in support of planned regional approaches that were disrupted in midstream. Concerns exist, too, about localities and regions being at the mercy of private corporations and about the market for waste disposal once local facilities are abandoned.

Finally, the last chapter highlights lessons learned and policy options for state and local decisionmakers interested in balancing values to advance regional interests—equity, efficiency, competitiveness, and community. Although well aware of the limits of generalizing from one case, even one so big and diverse, we conclude with a series of lessons drawn from the tri-state area experience on how to temper regionalism with realism. We find that in the American federal system regionalism's aims are often best advanced in state, not local, political arenas. Locally initiated reform of local political structures is possible—and we speculate about some options—but there are limitations. Experience in the tri-state region shows that problems are especially intractable for regionalists seeking structural change in large multi-state areas. National government involvement might be desirable, but experience suggests this is not likely for broad-scale, system-altering approaches.

A century of history in the tri-state region demonstrates that the creation of very large general-purpose local governments, organized regionally, is unlikely to achieve regionalists' goals. We suggest that this history, properly understood, also shows that citizens want to preserve community value as part of arrangements for regional governance, and therefore, this value is an essential consideration for regional reformers.

Large-scale regionalism in government has rarely been achieved as the result of planned efforts. Rather, it has arisen from exploiting political opportunities as they occur. We identify ways for state governments to advance efficiency as a value, on both regional and subregional levels. Much of our emphasis is on functions rather than overall structural consolidation. In a nutshell, we believe that efficiency, more than equity or competitiveness, is the value and approach that most successfully promotes region alism. Given the way local government is financed in America, economic competitiveness drives localities away from—not toward—collaboration, and as a general rule, social equity is best advanced as a by-product of regional reform, not as its focal purpose. Finally, we stress that regionalism is best regarded as a process—an approach to problem solving—rather than as a "magic bullet" solution for regional ills. The values of regionalism endure, but the means for effecting change evolve politically as society is transformed and economic conditions change.

CHAPTER TWO

The Values of Regionalism

In 1993 New Jersey sued New York for ownership of Ellis Island, the famous immigrant port of entry to America in New York harbor. The next year, despite the reservations of Solicitor General Drew Day, III, the U.S. Supreme Court agreed to a rare use of its original jurisdiction over cases "in which a State shall be a party" and took up the matter. Soon thereafter the Court appointed Paul R. Verkeil (who later became Dean of the Cardozo Law School in New York) as special master to advise it on this lawsuit. To serve the Court, Verkeil reached centuries back into the region's disputatious history to examine the basis for each state's claims.

Until they were defeated by the British, the Dutch maintained economic and political unity in their colonial governance of the region around the mouth of the Hudson. Following his victory in 1664, King Charles II of England deeded the region to his brother James, Duke of York (later King James II), who in turn granted the part of it that later became New Jersey to Sir George Carteret and John, Lord Berkeley. This decision to organize East Jersey as a separate colony "broke the political unity of the Hudson at the most critical point, and opened the estuary to competition for trade"—a circumstance that persists to this day.[1]

Boundary claims based on ill-defined initial land grants were further complicated by the brief Dutch reconquest of the region and the tumultuous English politics of the time. The economic stakes in boundary disputes in the region before and after independence were similar to those of modern business location decisions that generate bidding wars between neighboring states. As the colonies developed, however, New York dominated. It claimed and held all the islands in the Hudson harbor—Staten Island was a particular issue—and exercised jurisdiction over fishing and all maritime trade and commerce to the high-water mark on the Jersey shore.[2]

New Jersey rightly understood that it was in New York's interest, as long as it had control of the entire port, to hamper the development of facilities on the west bank of the Hudson. After independence New Jersey sought several times to negotiate a boundary that would give it control of port development on its shore, but New York would not come to the table.[3] The result in 1828 was New Jersey's first resort to the U.S. Supreme Court on the boundary question. New York initially resisted the Supreme Court's jurisdiction. The Court responded by affirming that its original jurisdiction, provided for in the U.S. Constitution, did not (as New York argued) require antecedent congressional action to make it operative. New York was encouraged by the Court to respond to New Jersey's second filing in 1831 and given considerable time, but it also was told that New Jersey's case would be heard ex parte, if necessary. New York chose the nonconfrontational path: in 1831 Governor Enos B. Throop advised the state senate that New York would be represented before the Court.[4]

Under the threat of adverse Supreme Court action (and perhaps because former New York governor Martin Van Buren's national ambitions caused him to seek political friends in New Jersey), New York agreed to a settlement in 1834.[5] The interstate boundary was placed in the middle of the Hudson and New York Bay. New York received jurisdiction over Staten Island, Bedlows Island (later Liberty Island), and Ellis Island; the waters of the bay and river; and the lands covered by these to the low-water mark on the Jersey shore. New Jersey received "right of property" to land under water on the western side of the bay and river and exclusive jurisdiction over improvements on its shores and over ships tied to its docks.[6]

When it was determined after these negotiations to be within New York, Ellis Island was about three acres in size. Its current size is 27.5 acres, reached in about 1936. After the island's designation in 1890 as the first federal immigration station, more space was needed. It was created by filling (supposedly with material taken from the tunnels excavated to build the New York City subways) on underwater land owned by New Jersey, and on this fact New Jersey subsequently based its claim.

In 1997 Special Master Verkeil decided that the original island (with a bit added on to make the outcome "practical, convenient, just and fair") was New York's, but most of the acreage resulting from filling was New Jersey's. The *New York Times* at first denounced New Jersey's original lawsuit as "unfriendly, unbecoming, un-American, untoward, unhelpful, unprincipled, unseemly, unwarranted, and underhanded."[7] Nevertheless, and perhaps belatedly mindful of its role as a *regional* newspaper, it found the special master's decision "Solomonic."

But the analogy was inapt: King Solomon *threatened* to divide the baby to identify the real mother and return it to her; Verkeil *actually* divided the island, and left both states unhappy. Each believed it had gotten too little. New York appealed only to receive its comeuppance. In May 1998 the U.S. Supreme Court awarded even more of Ellis Island to New Jersey than had the special master, leaving only the original 3.3-acre portion in New York. "This is a recognition of New Jersey's place in history. It is a matter of pride for the state," said Governor Christine Todd Whitman. New York's Governor George Pataki demurred, "Ellis Island will always be a part of New York in the hearts and minds of the millions of immigrants who came to America seeking freedom," he said.[8]

Pride. Place in history. This example illustrates that beyond economics there are other powerful reasons that state and local boundaries matter to people—and therefore to their elected officials. The Ellis Island fight, as Linda Greenhouse of the *New York Times* wrote, was basically about "bragging rights."[9] Toward this end millions have been spent by New York and New Jersey on litigation, money that might otherwise have been used for collaborative development of tourist facilities or to benefit the entire tri-state region in other, more concrete ways.

Persistence of Governmental Boundaries

The Ellis Island story shows not only that boundaries matter, but also that they persist. As the twenty-first century approached, New York and New Jersey were still disputing a boundary established in the seventeenth century! Indeed, a singular paradox is at the core of the Ellis Island dispute: namely, that the tri-state region's key geographical feature, the Hudson River, provides an unmistakable, convenient (though not always clear) political boundary between places while at the same time it is the economic focal point that integrates those places.

The persistence of political boundaries as barriers to economic and social integration has been a fundamental concern for regionalists in the last decade. For example, Neal Peirce, the leading nationally syndicated columnist writing exclusively about state and local government, asserts that it is neither cities nor states but regions that will be the key organizing units of future society.[10] Peirce coined the term "citistates" to describe America's regions, "consisting of one or more central cities surrounded by cities and towns which have a shared identification, function as a single zone for trade, commerce and communication, and are characterized by social, economic and environmental independence." We create regions, Peirce and other regionalists argue, as a by-product of how we conduct our daily lives—ranging widely and moving repeatedly across state and local lines as we travel back and forth to work and school, do business, shop, and visit family and friends. And we re-create these regions daily, too, as astonishingly rapid technological change allows us to challenge the limits that time and space formerly placed on these familiar daily activities.

But governance is not keeping up. Local boundaries rarely are altered to reflect the new social and economic realities, and state borders never change at all. Thus citistates exist as social and economic realities but not as polities.[11] The "great disability of American citistates," Peirce wrote in 1993, "is their common lack of coherent *governance*—either formal or informal. The result is that fundamental public decisions, on every question from air quality to transportation to solid waste disposal to assuring a competent work force for the future, are reached in piecemeal, often haphazard fashion."[12]

Regionalists agree with organizational theorist Peter Drucker that "any organization . . . needs to rethink itself once it is more than forty or fifty years old."[13] They know that general-purpose local government in much of the United States is delivered within boundaries largely determined generations, even centuries, ago, and they question why this is so and whether it is smart and must continue.

New Jersey, for example, finished creating its counties in 1857, nineteen years before Alexander Graham Bell made the first phone call; twenty-two years before Thomas A. Edison (a most famous Jersey man) invented the light bulb; thirty-five years before Henry Ford sold his first car; forty-nine years before the Wright brothers flew. All these century-or-more-old revolutions in communications, technology, and transportation transformed the geographical premises upon which all organizations in society are designed and built—except for general-purpose local government systems in the states. Furthermore, this does not even take into account the computer, photocopier, fax, Internet, all of the machines, media, and methods of the communications revolution of the twentieth century.

Peter Drucker also advises that "any organization, whether biological or social, that doubles or triples its size needs to be restructured."[14] When measured by how much it spends, local government has far more than doubled (and redoubled, and redoubled again) in size in recent decades. The Census Bureau reports aggregate local government spending of $59.5 billion in 1967, $172.8 billion in 1977, $465.4 billion in 1987, and $719.1 billion in 1994.

Regionalists realize that there have been changes in local government systems. While general-purpose governments have remained in place, special-purpose governments have been layered upon them. By the federal government's count there were 34,683 special districts in the country in 1997. According to the census these "are independent, special-purpose governmental units (other than school district governments) that exist with substantial administrative and fiscal independence from general purpose government."[15] Political scientist Kathryn Foster reports that while the average number of general-purpose local governments in U.S. metropolitan areas counted by the census increased by 8 percent in the third of a century between 1952 and 1987, the average number of special districts increased by 150 percent.[16] The Census Bureau reports that the number of these districts increased 5 percent between 1987 and 1992 and another 9.9 percent between 1992 and 1997. And these numbers do not include semiautonomous public authorities familiar to most citizens, such as solid waste and transportation agencies. This sort of adding on without replacement, with its attendant layering, overlap, and jurisdictional complexity, is hardly the kind of restructuring that Drucker had in mind. Nor is it the kind that private corporations did in the 1990s when they fought in the marketplace for their organizational lives.

Some of the strongest, most important voices in the regionalism movement—David Rusk, for example—argue for the creation, where possible, of region-wide general-purpose governments that would bring governmental boundaries into conformance with the way people actually live and work in places across the country.[17] However, Rusk and others have increasingly come to realize that even in places where local barriers are least frozen in state law, the creation of general-purpose regional governments is extraordinarily difficult.[18] A region that expands into more than one state enormously complicates the possibility of regional solutions. Even within a single state, local leaders who may be sympathetic to regionalism in principle are likely to get off the regionalism bandwagon as soon as they hear the words "metropolitan government." They know what it is, and it's not what they want. It threatens their jobs and, more importantly, the community identity of those they serve. "I am for regional approaches, but not regional government," declared Town Supervisor Carl Calabrese of Tonawanda, a Buffalo, New York, suburb.[19]

Four Values of Regionalism

The revival of the regionalism idea in the 1990s after decades in eclipse was driven by three values and had to accommodate a fourth. The first two, *efficiency* in delivering services and *competitiveness* in the world economy, are the same ones that have propelled corporate downsizing and restructuring in the private sector and privatization of domestic service delivery on the public side. The third core value for regionalists is *equity*. It has long been noted that although central cities try to compete within and outside their regions to retain their residents and economic bases, the jobs move farther and farther out from the center or leave the region entirely, diminishing these cities' capacity to serve the poor that concentrate within them (often minorities and new immigrants).[20] Regionalists seek to relieve older inner cities of this disproportionate burden and advance social equity by sharing over entire regions the cost of serving the poor.

Despite onrushing social and economic change and powerful forces demanding regional reform, local government boundaries persist, largely due to the success of citizens in defending them in the name of a fourth value, *community*. For advocates of regionalism, this is a compelling and important fact. Neil Peirce's focus is deliberately on regional *governance*, not regional *government*. The former is more inclusive and less defined. Perhaps reflecting the decade's general disenchantment with government, this formulation preserves a large role for the private and not-for-profit sectors. It suggests collaboration and cooperation, consensus building rather than winning political battles, and the value of partial rather than comprehensive solutions. And it is not threatening to existing localities and their elected leaders. Planned changes in the forms of government are important, but this is not an exclusive (or even primary) concern; informal regional action is included, too.

Though not a driving force in the regionalism movement—and in fact often a source of resistance to its proposals—the deep desire for community is a value regionalists must accommodate if their movement is to succeed. They know, as Margaret Weir has written, that "localism has long been a defining feature of American politics."[21] They also know from historical experience that American suburbs have become the strongest bastions of localism. In his book *Crabgrass Frontier* one of the nation's leading urban historians, Kenneth T. Jackson, describes the United States as "the world's first suburban nation." Jackson concludes, "For better or for worse, the American suburb is a remarkable and probably lasting achievement."[22]

The extent and force of this suburb-focused localism was brilliantly demonstrated by Richard Briffault in two landmark articles in the *Columbia Law Review*, published in 1990. Briffault recognizes suburbs, not cities, as "the principal form of urban settlement in the United States today." He shows that legal theories of state dominance notwithstanding, local power centered in suburbs is at the heart of modern American governing arrangements. "Local autonomy," Briffault concludes, "is to a considerable extent the result of and reinforced by a systematic belief in the social and political value of local decision making. Local control of issues central to local life has repeatedly been treated as desirable, as natural, indeed, as presumptive. State courts and legislatures appear to believe in the value of local control."[23]

Regionalists balance the core values of equity, efficiency, and competitiveness in various ways. All say that they favor social justice and enhanced economic competitiveness; all would like to see local government be more efficient, effective, and democratic; and all acknowledge that a sense of community must be preserved while enhancing regional connections. However, not all regionalists acknowledge that these core values may compete or even, at times, conflict. But they do, and therefore establishing priorities among them (or concealing the need to do so) becomes necessary. Thus in their writings the advocates of regionalism blend these values in different ways.

For purposes of clarity, we identify three basic approaches to regionalism: *redistributive metropolitanism* gives primacy to equity; *functional regionalism* emphasizes efficiency; *economic regionalism* places economic development or competitiveness first.

—Achieving *equity* between races and classes is the primary objective of one prominent group of regionalists, David Rusk among them. These "redistributive metropolitanists" seek primarily to aid the poor—often minority—residents of inner cities. Rusk has traveled the nation for almost a decade, calling for reunification of cities and suburbs where possible or advocating other strategies toward this end.

—The classic goal of delivering local services with *efficiency*, thereby making government work better, is the prime motivation of a second group of regionalists. "Functional regionalists" emphasize mastering such management challenges as governmental fragmentation, layering, and overlap. One of the main ways to do this is through what we call functional right-sizing: minimizing cost by assigning responsibility for major functions to governmental entities with the appropriate geographical reach.

—Assuring *competitiveness* is the main purpose for another group of regionalists. "Economic regionalists" believe that regions must grow or die, that the world economy will be organized around regions, and that outmoded local government organization in the United States is a barrier to regional competitiveness in the global economy. They attempt to identify and learn from places that have achieved some success in this direction. (Two examples, Chattanooga and Cleveland, are mentioned briefly below.)

Redistributive Metropolitanism: Seeking Equity

In his enormously influential book *Cities without Suburbs*, David Rusk advocates metropolitan unification wherever state law and political conditions permit. "The city," he writes, "must be redefined to reunify city and suburb. Ideally, such reunification is achieved through metropolitan government."[24]

Rusk, son of former secretary of state Dean Rusk, speaks from experience; he was once the mayor of Albuquerque, New Mexico. His landmark book was written in 1993 when he was a visiting scholar at the Woodrow Wilson International Center for Scholars, part of the Smithsonian Institution in Washington. To the surprise and pleasure of its sponsors, the book went through seven printings and was followed by a second edition in 1995. It was critical in reenergizing the regionalism movement. Taken together, its twenty-four crisply written lessons make the case for metropolitan area-wide structural reform.

Rusk's acknowledged purposes are greater class and racial integration in communities, together with shifts within regions in patterns of taxing and spending. He shows that aging cities struggle with concentrated poor (often minority) populations, diminished tax capacity, less intergovernmental aid, and higher costs. Meanwhile, formerly rural suburbs, largely white and middle class, seek to cope with the desire of new residents to have the range of services to which they were accustomed in the city, and with the need for enormous infrastructure investment to accommodate growth. Regional government, Rusk argues, is a way to bridge the racial divide, more equitably distribute the cost of central-city needs, and maximize the return from existing and new infrastructure investment.

His data show that "elastic" cities, which can more easily expand their boundaries through annexation and consolidation, are far less racially segregated and less economically stressed than those that are "inelastic." He urges structural changes in state and local law to allow inelastic cities to stretch the "rubber sheet" of local government over inner city and suburbs.

Perhaps because of the power and accessibility of its argument, readers have overgeneralized from David Rusk's work. He does acknowledge in *Cities without Suburbs* that metropolitan government may be neither feasible nor desirable for the largest, most complex regions in the United States, and he subsequently devotes an entire book to advocating ways for fragmented regions—places that cannot become one governmentally—to act as one in key areas of regional policy: land-use planning, provision of low- and moderate-income housing, and reduction of fiscal disparities through regional revenue sharing. But even in this later work, Rusk says, "Where annexation or consolidation is still feasible, my advice is 'Do it.'"[25]

Despite the battering it has taken on the shoals of local politics almost everywhere it was advanced during the last half century, the metropolitan government idea has always retained a cadre of advocates. Reducing the number of local governments and increasing the scope and powers of the remaining area-wide governments, metropolitan reformers traditionally argued, would simultaneously achieve economies of scale in service delivery and provide the wherewithal to build the infrastructure to undergird further growth. And, they also argued, it would improve equity in taxation and service delivery. It might even advance democracy by simplifying local government and making it more understandable to citizens.

Redistributive metropolitan government advocates emphasize racial justice and social equity. Like Nancy Burns they think that "the way in which Americans have constructed local autonomy means that we have created a space in American politics where race and class are embedded in boundaries."[26] Among the most prominent of this school is urban economist Anthony Downs of the Brookings Institution, who notes that members of minority groups, many poor and most living in central cities, will constitute an ever-increasing portion of this country's population. Yet, "the way the American metropolitan process works," he writes, "inevitably draws viable resources . . . out of the core portions of our metropolitan areas, into the peripheral portions, thereby leaving the core portions physically unable to perform their social functions in an acceptable manner." Downs continues, "A critical factor underlying the whole core debilitation process is the fragmentation of government."[27]

Redistributive metropolitanists are confident that planned and directed reform—large-scale government restructuring—can achieve social change. Moreover, they are deeply suspicious of the consequences of the recent devolutionary trends in American government. Witness Margaret Weir's recent criticism of "defensive localism," which she thinks seeks "to reduce domestic spending by the federal government, push responsibilities down to lower levels of government, and contain the social problems associated with poverty—and their costs—within defined spatial and political boundaries."[28]

Even the purest of the redistributive metropolitanists must acknowledge that their approach usually has failed to be adopted, especially in the largest metropolitan areas. According to David Walker, a lifelong expert on intergovernmental relations, during all of U.S. history "real regional reforms . . . have occurred in only about twenty-five instances, largely in medium or small metropolitan areas."[29] Most successful efforts at this kind of regionalization have been the result of special political circumstances. They typically were triggered by local crises: corruption scandals, massive service failures, growth pressure on infrastructure, or threats that in-migration posed to the established political order.

For example, a Republican takeover of Indianapolis city government in 1967, during a time when Indiana Republicans dominated state and local government at every level, presented a unique political opportunity for change. Newly elected mayor Richard Lugar (later a U.S. senator) successfully led reform efforts to combine the City of Indianapolis and Marion County to create "Unigov." For many services Unigov, although not a full-scale consolidation, combined agency operations and fostered a spirit of cooperation in the region. (Some services, however, were kept separate, such as schools and public safety, and some localities in the county chose not to be included in Unigov.)

The creation of Unigov brought thousands of suburban Republican voters into the city and was a crucial step in advancing Lugar's announced economic development agenda.[30] Although there is still widespread agreement that the Unigov aided the economy of the region, the Indianapolis-Marion County merger remains controversial; a 1997 effort by Democrats in the state legislature to authorize a referendum on its continuation narrowly failed in a straight party-line vote in the Indiana House of Representatives.[31]

There are several reasons why megamergers so rarely find support in metropolitan regions. The first and most important is that *people like their localities.* They live in communities they value. Citizens are heavily invested both emotionally and financially in existing jurisdictions. They buy their homes, shape their careers, develop community feelings, and in sum, build their lives around assumptions about the stability of local governmental boundaries, powers, and service arrangements.

Moreover, the power of politicians is rooted in an electoral mandate from a *place.* To get elected, one must have a base. Politicians speak of "my" district, town, city, or county. The law almost everywhere in the United States requires that a representative live in the district or jurisdiction he or she represents, and there are rules about time limits for changing residence if reapportionment removes a representative's residence from his or her district. Political career ladders are based on the size of the place a person represents; politicians move up the ladder by being elected to a position in a bigger place.

Thus while regionalists seek to define the region as "a community," that same word for citizens and those they elect most often means a neighborhood or a locality that has had the same general boundaries for generations. What is essential to realize—and what many reformers do not—is that these local impulses, based on the powerful value of community, are not necessarily racist, discriminatory, or negative. They arise from strong, deeply rooted, often positive forces in American life. In fact, Howard Husock of Harvard's Kennedy School of Government advances the view that independent jurisdictions are a crucial means by which a nation as diverse as the United States can develop a modus vivendi among peoples of sharply different values and widely varying backgrounds.[32]

A second related reason for difficulties with the metropolitan government approach focuses on poverty. It turns out that *both* urban blacks and suburban whites have been against consolidation. Suburban whites resist being joined to the cities that many of them have escaped, regarding them as centers of crime and decay. Racial bias may be part of the story for suburbanites, but it is not the whole story. They also want to protect the quality of services they receive and the communities they have adopted or constructed.

For blacks electoral politics has entered into the picture in an important way since the 1960s. Having wrested power away from whites in many cities after years of struggle, African American politicians want to keep that power.[33] This is the case despite the contention by proponents of regionalism that regional consolidation aids lower-income residents, many of whom are members of racial and ethnic minority groups.

For Myron Orfield, as for David Rusk, the objective of regionalism is to "stabilize central cities and older suburbs." Orfield is a lawyer and state legislator, a third-generation resident of Minneapolis, Minnesota, whose crusade for metropolitan reform in Minnesota has made his urban district increasingly safe for him politically. Orfield's priorities are quite similar to those of Rusk. In his book on *Metropolitics,* he argues that to achieve reform, six important substantive goals must be met: The top three are fair housing, property tax base sharing, and reinvestment. The second three—needed, says Orfield, to reinforce and institutionalize the others—are land-use planning and growth management, welfare reform and public works, and transportation and transit reform.[34]

Compared to Rusk, Orfield places less emphasis on integrated, unitary metropolitan government, though he does write that "these [six] reforms can be most effectively administered by an elected metropolitan coordinating structure." For him the key arena for achieving regional reform can be found at the state, not the local, level. A practicing politician, Orfield—unlike many other regionalists—is not after consensus. One of his major contributions to the regionalism discourse is his insight, dramatically illustrated in a series of multicolored maps, that core cities and older inner suburbs share many of the same problems. This provides the rationale for forming powerful winning coalitions at the state level between core cities and these suburbs; together they can achieve change in the key areas of action he has identified by overcoming resistant, more affluent, and recently settled suburban areas which have very different interests.[35] Orfield has, in fact, successfully assembled winning state legislative coalitions in Minnesota around major regionalist goals, although most changes have been blocked by gubernatorial vetoes.[36]

Functional Regionalism: Achieving Efficiency

Functional regionalists envision regionalism emerging locally, gradually, and function-by-function to solve specific service delivery problems. The changes they advocate may appear to be less dramatic than they actually are. For example, citizens might notice that the signs on their sanitation trucks or commuter buses have changed from "Town" or "City" to "Metro" or "Regional." However, these surface changes would also be accompanied by lower costs for the same level of service or better service for the same cost.

Regionalists in this category are suspicious of planned structural change. They accept the local governmental status quo as the result of a series of citizen choices over time. The local government system you see, they would argue, is the one people want.

Anita Summers, an economist and well-known regionalism researcher at the University of Pennsylvania's Wharton School, observed at the 1997 Chautauqua national conference that unified metropolitan government was "a matter of the heart." "Everyone seemed to favor the idea at conferences," she said, "but at the ballot box, no one votes for it." Although metropolitan governments are rarely created, Summers continued, regional service delivery has developed throughout the nation for transportation and other functions that can benefit from large-scale service delivery.[37]

Summers' criterion for optimally sizing public services is that "every service is delivered in a cost-minimizing geography." For public transportation, she noted, there is no choice but a large-scale, regional approach. Similar reforms in functional rightsizing are often applied to libraries and waste water treatment, services for which there are "clear efficiencies in the size of delivery areas." "It is hard to believe," she concluded, "that the opportunities for these kinds of changes have been fully exploited."[38]

John Kincaid, another proponent of this view, compares unitary regional government to an old, 1960s mainframe computer: too big, too centralized, and too slow. He believes that modern regionalism requires lots of small, freestanding local governments linked together for specific functions, like the networked PCs of the 1990s.[39]

In contrast to redistributive metropolitanists, functional regionalists are inclined to see existing local government arrangements not as fragmentation, but as an organic response to citizen preferences. More communitarian in their values and market oriented, they welcome devolution and distrust large-scale planning and universal solutions. "The desire to create some presumably 'rational' structure . . . remains strong among many advocates of metropolitan governance," Kincaid wrote, "but it is not clear that an exogenously built structure is . . . [preferable to or] more rational than endogenously built structures slowly emerging in metropolitan areas."[40]

Functional regionalism is sometimes achieved entirely outside of government. In recent years there has been a good deal of both privatization and "nonprofitization" in service and delivery. Privatization, of course, involves businesses competing to contract with government to do things formerly done by public employees. In this volume we discuss how this has happened with solid waste management, undoing planned regional solutions and transforming one of the most local of local government functions into a multibillion-dollar national industry in a brief quarter century.

Nonprofitization involves delegating public services to nonprofit organizations that receive the bulk of their money from various governmental agencies and programs. Increasingly, for a wide gamut of social and community development programs, it is employees of nonprofit groups, not civil servants, who actually provide services. This is true with respect to child care, services for the mentally ill and disabled, drug and alcoholism treatment, youth services, care for the elderly, neighborhood community development, construction and management of affordable housing, employment and training, and a wide array of health services.

What has been less than fully appreciated is that both privatization and nonprofitization are both ways of altering the scale of service delivery, function by function, without changing governmental boundaries. Some of these arrangements are very localized, involving coalitions of neighborhood groups. But on a larger scale, a vendor or nonprofit agency can contract with many governments to perform a single function throughout a county or metropolitan area, achieving economies of scale by doing so. Such outcomes are another dimension of what reformers who are committed to functional—or what might be called situational—regionalism care about.

Although many functional regionalists acknowledge the importance of social equity, they may question the appropriateness of redistributing wealth or income at the local government level. They are pragmatists, interested more in the better system they can have rather than the best system they can hope for. They seek to avoid knock-down-and-drag-out battles over consolidation, looking instead for approaches that work by altering the scale of service delivery. Writing in the same recent issue of *The Regionalist* as did Kincaid, Roger Parks of Indiana University concluded, "Careful study of what works in particular metropolitan areas and why, plus what doesn't work and why not, could inform a serious effort to improve on local governance in those areas facing real problems."[41]

Economic Regionalism: Assuring Competitiveness

"The first lesson of the global economy," writes Theodore Hershberg, professor at the University of Pennsylvania and director of the Center for Greater Philadelphia, "is that regions—not cities nor the suburban counties that surround them—will be the units of economic competition."[42] In fact, it has long been true that city and suburban economies were inextricably linked while their polities diverged. Perverse incentives militated against cooperation, and regional leadership was lacking. But now, Hershberg says, economic survival requires that cities and suburbs work together to develop human resources, lower the cost of services, and maximize returns from investment capital. "To compete effectively, regions have to be cohesive. . . . In a nation with precious few examples of regional government, this means that cities and suburbs have to find ways to work together for their mutual benefit."

Taking Hershberg's argument one step further, William Barnes and Larry Ledebur of Cleveland State University argue that the United States does not have a single national economy but rather a group of regional economies linked in a common market. Furthermore, they say, in no instance is a local government congruent with a regional economy. This necessitates collaborative partnerships for "governance to nurture the regional commons."[43]

Economic regionalists want to minimize intraregional competition to make regions more competitive nationally and internationally. They say that when competition occurs among governments within a single region, it simply results in a net reduction of resources available to local governments or a redistribution of the tax burden within localities, without any real overall economic benefit to the entire region.[44]

An example of what economic regionalists dislike was reported in the April 19, 1997, issue of the *New York Times*. New Jersey offered the Standard and Poor's company over $50 million in incentives to move its headquarters to Jersey City, New Jersey, just across the Hudson River from Manhattan. (Standard and Poor's, a subsidiary of McGraw-Hill publishing, had 2,000 employees in New York City and wanted to consolidate its operations in one location.) Supported by New York State, New York City offered a competitive incentive package to retain the company. After thinking it over, Standard and Poor's officers opted to lease almost a million square feet on fifteen floors at 55 Water Street in New York City's financial district—a major win for the then sagging downtown real estate market, but it was obtained at a big price.

This example is especially interesting because it demonstrates interstate competition reinforcing interlocal competition within a single metropolitan region. David Rusk has argued that "it is only at the state level that a local citizen's interests are placed in a framework that addresses his or her interests as a citizen of an entire state or a metropolitan region."[45] But, of course, such a role for the state is impossible where the region reaches into two or more states, as in the case of New York and many other places in the country.

Offering the classic economic regionalist perspective, Claude Shostal, the head of the Regional Plan Association, describes intraregional competition among governments in the tri-state area as "a zero-sum game." "The revenue lost to local government as a result of this competition," he added, "could be put into schools and transportation programs that would benefit everybody, and the whole pie would grow."[46] Dick Netzer, an urban economist at New York University, sees this kind of governmental intervention in the market to influence business location decisions as even worse—not a zero-sum game but a "negative sum game," reducing overall economic welfare in the region, and the nation.[47]

There is an alternative view. For example, Joe Mattey, an economist at the Federal Reserve Bank in San Francisco, thinks that the long-term benefits of interjurisdictional competition are likely to offset the costs of locational incentives. Lower marginal costs of delivering services are likely to ensue, he says, as demand for services increases with business development.[48]

The economic regionalism argument has appeal to businessmen and civic leaders used to competing nationally and internationally and to thinking in terms of markets rather than civil subdivisions. This kind of regionalism often emerges in response to a faltering regional economy. It is manifest in public-private partnerships to overcome barriers to economic growth.

David Crockett, a fifth-generation descendant of frontiersman Davy Crockett, is a retired businessman and a member of the Chattanooga, Tennessee, city council. At the 1997 Chautauqua conference, he described his efforts to promote regionalism as simply about "being competitive." Chattanooga reputedly had the worst air quality in the U.S. in 1969. The air was so dirty that businessmen who wished to remain presentable reportedly had to take two shirts to work and change in the middle of the day. Slides taken at that time showed ground level haze so thick that you could not see through it in broad daylight.

The early seventies was the take-off time for the national environmental movement. Federal and state air pollution control laws and regulations were tightened. The need to face the air pollution crisis in a way that preserved the local economy motivated the public-private partnership in the region that renewed the area economy while also making Chattanooga the "Environment City—a poster child for the livable city."[49]

The Chattanooga "Vision 2000" project, undertaken in 1982 with funding from the Lyndhurst Foundation, involved 1,700 people in a planning process that established a "commitment portfolio" of forty community goals. According to one local account, between 1984 and 1992, "the goals set forth at the Vision 2000 meetings generated $793 million of investment in the community. Three-fourths of that commitment came from the private sector, and one-fourth from the public sector. Major investments included downtown and riverfront development, low-income housing and social initiatives."[50] With many economic development objectives reached or well under way, Chattanooga's 1993 "revisioning" initiative focused to a greater degree on social goals such as education and job training.

The Cleveland region's experience was similar. An environmental laughingstock when the Cuyahoga River caught fire in June 1969, the city of Cleveland entered bankruptcy in 1978.[51] Recruited by the city's business elite, Republican Lieutenant Governor George V. Voinovich ran for and won the mayoralty. With broad community backing from across the region, the new mayor established a number of public-private partnerships to take the lead in urban revitalization efforts. Between 1982 and 1986, a "civic vision" proposal was enacted to guide downtown and neighborhood development. As a result over $3 billion has been invested in the infrastructure of Greater Cleveland since 1983. "Office towers have been renovated and new ones constructed. The theatre district has been restored. On the lakefront site, there is a new Science Center and the Rock and Roll Hall of Fame. The huge, stodgy Municipal Stadium came down, and in 1997 the National Basketball Association and Major League Baseball All Star Games were played in sleek new facilities right in Cleveland's downtown."[52]

The Cleveland area's comeback has been remarkable; but here, as in Chattanooga, work remains to be done. For example, in 1995 a federal circuit court judge, Robert B. Krupansky, found Cleveland's schools to be in crisis and previous city efforts at improvement ineffectual; he transferred their control from the elected school board to the state government.[53] In the preface to a volume prepared in connection with the city's bicentennial in 1996, David Sweet and Kathryn Wertheim Hexter acknowledged the city's successes but found the Cleveland region still characterized by political fragmentation, racial division, large income and education differentials, and interjurisdictional competition. "The bottom line," they continued, "is a lack of a shared sense of community and common destiny."[54] Most recently Richard Shatten, professor for the practice of regional economics at Case Western Reserve University, has argued that organizational disarray in local government and civic leadership systems remains a barrier to economic development in the Cleveland region.[55]

In both Chattanooga and Cleveland, ballot proposals to create unitary regional governments had previously failed. Regionalism's successes were not initially based on government restructuring or social reform. The motivating force in constructing public-private partnerships that worked was economic crisis, and the primary goals of these efforts were economic renewal and development. Only after major economic achievements did these cities and their regions begin to give primacy to social goals. And local boundaries persisted, and mattered, even in the face of successful reform efforts.

PART TWO

Regionalism and the New York City Experience

CHAPTER THREE

One Grand and Glorious City

On New Year's Eve in 1897, William Randolph Hearst, then the nation's most flamboyant publisher of newspapers in New York and other major cities, organized a spectacular party to celebrate the consolidation of Greater New York City.

> Choral groups from the city's ethnic societies and organizations sang before a panel of judges. . . . Floats and marching bands paraded under gleaming white magnesium searchlights . . . [including Hearst's *New York Journal*'s] . . . "oblong square of electric lights eighty feet long by forty feet" arranged in the Stars and Stripes. At midnight, the singers joined together in *Auld Lang Syne;* Henry J. Pain, the nation's most celebrated fireworks expert, set off a dazzling display of skyrockets, a battery of guns fired a deafening hundred-gun salute, and from three thousand miles away, Mayor Phelan of San Francisco pressed a magic button which sent an electric signal across the nation to city hall park and "propelled the blue and white flag of Greater New York whipping up the staff of the city hall cupola."[1]

Today, creation of a single big city from what is now the New York region would be regarded as an enormous and unlikely victory for metropolitan reformers. So it was when Greater New York was established a century ago.[2] The Greater City resulted from the joining of a Democratic reformer's visionary persistence with a Republican boss's brute political strength at a unique historical moment. The Democrat was Andrew Haswell Green; the Republican was Thomas Collier Platt. Their time was one in which bigness was valued, politics was disciplined, and the structure of local government could be imposed, relatively unimpeded, by the state.

"I do not believe that we should realize our idea of a united and homogenous city," Greater New York's first comptroller, Bird Coler, wrote in 1900, "until all divisional lines have been forever obliterated, and there is no Manhattan, no Brooklyn, no village by the sea, no localized settlement upon the Sound, no isolated community upon the hills of the Hudson, but one grand and glorious New York."[3] In this chapter we show how both the original governmental design of Greater New York and its periodic restructuring over the ensuing century resulted from struggles between those, like Coler, who wished to centralize and those who wished to decentralize power in the government of the metropolis.

The values at the core of these struggles—efficiency in government, competitiveness, equity, and community—were not always defined in precisely the same way in each era, but they remained remarkably constant and have become a legacy for contemporary regionalists. Centralizers advocated concentrating responsibility for governmental functions in citywide departments and a strong mayor; decentralizers promoted empowering the boroughs and later, newly created community boards and community school boards. Over time and not without setbacks, the centralizers won. However, the persistence of this debate in the daily life of the city, detailed here and in the chapter that follows, demonstrates that the city's residents desire real local government within the framework of the larger metropolis. This is an important, unresolved governance problem for Greater New York and must be considered in any proposed approach to regionalism.

The Vision: Development and Efficiency

Greater New York as "one big city" was the vision of Andrew Haswell Green. Born in 1820, Green was a leading reform Democrat of nineteenth-century New York. Like his law partner Samuel J. Tilden (who was elected governor in 1874 and was deprived of the U.S. presidency by the "corrupt bargain" in the electoral college two years later), he came to prominence as an opponent of the notorious Tweed ring. Green first recommended consolidation of New York, Brooklyn, and the surrounding counties in 1868, while serving as treasurer and comptroller of the Central Park Commission (an agency created by the Republicans in Albany to keep control of park development for themselves and out of the hands of city Democrats). He was so constant and consistent an advocate of the idea over the following decades that in New York the cause of consolidation came to be called "Green's Folly." Vindication came almost three decades later, in 1896 when the state legislature adopted the plan, drafted by its Consolidation Inquiry Committee, which created Greater New York. Andrew Haswell Green was that committee's president.

Central to Green's vision were two of the four values currently at the heart of the regionalism movement: competitiveness or economic development and efficiency in local government. Creating a single government around the great port at its economic center, he thought, was essential to preserve New York's status as the nation's preeminent city and engine of the national economy. The late nineteenth century was an era of manifest destiny and corporate consolidation; bigness was valued. New York City leaders, feeling pressed by Chicago's growth, wanted to cement their number one position in population size once and for all. (In fact, by 1920 the population of Chicago surpassed that of the old city of New York, that is, the city before its boundaries were expanded.)

Green's economic development arguments were compelling for landowners (and speculators) in still-rural parts of Brooklyn and in Queens and Staten Island towns surrounding New York City because the city's tax base and borrowing power would be available to finance the roads, bridges, sewer and water systems, and mass transit that would attract buyers for abundant undeveloped land. In the brief period in 1897 between passage of the charter for the consolidated city and its effective date, local leaders in cities and towns that would cease to exist when the Greater City came into being took advantage of this window of opportunity. According to Bird Coler (who later became Democratic candidate for governor), "Local public improvements, on a scale impossible under the conditions about to pass away, were undertaken, and bonds were hurriedly issued and sold, with complete disregard for the consequences."[4] One contemporary historian described the time as "an orgy in Queens of lavish expenditure and debt incurring obligations."[5] The idea was, buy now, let somebody else pay later.[6]

Creating one big city, Green also thought, would bring sound business principles to local government management, overcoming pandemic corruption. Of the New York region in 1890, he wrote that "there is . . . no other area of a hundred and fifty square miles whose welfare could better be prompted by one general administration."[7] Certainly this champion of the Greater City would be categorized today as a pure metropolitan reformer.

The creation of Greater New York was not without popular support. In an early advisory referendum held in 1894, majorities in every county involved did favor consolidation. But the margin in Brooklyn—itself just consolidated between 1894 and 1896, when the towns of Flatbush, Flatlands, New Utrecht, and Gravesend were annexed—was a thin 277 votes out of 129,000 cast.[8] In addition, majorities were not obtained in all of the local jurisdictions facing absorption. (By a margin of 1,034, those living within the borders of the pre-1894 city of Brooklyn opposed the plan.) However, in contrast to subsequent situations, such majorities were not required to authorize consolidation. In the end it was an exercise of sheer political power, not the popularity of the idea, that produced Greater New York.

The Power: Development and Spoils

For Thomas Collier Platt, styled the "Easy Boss" of the powerful state Republican party for his soft, decorous, consultative manner, the real reason for consolidation was to capture the patronage and wealth that would flow in ever-growing streams from an enlarged New York City government once the great metropolis was created. Born in Owego, New York, Platt came to New York City in 1880 and soon parlayed his power as state Republican chairman into election to the U.S. Senate (at a time when senators were still elected by the state legislature). Platt dispensed patronage and preferment from his headquarters in the luxurious Fifth Avenue Hotel. Regular Sunday meetings there with legislators and local party leaders came to be called "Platt's Sunday School"; the corridor outside the GOP boss's door became famous statewide as the "Amen corner."[9]

Several times in the late nineteenth century, Republicans in Albany established special districts to perform specific local functions—police, parks, public health—in the downstate region. By taking these functions from New York City and other existing localities and giving them to these new, larger districts, Republicans were able to seize control of patronage from Tammany Democrats and use the city's wealth to pay for services in surrounding areas. Generalizing from these successes, Boss Platt assumed that permanently expanding the city's boundaries would allow the Republicans to wrest control of all of city government more or less permanently from Tammany Hall.

Platt also faced a powerful reform insurgency within his party, based in Manhattan. The Republican victor for mayor in 1894, William Strong, was only reluctantly accepted as the party nominee by the Easy Boss. Strong, a wealthy businessman, was first backed by the bipartisan Committee of Seventy, organized in reaction to Lexow Commission investigations, which revealed the police and municipal corruption under Tammany control.[10] Once elected, Strong resisted Platt's patronage recommendations in the city. In Albany he battled the state boss in the "Platt–Strong War" to get reform legislation through the legislature. In light of these events, consolidation of the Greater City may have been not only a means for Platt to overcome Tammany, but a way to dilute the strength of fractious reform Republicans as well.

In any event, the consolidated city became Thomas Collier Platt's obsession. The rules were different a century ago. The New York State Legislature had clear authority to consolidate local governments, even against their will.[11] In Albany powerful state party leaders like Platt, directing hierarchical, disciplined political parties, could force governors and legislators to adopt the local structural arrangements they favored.

Platt cajoled and intimidated two governors to achieve the reformers' dream. In anticipation of the 1896 national Republican convention, he used Governor Levi Morton's presidential ambitions to secure his public support for the 1896 Consolidation Bill that created the Charter Commission for Greater New York. After the bill's passage, according to historian DeAlva Stanwood Alexander, Morton's "detestation of the scheme revealed itself so plainly in letters and interviews that Platt found it necessary to rowel him again with a fierceness that hurt" in order to gain the governor's signature.[12]

The resulting charter was reluctantly signed into law the next year by the newly elected Republican governor, Frank Black. Black's nomination was engineered by Platt precisely because he was expected to be manageable on the consolidation question. Alexander wrote that Governor Black "yearned" to veto consolidation. "He thought it bad politics . . . but fear of Platt's combine and the failure of a renomination finally broke him. . . . So he signed the Charter without giving his reasons, and sent the pen to Senator Platt as a symbol of his vassalage."[13]

It took four affirmative votes in the state legislature to create the consolidated city. An early form of home rule in New York State's 1894

Constitution gave mayors a "suspensive veto" that could halt implementation of state legislation applying specifically to their city until it gained second passage by the legislature. Mayors William Strong of old New York and Frederick Wurster of Brooklyn both vetoed the bill creating the charter commission in 1896. The next year Strong opposed the resulting consolidated city's charter. Both times, in secret alliance with Tammany Hall, Platt provided the majorities for first passage and to overturn these vetoes.

Harper's Magazine denounced the act that created America's leading metropolis as a "Platt–Tammany robber partnership." In truth, and not atypically, both parties saw potential advantage in the same result. Just as the Republicans sought to control the city, Tammany desired inroads into Brooklyn and Queens. Viewing the likely consequences far differently than did Platt, the Democratic machine provided the needed votes in Albany for the consolidation of Greater New York. "We wanted it all the time," boasted John Sheehan, temporary head of Tammany Hall, after the charter passed. "Our . . . opposition was simply a blind."[14]

The Loser: Smaller-Scale Government

What we have called the value of community, or localism, meant little to both Thomas Collier Platt and Andrew Green. The strongest Greater City advocates wanted "one big city." They saw no need to retain preexisting smaller units, such as neighborhood or community governments, for service delivery or to give localities a voice. Indeed, the continued existence of these localities within the larger whole was seen as a threat to their plan. For them, preexisting cities, towns, and villages (surviving for today's New Yorkers only as subway stops, place names, or neighborhoods) were to be purposely subsumed to strengthen the new metropolis.

Thus those who defended the value of community against the all-encompassing city were not the metropolitanists but their adversaries on the first charter commission. And those who sought equity between classes and races were not even in the conversation. When the issue of equity arose, it concerned attempts to ensure that each part of the new metropolis would be fairly represented in its government and would get its share of public spending devoted to its needs.

Preexisting, small scale municipalities were given some recognition in apportionment and districting for both houses of the bicameral municipal assembly established by the 1897 city charter. However, these arrangements were forgotten almost immediately when the unicameral city council was constituted in the second charter in 1901. As a small concession to localism, the first Greater City charter did include twenty-two local improvement boards. Based on state senate district lines (and not community boundaries arising from previous local governmental arrangements), the improvement boards were composed of the borough presidents and municipal assembly members from each district. Their power was limited to making recommendations to the central city government, most of which were ignored.[15]

The Boroughs

Much as the eighty-seven French prefectures replaced historic provinces just after the revolution, allowing a fundamental restructuring of government, boroughs replaced existing localities in Greater New York at the turn of the century, permitting a similar reordering. New boundaries were used to subsume old loyalties to established localities, which became mere neighborhoods with no governmental presence. The unfamiliar name "borough" was consciously used to emphasize the new and different nature of the city's subregions.

The city of Brooklyn was an exception; it was the only previously existing governmental entity that retained its boundaries within the consolidated city. In fact, it was largely because of the need to satisfy Brooklyn's partisans that modern New York City has any boroughs at all—and that there are five of them. Andrew Haswell Green went to his death thinking boroughs were a big mistake, "a folly . . . that should never have been adopted."[16] But a majority of the 1897 charter commission thought otherwise.

The consolidation statute provided for a geographically balanced, fifteen-member commission to write the Greater City's charter. Green was expected to chair it, but he became ill and the task fell to Benjamin Tracy of Brooklyn, a former secretary of the Navy and close political ally of Boss Platt's. In addition to the mayors of each city, three charter commissioners were to be from Brooklyn and four were to be from the old city of New York. One of Governor Morton's appointees was Seth Low, president of Columbia University, formerly mayor of Brooklyn.

Given the commission's composition and Green's illness, those who favored "one big city" yielded to borough advocates, but then they sought to minimize the number. In one of Low's early drafts of the Greater City charter, nine boroughs were proposed. Five were finally settled upon as the minimum possible consistent with keeping Brooklyn whole within the Greater City. "Smaller, more coherent local units were rejected," historian David Hammack has written, "as inconsistent with Brooklyn's preferences."[17]

Preservation of Brooklyn's unity was the main reason that its mayor did not veto state legislative passage of the charter of 1897. The coterminality of Brooklyn's city boundaries with those of King's County, New York, had only just been achieved in 1894, when the towns of Flatbush, Gravesend, and Flatlands were included (figure 3-1). Thus the city of Brooklyn was hardly a well-established entity when the Greater City was created.

A myth later arose that the boroughs were somehow parties to a bargain in the creation of Greater New York. Indeed, this constituted a part of the argument offered before the U.S. Supreme Court in 1988 for the retention of the Board of Estimate (see below)—on which the boroughs were equally represented—as a core institution of city government. But it was not so: the truth is that there were no boroughs until there was a Greater New York. Until 1914 when Bronx County was created, there were five boroughs (subunits of the city) but only four counties (subunits of the state) in the Greater City. (The territory subsequently included in the Bronx had become part of New York City through earlier consolidations and was still, after consolidation, retained as part of New York County.) In Queens the creation of the Greater City led to the demise of one city—Long Island City—plus nine towns and seven incorporated villages. On Staten Island (Richmond County), five towns and five villages went out of existence with the birth of Greater New York. Additionally, a number of other localities were absorbed as a result of the earlier consolidations that created the cities of New York City and Brooklyn, themselves then consolidated into Greater New York.[18]

Centralizers versus Decentralizers: Revolt of the Boroughs

The boroughs were created in the first city charter; they were empowered in the second. Green and the other metropolitanists, the "one big city" advocates on the 1897 commission, substantially accomplished a concentration of governmental powers in citywide officials and institutions at least as great as that which obtained at the consolidated city's centennial. Reflecting this outcome, a state assembly investigating committee (the Mazet Committee) reported in 1900 that "under the present system we

Figure 3-1. *Governmental Genealogy of Greater New York City*

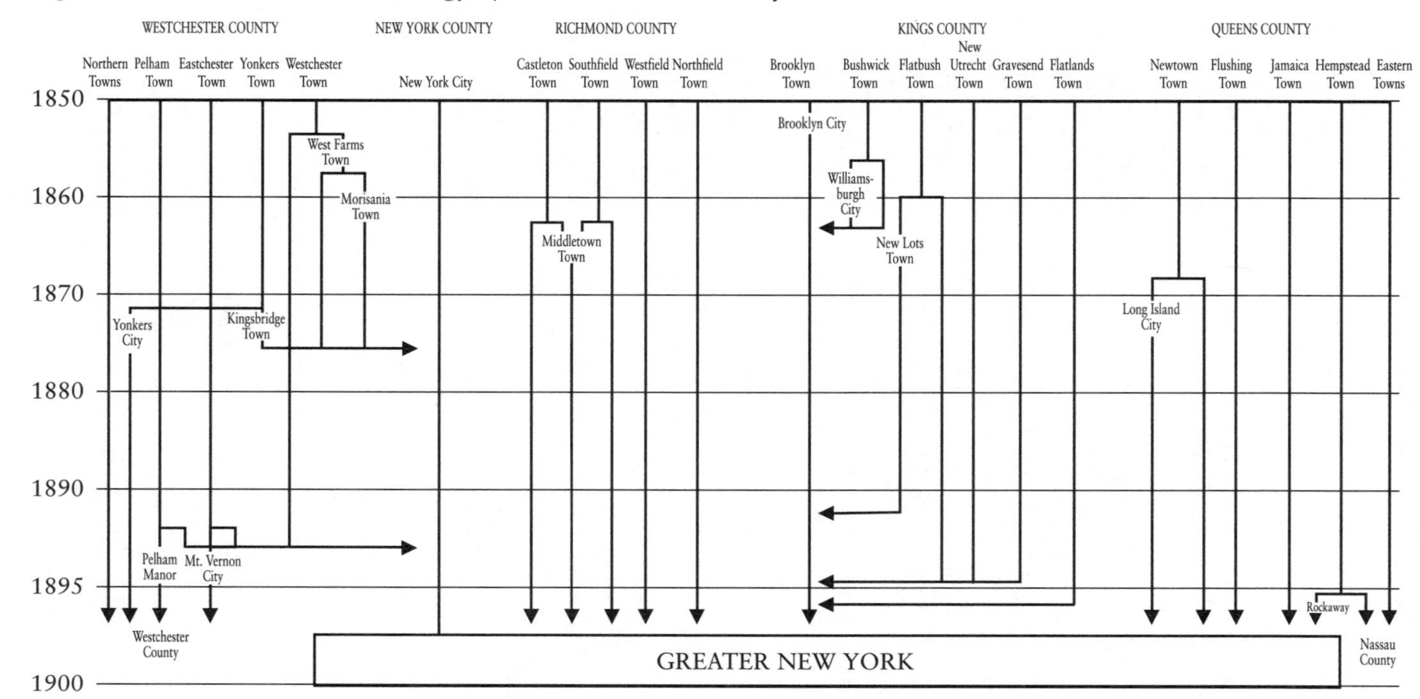

Source: B. Bruce Briggs, "Abolish New York," *New York Affairs*, vol. 5 (Spring 1979), facing p. 9.

have presidents of each borough . . . for whom . . . very little has been found to do."[19]

The Mazet Committee was created by Platt's Republicans in reaction to the Democratic sweep, against divided opposition, of the newly consolidated city's municipal elections in 1897. That Tammany triumph, and the Citizens Union–led fusion movement's victory at the polls in 1901, made the GOP organization in Albany receptive when presented with the "revolt of the boroughs," the first major political effort to decentralize power in New York after its expansion in 1898.[20] Widespread complaints arose from areas newly included in the city that they were getting insufficient attention and resources from city hall. The rejoinder of those at the center, such as Comptroller Bird Coler, was that the outlying areas had nearly bankrupted the city by their excessive borrowing during the transition to the Greater City.[21]

This equity case was made by the metropolitanists' adversaries, the advocates for local interests within the city. The metropolitanists continued to argue that "if Greater New York is to become the imperial city contemplated by the men who conceived the plan and worked it out . . . there can be no dividing government within its limits, no placing one section as the rival of another. Divisional lines must be obliterated forever."[22]

Now realizing his miscalculation, Boss Platt supported the Mazet Committee's proposals to decentralize power to the borough presidents. Governor Theodore Roosevelt resisted this immediate response as too overtly partisan; instead he appointed a second charter commission chaired by George Rives, a former Democratic assistant secretary of state. The Rives Commission did decentralize power. It recommended a new charter, adopted by the legislature in 1901, that abolished a number of central city departments and made the borough presidents "submayors," with control over numerous major functions in their jurisdictions: highways, sewers, public buildings, construction, lighting, and supplies.[23] (In Queens and Richmond they were responsible for street cleaning as well.) Additionally, these officials were to sit on a newly constituted Board of Estimate, now composed entirely of elected officials, that was to exercise citywide authority over capital projects.

Albany-based Republicans were political pragmatists, not ideological metropolitanists. Especially because of the omnipresent factionalism in the GOP generated downstate by progressive reformers, Tammany proved more accurate than they were about which party organization was likely to control the Greater City. When centralizing power within the city failed to serve their political ends, these Republicans subsequently delegated key city functions—and thereby, jobs and patronage—to the borough halls, where their power still might prevail. This is important because with these resources shifted, the boroughs became much bigger political prizes. If New York, Kings, and (what was later) Bronx counties had been separate cities, they would have ranked among the state's five biggest in population at the turn of the twentieth century. Queens and Richmond would have been among the next five—and their growth was just beginning.

For the rest of the century, politicians and reformers struggled over the degree to which Greater New York was to be "one big city" run by the mayor and his appointees.[24] Those who favored further decentralization to the boroughs were held at bay, in large measure because of an endless string of scandals in borough presidents' offices. Proponents of centralization, on the other hand, were blocked by the power of county political organizations, both Republican and Democratic, that controlled the nomination of borough presidents and other county-based elected officials and thrived on the patronage these offices dispensed.

The key to the role of the boroughs in city government lay in the way politics—not government—was organized in the State—not city—of New York. A glimpse at the state election law reveals that counties are the state's principal units for political organization. As we have noted earlier, the Greater City's borough lines were not coterminous with the state's county lines; there was no Bronx County. This disadvantaged Bronx Democrats; it made them a mere appendage to Manhattan-based Tammany Hall. Bronx County was created in 1914 to fix this situation, establishing complete coterminality between the state's political organization and the city's principal subunits.

To this day there have never been citywide political organizations in Greater New York; politics in the city has always been county based. County bosses in both parties valued the boroughs, protected them, and sought to have important city functions administered by borough presidents. Citywide governmental organization required the borough-based political organizations to negotiate with the mayor for patronage and preferment. The mayor had his own friends to reward and his own priorities, and he could gain leeway by arguing for citywide needs and playing one county leader against another (as Al Pacino did in the movie *City Hall*). In contrast, borough-centered government and employment created opportunities for heads of county political organizations to directly influence the distribution of jobs and contracts.

Functional Regionalism and Recentralization of Power

Well into the 1930s, former governor Alfred E. Smith, Samuel Seabury, and other reformers denounced the borough system as wasteful and unnecessary, the result of a pure political deal. But by then the boroughs were entrenched in New Yorkers' hearts and minds; their removal was politically impossible. Therefore, efforts to restructure city government focused on shifting *functions* to mayoral control, while leaving borough *structures* in place. As a result of the Thatcher Commission recommendations in 1936, borough presidents were removed from the board of aldermen (later the city council), and some of their responsibilities were shifted to a citywide public works department and the city's planning commission. Twenty-five years later the Cahill Commission recommended and the voters accepted charter changes that took responsibility for streets, highways, sewers, and assessments for local improvements from the boroughs and gave it to citywide agencies.

Attempts to reverse these changes in 1975 failed, and further devitalization of the boroughs as community governments within the city soon followed. Although bereft of virtually all their responsibilities as submayors, borough presidents still had substantial influence in city governance as members of the eight-person Board of Estimate formed in 1901. Over the history of the Greater City, this board gained considerable budgeting, land-use, franchising, and contracting authority, in addition to control over acquiring and selling city property. Each of the three citywide elected officials—the mayor, the comptroller, and the city council president—had two votes on the Board of Estimate, and each borough president had one vote. By acting together to leverage their power, the borough presidents could moderate citywide policies that had impacts in their jurisdictions.

Eventually this power, too, was taken away from the borough presidents by a successful legal challenge. In the 1989 case of *Morris* v. *Board of Estimate*, the U.S. Supreme Court upheld the claim by the New York Civil Liberties Union and others that some citizens of the city were unequally represented on the board. The board was found to be, in effect, a "legislative body" in which residents of Staten Island, with 379,000 people, had the same representation as those of Brooklyn, with a population of 2,301,000. This, the Court said, violated its one person–one vote apportionment standard.[25]

After considering a range of options, a New York City charter commission appointed by Mayor Edward I. Koch and chaired by Fritz Schwarz decided that the only way to comply with the Supreme Court's decision and avoid new problems under the Federal Voting Rights Act was to abolish the Board of Estimate in the new city charter they had been preparing in anticipation of the *Morris* decision. Thus the last sphere of influence for borough presidents in citywide government was removed. Although these offices remained in the new charter, they were left with few significant functions.

The drafters of the 1989 charter might have tried to abolish the borough presidencies entirely, but they did not. Instead they left the borough presidents where they began in 1897, with a title, a salary, and an advocate's role, but precious little real governmental work to do. Each borough president is paid $114,000 a year; collectively their offices cost the city $32.5 million in 1996 and employed 442 people. Under the city charter now in force, they have authority to appoint members to community boards, the Board of Education, and the City Planning Commission; preside over the borough boards; have some say in the siting of public facilities; and play a small role in capital and expense budgeting.[26]

In opposing abolition of the Board of Estimate, Howard Golden, Brooklyn borough president since 1977, argued that without the power that board membership gave it, his office would become a "vestigial organ."[27] Golden was right: the resiliency of the boroughs preserved them as *structures* into the 1990s, but the triumph of functional regionalism left them largely bereft of consequential governmental *functions*.

A few years later, when the question of the continuation of Staten Island as part of New York City was put to a referendum there (see chapter 4), Golden urged that the state legislature create a commission on borough governance. Finding ways to empower the borough presidents, he argued, was one means to moderate the centrifugal forces pulling the city apart. Mayor David Dinkins was unenthusiastic and so was City Council Speaker Peter Vallone. The idea was a nonstarter.[28]

One attempt to reempower the borough presidents was a mid-1990s proposal for a state law that would create, and give them control over, borough-based industrial development agencies (IDAs). Operating citywide within New York City and at the county level elsewhere in the state, IDAs offered tax and other incentives to attract business and jobs. The idea was first advanced by Bronx Borough President Fernando Ferrer, who argued that the citywide IDA in place since 1974 had neglected his borough. Strongly opposed by Mayor Giuliani, a law creating these agencies under the borough presidents' control (and leaving the city's chief executive with only veto power over their decisions) passed both houses of the state legislature in 1996. But then it was vetoed by Governor George Pataki, who feared competition between boroughs that might result in "a bidding war for projects that could escalate the size of tax exemption packages to the detriment of the city's and state's budgets."[29]

The assembly sponsor of the borough IDA legislation, Roberto Ramirez of the Bronx, characterized the governor's veto as partisan. He and Ferrer were Democrats; Giuliani and Pataki were Republicans. But in fact it was one more example of the contest in the Greater City between centralizers and decentralizers, with the chief executive at the center of the state's government supporting the chief executive at the center of the city's government.

As the consolidated city approached its centennial, the borough presidents behaved far less like people with power and more like people trying to influence the powerful. Their tools were lawsuits and press conferences, not votes and decisions. In 1993 Fernando Ferrer sued the city to pressure it to fill potholes and clean up the main thoroughfares in the Bronx. In 1994 Ruth Messinger of Manhattan had difficulty getting Mayor Giuliani just to allow his commissioners to attend her borough board's hearings to answer questions about the preliminary budget. In 1996 Claire Schulman attributed the designation of the Flushing Town Hall in Queens as an official city "cultural institution" not to her power as borough president but to her capacity to "badger the hell out of the city."[30]

Finally, Guy Molinari, the Staten Island borough president, showed what he thought about the office in 1995 when he ran against the incumbent Democratic district attorney in his county (Richmond County) in order to escape it. He was after a job with real power (and because the terms of the two offices overlapped, he did not have much to risk). Molinari lost and remained in the Staten Island borough presidency.

Professor Mitchell Moss of New York University has called the borough presidency a "junior varsity for up-and-coming politicians."[31] He is right: the primary function of the five borough presidencies in New York City today is political, not governmental. These offices are an intermediate rung on the ladder of political succession, allowing ambitious politicians to develop visibility and support for a potential run for citywide or other higher office. Both Robert F. Wagner and David Dinkins served as Manhattan borough president before becoming mayor. Ruth Messinger, Rudy Giuliani's Democratic opponent for mayor in 1997, had also served as Manhattan borough president. Fernando Ferrer, one of her early rivals for the nomination, continued as the borough president of the Bronx.

Borough presidents defend their role as a voice for New York City's communities in the larger city government. "There is a need to have some central person who is local," former Manhattan borough president Percy Sutton has remarked, "to plead the interests of the citizens in that borough." But this presumes that each borough constitutes a community with a consistent interest, and that is just not so. It cannot be—because, as Sutton also notes, the smallest borough in population is bigger than most cities in the United States.[32] If Staten Island had become a city, it would be the second largest in the state and the fortieth largest in the country. (See chapter 4.)

Recentralization of the Schools

New York City conducted community school board elections in May 1996. Two weeks after the vote, the results of the complex, proportional representation voting system (employing a paper ballot) were still unknown. As usual, voter participation was minuscule. This allowed powerful interest groups (teachers' unions and local and church-based organizations) to dominate the process. Despite the formal separation of education from the rest of city government, local political organizations also were drawn in. As Vito Lopez, a Brooklyn assemblyman whose political organization fielded a school board slate, explained in the *New York Times*: "The local school boards have more patronage than any political club in New York City."[33]

As with the boroughs, scandals in local school boards have periodically elicited demands to shift power from community-level elected officials to a more distant central authority. The *New York Times* printed a major exposé on the 1996 community school board elections, spotlighting fiscal mismanagement, corruption, election fraud, nepotism, partisan hiring, drug abuse, and out-and-out theft in ten community districts, all of which depleted already scarce resources needed to educate the city's children.[34] The paper called for reform, but the editors might not have realized that they were taking one side in what educational historian Diane Ravitch calls the "Great School Wars" of New York City. This debate between centralizers and decentralizers—the advocates of efficiency versus those of community—has been ongoing more than a century. "Time and again," Ravitch wrote in her 1974 book of that title, "the central board and local boards [within Greater New York] . . . fought over the power to appoint and dismiss teachers, to procure supplies, to determine salaries, to establish holidays, [and] to control expenditures for repairs, cleaning, building, fuel and every other kind of outlay."[35]

The most recent New York City school debates over decentralization reach back to the late 1960s. With the proportion of minority children in the schools rising, the performance of the city's educational system falling, and racial integration seen as a failed strategy, pressures for decentralization and community control came from several quarters, leading to the creation of the current arrangements. The implicit model was school governance in suburban and rural areas.

In 1968 a commission appointed by Mayor John Lindsay and chaired by Ford Foundation President McGeorge Bundy recommended creation of forty to fifty community school boards with powers over local school personnel and spending.[36] In the year after the report was issued, racially charged confrontations occurred in three special "demonstration" districts funded in part by the Ford Foundation, and teacher strikes closed schools throughout the city twice. Ultimately the state legislature enacted a law creating a system that "had enough protection to satisfy the union, and enough local autonomy to satisfy the minority lawmakers."[37]

Although minorities pressed for community control, it was conservative state legislators from the city—worried far more about protecting community than about achieving equity in service delivery—who were the decisive voting bloc. They signed on because decentralization seemed to offer greater protection of neighborhood schools. Thirty-one local, elected community boards were given substantial authority over all education up to high school, but final control was placed in the hands of a chancellor accountable to a citywide board of education, with members separately appointed by the mayor and the five borough presidents (figure 3-2).

In response to the uproar after the 1996 school elections, three distinct reform plans for the governance of education in New York City were advanced in the state legislature.[38] All reflected the classic century-old clash of values over structuring city government. Centralizers wanted consolidation and control to overcome corruption and achieve greater efficiency. Decentralizers questioned the effectiveness of a citywide school system,

Figure 3-2. *New York City Community School Districts, 1993*

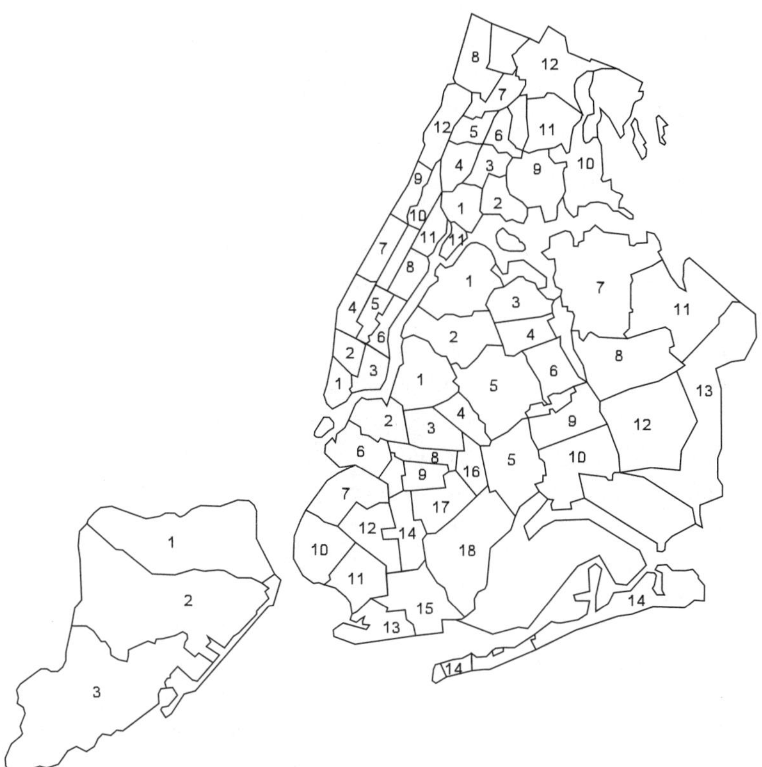

Source: New York City Department of City Planning, *Public Schools by Community District and Community School District by Borough* (1993), p. 2.

and sought greater accountability and responsiveness to parents and communities at the school level.

The Democratic state assembly would have created an elected citywide school board while abolishing the community school districts and giving local power to school-based councils of parents, teachers, and administrators. In contrast, the plan initially offered by Mayor Giuliani and Republican state senator Guy Velella of the Bronx called for elimination of the citywide school board and for mayoral appointment of a city commissioner of education. Additionally, it proposed creation of borough-level school boards and retention of community school boards. Finally, two other outer-borough Republican senators, John Marchi of Staten Island and Frank Padavan of Queens, recommended eliminating the metropolitan level of school governance entirely and replacing it with borough-level school boards. Under their plan, too, community school boards would be retained.

The compromise that was finally forged in a December special session of the legislature recentralized power in the hands of the existing chancellor but without giving the mayor control of the schools.[39] Authority to hire district superintendents was taken from elected community school boards and vested in the chancellor, an appointee of the citywide board. The chancellor also gained greater power to intervene in schools that were not producing acceptable educational results in accordance with state standards.

A historic pattern thus repeated itself. The *New York Times* hailed the outcome editorially as "a triumph for city schools" and praised state and city leaders for "coming together on a contentious, highly politicized issue, and producing an important and useful agreement."[40] Yet it is hard to imagine such an outcome, so damaging for local communities, resulting from reform efforts that focused on suburban rather than city schools. Would the state pass a law requiring that district school superintendents in Westchester or Long Island be appointed by an expert professional—say, the state commissioner of education or his regional deputy—rather than by the locally elected school board? To ask the question is to answer it. Moreover, experts in education almost immediately expressed reservations about the dissonance between the direction taken by the state—centralization to combat corruption and achieve that classic goal, "removing politics from education"—and the decentralization to the building level that their research said was needed for improving educational outcomes.[41]

Community, Equity, and Community Boards

Urbanologist Louis H. Massotti once observed that "people live in neighborhoods, not cities."[42] Many professional planners use a circle with a quarter-mile radius "as the defining element for a neighborhood."[43] Tony Hiss, one of the coauthors of the Third Regional Plan, estimates that a neighborhood in the city is "about a 15 minute walk wide, everywhere we can get to and bring stuff home from before our feet get too tired."[44] According to the *Encyclopedia of New York City*, "The number of neighborhoods in New York City is impossible to measure precisely but is almost certainly greater than three hundred."[45] By any of these standards, there has never been neighborhood-level government—government, not politics—in New York City.

There was neighborhood-level politics. When metropolitan New York was created a century ago, political party organizations were strong, and connecting ordinary people in the metropolis's neighborhoods to the citywide government was their task. In his widely accepted analysis, historian Samuel P. Hayes explained that Progressive Era municipal reformers, who said they were interested in the good of the city as a whole,

> objected to the structures of government [partisan ward- and district-based elections] which enabled local and particularistic interests to dominate. . . . These particularistic interests were the focus of a decentralized political life. City councilmen were local leaders. They spoke for their local areas, the economic interests of their inhabitants, their residential concerns, their educational, recreational and religious interests—i.e., for those aspects of community life which mattered most to those they represented.[46]

Another classic analysis, by the sociologist Robert Merton, also showed that before government provided public assistance, people got the help they needed through the urban political machines.[47] Relationships were personal, neighbor to neighbor. The clubhouses' hierarchy of district and block captains reached into every street and building of the city, identifying and responding to local needs and, of course, creating obligations that could later be translated into votes. Thus an important reason why community and equity were given less attention in the original structure of metropolitan *government* was that these values were addressed in the structure of metropolitan *politics*.[48] Moreover, for reformers, weakening the hold of these values, not strengthening them, was a primary goal.

The emergence in the 1970s of community-based governance structures paralleled the decline of party organizations in New York City.[49] With the parties decreasingly vital, advocates of community control sought a restructuring of metropolitan government that would advance the values of community and equity. Although they fell short of their most ambitious goals, major changes were made in the organization of city government in the 1970s in response to this movement. But both before and after these changes, the community-based structures within citywide government have not always advanced the interests of the poor or minority groups. Furthermore, community units have never been neighborhood sized. And affluent city neighborhoods have a much greater capacity to protect their interests, similar to that of affluent suburbs in surrounding counties.

As early as 1947, the Citizens Union called for creation of "home town" governments within the metropolis.[50] Community planning councils first appeared in 1951, established by Manhattan borough president Robert Wagner both to enhance neighborhoods and help him build his political base. Later on, charter changes made during Wagner's third term as mayor established sixty-two community planning boards (precursors to the current community boards) throughout the city, with members appointed by the borough presidents.

Shortly thereafter, the federal government's Community Action Program of the mid-1960s (part of Lyndon Johnson's War on Poverty) also attempted to build grassroots political entities in the city, in this case outside the structure of city government. These efforts ultimately foundered because of the opposition of those they sought to bypass, namely, elected political leaders. Mayor Wagner's Republican successor, John Lindsay, followed with an outreach strategy of his own, gathering information through neighborhood "little City Halls" and urban action task forces that might allow him to respond to needs at the community level. Building on this experience, Lindsay also pursued administrative decentralization by appointing district managers and district service cabinets. Existing community planning district boundaries were used as the basis for this approach to coordinating city services, which was initially tested in eight demonstration districts. Linkage to the city government was through the special Office of Neighborhood Government at city hall.

The boroughs, bastions of the diminished but still extant Democratic Party organizations, were at first left out of the loop. Then Lindsay issued an executive order in 1973 adding city council members and borough presidents to his district service cabinets.[51] Democrats saw these initiatives as a way for the Republican mayor to use city resources to build a political base in the neighborhoods; hence they resisted them. So did some centralized bureaucracies in city government, although, interestingly, not those agencies (such as fire and police) that were already organized on a decentralized basis for service delivery.

The point man for the Democratic opposition was City Comptroller Abraham Beame. When he became the next mayor, the Lindsay system was dropped. According to one observer, under Beame administrative decentralization was turned into another source of party patronage.[52]

Meanwhile, in Albany the legislature created a charter commission chaired by Republican state senator Roy Goodman and charged with enhancing citizen involvement in city government and assuring effective local self-government. It considered but rejected both returning power to the borough presidents and a radical shift of focus of New York City government to the neighborhood level. Instead, it proposed coterminous local service delivery cabinets, based on the Lindsay model. Under its plan district managers were to be selected by community boards appointed by the borough presidents (not the mayor) and given enhanced power to advise on budgetary and land-use matters. This proposal was adopted by the city's voters in 1975.

Two decades later Robert Pecorella of St. John's University concluded that the charter changes of 1975 were moderately successful.[53] In the critical area of land use, where decisions define the look and feel of neighborhoods and vastly affect the quality of life within them, Pecorella shows that community boards have won concessions from developers. They have, he writes, "made it more difficult to alter fundamentally the character of city neighborhoods without extensive and public consideration of proposed changes." But these boards did not bring a higher degree of equity to city government. Pecorella found that "the better functioning boards represent middle class community districts, while the weaker boards were in the poorer communities."[54]

In her study of the North River Water Pollution Control Plant in West Harlem, Vernice Miller argued that if residents of that neighborhood had more control over land use in their local area, they might never have ended up with this plant.[55] Similarly, research by Richard Rodgers showed more generally that lower-income neighborhoods tended to receive a greater share of "negative facilities," such as trash incinerators, while "positive facilities," such as police stations and libraries, were concentrated in wealthier neighborhoods.[56]

In an attempt to implement provisions of the 1989 charter that sought to bring greater equity to land-use decisionmaking, the mayor and the city planning commission adopted in 1991 a set of administrative guidelines for facility siting called the "fair share criteria." Acting under these, the Dinkins administration then tried to close several large homeless shelters and open twenty-four smaller ones distributed throughout the city. The plan immediately ran into trouble. Residents of white, middle-class neighborhoods moved to block attempts to locate shelters in their areas. Ultimately the administration was forced to abandon its plan.[57]

Consolidationists argue that regionalism is desirable not only for the sake of equity but also on account of the greater efficiency it achieves. Yet here again the New York City experience raises questions. Whatever his or her role or responsibility, it is hard to imagine that any participant in the city's Byzantine land-use decisionmaking process—which seeks to square metropolitan and community-based values and needs—would describe it as "efficient."[58] The viewpoint of Donald Trump, one of the city's most famous developers, is typical: "You go through so many groups, and everybody takes a slice. It would be nice if it could somehow be consolidated, so that there is one bite out of the apple, instead of three or four or five or six."[59]

Vernice Miller also challenges the efficiency of the results of citywide (that is, regional) land-use decisionmaking in her case study of West Harlem.[60] She argues that the pollution control plant was sited in this African American neighborhood not because it had the best location—other, more efficient locations had been identified—but because residents in areas that did not want the plant had the power to stop it. To get *any* plant, the city had to pick a less efficient location.

Conclusion: Metropolitanism Subsumes Localism

The values promoted at the creation of modern metropolitan New York one hundred years ago were remarkably similar to those championed by regionalists in the 1990s: efficiency in government, competitiveness, equity, and community. Of these, efficiency and community were most important a century ago. Competitiveness arguments were crucial in justifying the creation of Greater New York, but they were less important in ongoing debates over internal governance, once the metropolis was established. Early equity concerns centered on the fair distribution of the metropolis's resources among its boroughs and neighborhoods; not until later did the differential treatment of races or classes within the city become a central element in public debates about governance. But over the entire hundred-year history of the Greater City, choices concerning the structure of government repeatedly necessitated balancing the requirements of efficiency with the need for localism and local control—that is, community.

Centralizers advocated economy, efficiency, professionalism, and mayoral authority. They struggled against decentralizers, who were advocates for community, for the prerogatives of borough- and assembly district-based political party organizations and for the power of locally elected officials. Each side's goal was to organize the Greater City's government to its own advantage.

The centralizers wanted "one big city," hierarchically organized and run largely by the "best men," credentialed professionals accountable to the mayor in city hall. The decentralizers focused on the boroughs: first on their creation, then on their empowerment, then on the retention of their elected offices and operating functions, and finally (after decades of erosion) on the preservation of their remaining role in central city governance.

As the boroughs grew in population and declined in functional power, and as political parties atrophied, other structures were sought to address the need for community in city government. Mindful of how suburbs seemed to be governed, decentralizers tried to create and empower new local institutions within the city—the community boards and community school boards. In the 1960s and 1970s, centralizers gave ground, but grudgingly and in a limited way. The resulting community-based entities, bigger in population than most other local governments in the region, have operated with decidedly mixed success. Certainly they have not provided within the city the kind of local government that suburbanites take for granted, nor have they achieved greater equity between classes and races.

Over time, the centralizers in the Greater City have mostly had their way. Abolition of the Board of Estimate and recentralization of control over the city's schools were recent victories for them. However, efforts to disassemble the Greater City, such as the Staten Island secession movement (discussed in chapter 4), and similar proposals for Queens and Brooklyn, suggest that the decentralizing impulse in the metropolis is still alive.

From this review of the New York City experience, two clear, general lessons emerge for the "new metropolitanist" school of regionalists:

—Creating a metropolis does not automatically reconcile the core values that regionalists seek to advance. Even when a city without suburbs is created, there is an ongoing need to balance these values. The establishment of one big government in New York City simply changed the *locus* of conflict: issues that once pitted the city against its outlying areas now generate confrontations within the Greater City itself.

—Creating a metropolis is likely over time to downgrade, not advance, community as a value without necessarily achieving the equity that modern regionalists seek. In the case of New York City, the economic imbalance between the city and its wealthy suburbs reflects the problems involved in more fully incorporating equity as a value in organizing the political structures of the metropolis.

In New York some would promote community by deconstructing the city. The real challenge, however, is to find ways to simultaneously preserve the metropolis while creating real community-based local government within it. This is the problem that we next attempt to address.

CHAPTER FOUR

Creating Real Local Government in New York City

To regard the government of New York as a local government," the noted political scientist Robert Dahl once observed, "is to make nonsense of the term."[1] The city's government was too big, complex, and different, he argued, to be placed in the same class as other localities. Based on what he viewed as a close linkage between smaller size and greater democracy, Dahl proposed making New York a city-state, divided into subunits the same way as states are, thus enhancing opportunities for self-governance. For those familiar with the city's history, Dahl's idea was not new. In the metropolis that has become modern New York, demands for stronger local governmental institutions within the Greater City have emerged with regularity. However, like the city's founders, generations of reformers mostly have sought to weaken localism, not strengthen it.

Boroughs, reluctantly accepted in 1898 by those who wanted "one big city," flourished for a while as powerful subcity entities headed by elected officials but over time lost standing under pressure for centralization of politics and delivery of services. Two types of intermediary entities—community school boards and community boards—were added on to the city's governmental structure in the 1960s and 1970s to meet the demand for small-scale units. However, they also were large (each encompassing many neighborhoods), their powers were limited, and their problems with parochialism and corruption have elicited calls for recentralization.

At the consolidated city's century mark in 1998, it was fair to say that the one-big-city advocates had won. The metropolis they had formed was a centralized government; the boroughs were empty shells. The most recent reforms have kept community school boards in place, but with substantially diminished authority. The community boards have had some successes, but few would characterize them as important centers of subcity governance.

Yet support for more activist local government within the city continues to surface. In focus groups organized by the Port Authority in the mid-1990s as part of its Prospects and Strategies for the Twenty-First Century program, city residents "expressed strong feelings of disenfranchisement from New York City, in the sense that they had little voice in how the city was run." In contrast, one participant from Montclair, New Jersey, said that in this suburban community "you have a voice in the government. They listen to you."[2] On the occasion of the centennial in 1998, John Tierney, writing in the *New York Times*, approvingly revisited a proposal made during Norman Mailer's unsuccessful 1969 mayoral campaign to "give every opportunity to neighborhoods to vote to become townships, villages, hamlets, subboroughs, tracts or small cities."[3] At the same time, Paul Kerson, a Queens lawyer who has been an elected village official in Westchester, suggested that the fifty-nine community boards be transformed into local governments with elected leadership, tax bases, and authority over local services. He urged that regional functions—water supply, highway construction, felony policing, and fire control—be left at the city government level but suggested transferring "public schools, zoning, street maintenance, sanitation and misdemeanor policing . . . to smaller entities."[4]

These are straws in the wind. Two recent movements for structural change in city government offer even more substantial evidence of the desire within the city for local government. The first is the Staten Island secession movement, along with half-serious proposals that arose in its wake to restore the City of Brooklyn to its preconsolidation status and to let Queens go its own way as well. The second development is the creation and expansion of business improvement districts (BIDs) that emerged in the city's commercial neighborhoods during the 1980s. BIDs are community-scale, multifunctional governmental units that are established, financed, and controlled locally. They are not without flaws, but with some restructuring they could provide a model for effective community-level entities.

The "City" of Staten Island

Staten Island leaders advocated separating their borough from New York City and making it an independent city long before the adoption of the 1989 charter, as described below. Many residents regarded their attachment to New York City in the first instance as the result of an unfortunate historical accident.[5] They said they wanted to leave the city because they felt their community was more suburban than urban, more like Nassau and Westchester counties than Brooklyn, Queens, or the Bronx.

The goal of making a city out of Staten Island was ambitious. In fact, villages aside, there have been no general-purpose governments established in New York State for more than half a century.[6] This is not an accident; it has been long-standing state policy to prevent this kind of governmental proliferation. The last city to be created in New York State was Rye (in Westchester County) in 1942.

The effort to make Staten Island a separate city arose in earnest shortly after New York City's Board of Estimate was found unconstitutional, and resulting charter changes left borough presidents without real power in the central city government.[7] With a major effort by John Marchi, Staten Island's long-time Republican state senator, a bill was passed in Albany to allow a referendum on setting up a charter commission to grant Staten Island its independence—but only after an amendment was added that brought the result back to the state legislature for approval before being implemented.[8] The commission was created and produced a new charter for an independent Staten Island, which passed overwhelmingly in a local referendum there. However, the Democratic assembly majority, dominated by members from New York City, was having second thoughts about "the first significant subtraction of territory from a major American city."[9] The city had long been the Democratic party base in state politics. Their reservations were joined by those of the Republican mayor, Rudolph Giuliani, whose narrow first victory in 1993 was made possible in part by overwhelming support from Staten Island.

Even before these second thoughts were voiced, New York City had sued to block the Staten Island breakaway, claiming that the state constitution's home rule provision (much stronger than that in force in Thomas Collier Platt's day, that is, more protective of local power) gave it the right to protect its territorial integrity.[10] The city argued that any state government action altering its boundaries affected its "property, affairs or government" and therefore required a request from the city council. Following the practice in New York of construing home rule provisions narrowly and state powers broadly, the appellate division disagreed. It found that the Staten Island secession legislation dealt with a "matter of state concern" and therefore was constitutional, its impact on local interests notwithstanding.[11] The court allowed the Staten Island secession process to go forward without judging the merits of the matter. In later deciding on a challenge by New York City to the state school aid formula, Judge Levine of the Court of Appeals (the state's highest court) reasserted state supremacy: "Constitutionally as well as a matter of historical fact, municipal corporate bodies—counties, towns, school districts—are merely subdivisions of the State—created by the State for the convenient carrying out of the State's governmental powers and responsibilities as its agents."[12] However, despite the action of the courts, Assembly Speaker Sheldon Silver of Manhattan's Lower East Side effectively killed the Staten Island bill in 1995. Silver obtained a ruling from the assembly's home rule counsel (who reported to him) that this legislation could not be passed without a request from the New York City Council, which, of course, had not been made.

The Staten Island case shows that more than a century after its creation, the issue of the size and boundaries of the consolidated city is not resolved in the minds of many of its citizens. It is interesting that Staten Island's expressed desire to leave the city was echoed in statements by leaders in Brooklyn and Queens. For example, Brooklyn borough president Howard Golden wrote on the eve of the centennial that the occasion was no reason to celebrate: "If consolidation had not taken place . . . continued independence for Brooklyn, Long Island City or Queens and New York would have fostered intense competition among the municipalities, resulting in dynamic economic growth and an even stronger metropolitan region than we have today."[13] Writing in agreement in the *New York Times Magazine*, John Tierney stated that consolidation unavoidably led to Brooklyn's subordination and made its social and economic decline inevitable.[14] But these were just musings. Overall, the lesson is that consolidation unleashes powerful forces for governmental centralization, which diminish the ability of subsumed localities to exit or act on their own.

Business Improvement Districts

In some areas of Greater New York, property owners are levying additional taxes on themselves to finance supplementary, community-based governance structures and services to meet local needs. According to the New York City Office of the Comptroller there are currently 41 business improvement districts (BIDs) in New York City and more are in the planning stage.[15] A report by this office for fiscal year 1997 stated that "BID assessment totaled $46.1 million—$8.3 million more that the combined fiscal year 1997 budgets of the five Borough Presidents and 59 Community Boards."[16]

Building a BID

In the mid-1970s New York State adopted legislation to create four special assessment districts, predecessors to BIDs, to pay for pedestrian malls and other improvements in Queens, Brooklyn, and Manhattan. By this means the state was reinstating a practice, employed in the early days of the consolidated city, of charging the immediately benefiting property owners for capital expenditures. In 1980 all cities in New York State were given authority by the legislature to create BIDs; these were authorized in New York City by a local ordinance in 1982.[17]

To establish a BID, a district plan must describe the geographical area to be covered, the services and types of improvements to be provided, a proposed budget and method for added property tax levies, and the governance arrangement for the BID. This planning process can be initiated by the local government or on petition from a majority of property holders owning more than half the assessed value in the affected area. The Department of Business Services, which oversees the application process, requires evidence of extensive outreach to the affected property owners and commercial tenants.

After hearings by the city council finance committee, a 30-day period is provided by statute to property owners to object to a BID's creation. At least fifty-one percent of the owners of benefited real property within the boundaries of a proposed BID have to file objections with the city clerk's office in order to disapprove it. Proposals to create BIDs along 86th Street in Manhattan and in Greenpoint in Brooklyn were blocked in this manner in 1997. Mayoral approval and a subsequent sign-off by the state comptroller are required as the final steps in creating a BID.

Once a BID is created, participation is mandatory for all property owners in the area. For some of them, receiving a tax bill including a BID assessment turned out to be a rude awakening. Some property owners protested that they did not learn about a proposed BID in time to object to its creation; this led in 1997 to a proposal by the city council's Committee on Finance that an affirmative approval of at least 60 percent of the owners of benefited property be required to create a BID.[18] This would be a big change, putting pressure on proponents to gather wide support in the neighborhood rather than on opponents to defeat it.

BIDs are paid for by additions to the property tax collected by the city's Department of Finance and paid out by the Department of Business Services to the BID. Large-scale property owners bear the bulk of the cost, but these charges may be passed on to renters through the provisions of commercial leases. Elected city officials are represented on BID boards and in most cases so are the officials of community boards. Voting rights in BIDs, however, are based on ownership, which is not the case, of course, for municipal corporations.

BIDs are not unique to New York. A 1999 report by Jerry Mitchell of Baruch College identified 404 BIDs nationally and noted further that "since new BIDs are created all the time the population of BIDs may have changed as this research was ongoing."[19]

In addition to BIDs in commercial areas, the number of private *residential* communities across the United States performing local government services is also burgeoning. According to Robert J. Dilger, there were 150,000 residential community associations in the United States performing government-like functions in the late 1980s, "straining the distinction that normally exists between public and private associations."[20] He reported that the Community Association Institute expected 250,000 such "privatopias" to be created by the year 2000 with 50 million people living inside their jurisdictions.

Community versus Equity

As with the debate over community school boards, the rise of BIDs produced tension between the values of community and equity. Opponents criticize citizenship based on ownership; they see serious equity issues raised by basing the level of services on an area's willingness to pay more taxes. Business improvement districts, it is argued, balkanize the city: not only do richer areas get better services as a result, but they can maintain these services from their own resources even in times of austerity when the overall city budget is being reduced. People who hold this view maintain that even if there is equity in the distribution of citywide resources (and this, of course, is not always the case), neighborhoods without BIDs—typically in poorer areas of the city—are likely to suffer.

BIDs in the city do more than augment traditional public services. Some have borrowed money to finance capital improvements; others have built parking facilities and offered neighborhood tours to attract shoppers, as well as paying for advertising and promotion to generate business activity. The Times Square BID runs the annual New York City New Year's Eve celebration and sponsors other events. It led the efforts to rid the area of three-card-monte dealers and was among the leading organizations promoting reinvigoration of the "Great White Way." BIDs do research and planning for community reconstruction and engage in advocacy vis-à-vis the city on such matters as code enforcement, redevelopment, and zoning issues. In sum, they provide property owners with a focus for joint action on common concerns.

Public officials, strained for cash and interested in getting help to promote economic development, often welcome the work BIDs do but worry about their governance. In 1998 both the city and private businesses drew back from contracts with the Grand Central Partnership to provide outreach and social programs after widespread publicity was given to allegations that the partnership's workers were roughing up homeless people to get them to move out of the area. The partnership also got a black eye in the press for the high salaries paid to its top employees. A 1997 report by the city council's finance committee concluded that BIDs could do better at measuring performance and member satisfaction and criticized their administrative practices. An additional issue was that BIDs, once established, go on forever. The finance committee's proposed legislative remedy was to require a 60 percent level of approval by property owners every five years, that is, when a BID's contract with the Department of Business Services is up for renewal.[21]

Despite these concerns, many people are impressed by BIDs. Finance Committee Chair Herbert Berman, who sponsored the 1997 city council study, told the *New York Times* that although he was concerned about the accountability issue, "BIDs are a significant reality, especially at a time of fiscal restraint. I've always encouraged them. A majority do an effective job in an honest way."[22] Defenders of BIDs cite their voluntary nature, exemplification of local control, roots in private initiative, and the freedom they embody from bureaucracy and process-style regulations. BIDs in the city, they claim, have made many business areas cleaner, safer, and more fun to work in and visit. The beneficiaries have been not only property owners but people who use the streets, parks, and other public spaces. "We control money, we get things done, and we are outside of democratic oversight and accountability," the head of one New York City BID told a reporter.[23] BIDs are not bound by civil service rules or city bureaucratic processes; their capacity to act relatively quickly is highly prized.

BIDs as Real Local Governments

Business improvement districts do bring local government to neighborhoods. They are not confined to a single function; although constrained by law in what they can do, BIDs are in some ways like suburban or rural villages. Once statutory minimum standards for their creation are achieved, their authority reaches all who live within their boundaries. (See chapter 8.) BIDs, like villages, raise their own money through property tax levies and provide their services as additions to what other local governments serving the same people and places provide. As with villages the governance of BIDs is by boards; however, in BIDs a majority of board members are elected by property owners (and in some cases by commercial and residential tenants) in the district. In addition, some city government officials serving as BID board members are appointed by elected city officials.

The fact that BIDs have provoked attempts from the center to limit and control them is undoubtedly a sign of their vitality as instruments of local governance in New York City. In the spring of 1998, in another round in the struggle between centralizers and decentralizers in city government, Mayor Rudolph Giuliani's office announced that "all [BID] activities and initiatives must be discussed with the Department of Business Services at the first opportunity and prior to their development." The mayor, who had previously been a booster of business improvement districts, now dismissed them as an approach for a "different time, when the city wasn't functioning as well." In reaction some BID board members suggested that they might go out of business rather than accept being treated like a "subagency of city government."[24] This time the *New York Times* spoke up for BIDs.[25] "Smothering the BID's with a blanket of new bureaucracy," the paper editorialized, was a "strange and unwelcome" stance for a mayor who "preaches the gospel of lean government, privatization and keeping power and responsibility as close to the grassroots as possible."[26]

Suggested Agenda for a New Charter Commission

Ever since the creation of Greater New York, residents have debated the structural issues presented by centralizers and decentralizers. Despite the persistent desire for meaningful local government within the city, power has increasingly been concentrated in the center. The boroughs and other board structures that do exist are the enervated remains of failed attempts to include community as a value in the governance of the metropolis. The lesson suggested by our analysis is that if the community value is to be incorporated into the structure of city government, then consideration must be given to replacing these residual institutions—not just adding on new ones. By doing this—replacing the old with the new—the blocking power of vested interests is avoided. So long as old structures remain, their existence is a psychological barrier to the success of new and more viable alternatives suited to current conditions and needs.

Changes such as the replacement of the boroughs by town government within New York City (as discussed below) could be achieved by amending the city charter. The charter commission, created by either state or local initiative, is the mechanism provided in state law for restructuring city governments in New York State. Five such commissions have operated in New York City since World War II, four appointed by the mayor and one by the governor.[27] At the city level, a commission to propose such changes may be created either by the mayor or the city council.[28] Charter commissions created by the mayor are limited by law to fifteen members appointed by the mayor. For commissions created by the city council, the size of the commissions is defined by the council, and the commission may include elected officials as members. The council also has the option under state law to ask voters whether they want to create a charter commission. Calling such a referendum is a way of testing whether there is support for this top-level political attention to designing new forms of local government for the city.

Ideally, the mayor and council should take the lead in advocating new forms of local government in the city, but even if they do not act, change is possible. The governor may take leadership, as Nelson Rockefeller did when he appointed the Goodman Charter Commission in 1972. But even without an initiative from the top, state law allows holding a referendum on the creation of local charter commissions. Citizens may petition for submission of such a referendum to the electorate.[29] A referendum advanced in this way can include the names of the persons to serve on the commission. Although it would be unusual, naming potential members in advance might demonstrate seriousness of purpose and provide assurance of the legitimacy of the reform effort. Under this procedure, support from a majority who vote on the question at referendum launches the reform process.

To be successful, history suggests that such a group must be composed of prominent citizens widely representative of the city's diversity and be broadly consultative with leaders and groups throughout the city, both within and outside of city government. Establishing a new charter commission now could bring fresh ideas and the highest level of attention to the ways in which the delicate balance between regionalism and community could be recalibrated in New York City. A good way to dramatize the role of such a commission would be to charter it with the proposition suggested by our review of the governance history of the city, namely, that the boroughs have become vestigial and should be eliminated. With this as a high-visibility starting point, a charter commission could then consider recommendations for the creation of new alternative structures of local governance within the "one great city."

Once created, a new charter commission would need considerable time and resources to do its work. Public hearings would be required, and a range of alternatives would have to be developed concerning not only structural questions, but also the responsibilities of new local entities, the resources they would need to fulfill them, and the way those resources would be obtained and distributed. The process would have to be informed by studies of the history of local governing arrangements in New York City and perhaps also of approaches used in other cities. Below we present eight agenda items that such a new charter commission could consider. These suggestions are not meant as a program of change; rather they are advanced to indicate the kinds of changes that a charter commission could consider. In short, the purpose of our analysis of the history and character of local government in New York City is to suggest a process, not a program, for change.

ABOLISH THE BOROUGHS. The proposition that could dramatize the work of a new charter commission is that boroughs no longer have substantial governmental functions but still take up institutional space. They are too big and unequal to provide genuine and effective local governance in the city. Although they are political bases for midlevel elected officials, there are other offices that could perform this function in a reconstructed city government. Boroughs as counties could continue for state purposes. This would preserve their place names, much as town or village names within the city have been preserved as neighborhood names even after they were abolished.[30]

ABOLISH THE COMMUNITY BOARDS. The role of community boards also has become limited. Their influence is unevenly distributed, both functionally and geographically, and they are fundamentally hampered by a lack of rootedness in cohesive communities.

ABOLISH THE COMMUNITY SCHOOL BOARDS. Likewise, the standing and viability of community school boards have been undermined. Corruption scandals and the patronage practices of school bureaucracies have caused wide resentment and undermined their legitimacy. Recent proposals for recentralizing education have further devitalized community school governance. The school election process is hopelessly complex and as presently constituted undermines local democracy.

CREATE TOWNS WITHIN THE CITY. This is the most far-reaching agenda item that we suggest for a charter commission. Many issues would be raised about creating new towns-in-towns—boundaries, functions, and finances. As in Connecticut and New Jersey (but not suburban New York), the same boundaries could be used for education and for general-purpose governmental services. Such a combination of responsibilities within the same boundaries would make local government within the city more important and more visible.

The boundary-setting function is a sensitive, crucial, and difficult one; once established, boundaries are the key to shaping communities and creating a sense of community responsibility. Town boundaries could be established by a bipartisan commission constituted in the same manner as currently for the apportionment of city council districts. Appointment to this boundary-setting commission could be by the mayor from lists supplied by the two major party caucuses in the city council. Like the Districting Commission, its mission would be "to the extent practicable . . . [to] . . . keep intact neighborhoods and communities with established ties of common interest or association, whether historical, racial, economic, ethnic, religious or other."[31]

The boards of the new towns could be elected, and they could then choose their presiding officer. Partisan election with nomination by the methods currently prescribed in New York law could be employed for town boards, with nonpartisan election for school boards (see discussion of these below) as is the case now in New York State outside New York City. Doing this would make town politics a launching point for political careers in the city, just as it is for such careers in suburban and rural areas.[32]

The boards could assume the current functions of both boroughs and community boards, including those involving capital and expense budgeting and land use. Boards could have the power to hold hearings, assess needs, review the performance of the city government within town boundaries, and make recommendations to the mayor and city council for policy and administrative changes. A chief executive for each town could be appointed by the mayor with the advice and consent of the town board. This person could function both as a town manager in overseeing town government operations and as a liaison with the city government.

Towns need not have taxing authority; the city government could provide funds for town governments on a formula basis. This could be done in part by using money recaptured as a consequence of replacing boroughs and community boards. (Borough office operations alone now cost the city over $32.5 million a year.) A charter commission could suggest a level of funding for town government, and towns might be empowered to seek governmental or even nongovernmental funds from other sources, including state grants and contracts. Representatives from each town could meet annually at a council of towns that could act in an advisory capacity, communicating formally with the mayor and the city council to assist in the preparation of the city's capital and expense budgets.

USE THE SAME TOWN-SIZED DISTRICTS FOR SCHOOL GOVERNANCE. The most conspicuous failure of local government nationally and in New York City is school governance. The clash and clang over education budgets and basics can be viewed charitably as democratic government dealing with difficult, emotional, and immensely controversial issues. But even with a democracy discount, school governance needs to clean up its act. Within New York City, recent recentralization changes in response to corruption and scandals are under way as we write, and there have been major changes nationally as other large cities have placed school systems under direct control of the elected chief executive. Here are three ideas that might be considered by a new charter commission trying to balance efficiency and democracy in school reform in New York City:

—Achievement of greater strength and accountability at the center requires involvement of local citizens in school governance. This could happen through elected town boards or specially elected local school committees. A charter commission might consider allocating a specific portion of school resources to such local groups for program enhancements, using a formula that gives consideration to the social and economic needs of a given school district.

—In creating new structures for town-based or other involvement in school governance, it could be stipulated that town-level school committee elections (as distinct from elections for the town board) be nonpartisan.

—A charter commission could also address the widely acknowledged need for politically insulated school elections. Candidates for town-level school boards could be vetted by selection-review panels whose criteria, though not strict, could include demonstrated participation in school affairs, familiarity with school finance and policy matters, and experience in government or civic life.

ENCOURAGE FURTHER DEVELOPMENT OF BIDS IN BUSINESS NEIGHBORHOODS, BUT DEFINE THEIR ROLE MORE CLEARLY TO ENSURE ACCOUNTABILITY. To increase accountability by BIDs, a charter commission could require that a referendum be adopted every five or ten years to reaffirm participants' commitment to a BID and its operations.

CONSIDER CREATION, ON A VOLUNTARY BASIS, OF ENTITIES LIKE SUBURBAN VILLAGES IN RESIDENTIAL NEIGHBORHOODS. "Queens is made up of a lot of small villages" according to New York City Council Speaker Peter F. Vallone (who himself is a resident of Astoria, an actual village in the nineteenth century). "It's like everyone is from a small town, where everybody knows everybody."[33] A new charter commission for New York City could invent entities that on a voluntary basis could give neighborhoods opportunities to undertake special projects for their area. An interesting way of thinking about this is as an analog to BIDs but for residential areas. They might actually be called neighborhood initiative districts, or they could be described as villages, which have a more formal legal status.

Approval by a majority of voters within defined boundaries could be required to create a village or a neighborhood initiative district; revenue could be raised by a supplementary property tax levy (collected by the city) that would be obligatory but could not exceed a ceiling set in law. A ten-year reaffirming referendum could be required. Neighborhood-level entities along the lines suggested need not be direct service providers. With available, though limited, resources, they could be authorized to contract with the city government or with public, private, or nonprofit providers for augmented service levels.

Of course, the creation of such entities raises very important equity questions. One obvious concern would be that citizens in richer neighborhoods in the city might adopt additional taxes, while those less affluent would not or could not do so. More affluent places might then augment services, creating even greater distance between haves and have-nots. Another concern is that the creation of such entities in New York might contribute to balkanization and increase racial and ethnic tensions.

There are, however, counters to these arguments. Neighborhood entities would more likely be created in less affluent neighborhoods, where many people are renters and therefore do not pay property taxes directly. The powers and resources of these neighborhood entities could be set forth in legislation, with oversight responsibility assigned to the appropriate city government agency. Unlike villages outside the city, urban villages could be precluded from having a say in land-use decisionmaking. A 1999 report indicated that the multiplicity of new immigrant groups and their settlement throughout the city have made them "fractured and dispersed . . . [and] . . . more difficult to unite into political movements."[34] The creation of new neighborhood entities could provide governmental experience and political bases for leaders of these groups that are not available now, enhancing their access to positions of influence in citywide government and politics.

RECOGNIZE NEW TOWN BOUNDARIES IN APPORTIONMENT OF CITY COUNCIL DISTRICTS. In theory communities within the city would be strengthened the most if city council members were elected from districts coterminous with the towns.[35] In an era of term limits for the city council, this would increase the chance that some council members would return to local elective office in towns after serving eight years at the citywide level. They would bring their experience back into the community, to its benefit and that of the city as a whole. Such an arrangement would also provide a training ground for future city council candidates. However, as a practical matter, one person–one vote requirements probably preclude a city council based strictly on town lines: town boundaries would have to be enduring, whereas council district lines must be changed with every decennial census. Once towns are created, however, it should be possible to modify the charter to require consideration of town lines when delineating districts for council members.

CHAPTER FIVE

The Limits of Metropolitanism

New York City was the nation's first great metropolitan experiment. At its birth in 1898, the Greater City contained over 90 percent of the population of its region as then defined.[1] New York was America's great metropolis before the U.S. Census Bureau first reported data on metropolitan districts in 1910; before planners started to think about metropolitan regions in the 1920s; before social scientists began writing about metropolitan reform in the 1930s; and before the push for metropolitan government came with the burgeoning suburbanization of the post–World War II period.[2] Still today in this same spirit, many advocates of regional reforms seek one big government over a socially and economically integrated region in order to achieve the regional values of equity, efficiency, and competitiveness while preserving community. The previous chapter examined how the value of community was sacrificed in the creation and development of New York City government. But how have the values of equity, efficiency, and competitiveness fared?

New York City has been a metropolis for more than a century, and its experience suggests the need for a healthy dose of skepticism about the ability of regionalism to achieve the goals its advocates seek. As a general matter, the metropolitan model is limited for two reasons. First, in the American political system, metropolitan governments are local and hence inherently constrained in their capacity to serve the values that advocates of regionalism espouse. Second, as regions grow, newly created metropolitan boundaries are as resistant to change as those of the municipalities that anteceded them. In fact, the very creation of the metropolis is likely to establish political conditions that resist its further expansion.

The New York experience also reflects the special difficulties of pursuing metropolitanism in multistate regions. The federal nature of our system is again limiting: integrated, general-purpose metropolitan governments cannot be created across state lines. A regional economy in a multistate region, rather than being an integrating force, necessarily becomes an arena for competition between states for equity—for "fair shares." And while incapable of political and governmental unity, the region remains a source of political division for each of the states that constitute it.

Limitations of Metropolises as Local Governments

The U.S. Constitution is silent on local government; the subject is left entirely to the states. Because metropolitan governments are considered local governments, the law treats them like all other localities. They operate within states, under state-granted charters, with defined and delimited powers; they are the states' legal creatures.[3]

Equity and the Absence of Home Rule

After it was established, Greater New York City, like other localities in New York State, remained subordinate to the state legislature, not sovereign like the state itself. City officials in Greater New York worked for decades, both before and after consolidation, to place home rule powers for local governments in the state constitution, on the theory that this would both empower New York City and restrict state intervention in its affairs. Their efforts came to fruition in the first quarter of the twentieth century through a series of increasingly strong home rule provisions added to the state constitution.[4]

But alas, what was gained in the constitution was lost in the courts: judges gave home rule a legalistic and restrictive definition that allowed, even encouraged, state intervention.[5] State constitutional home rule protections notwithstanding, the legislature, with far more members from outside than within the city, could still keep the metropolis from doing things it wanted to do, force it to do things it didn't want to do, and exact tribute or trade-offs in exchange for fulfilling the myriad city needs that could be met only through changes in state law.

The power of the state legislature over the governance of New York City was dramatically demonstrated to its residents in 1997. The Republican majority leader of the state senate, Joseph Bruno (whose district is in the Albany suburbs), proposed eliminating the system of rent regulation in New York City that had been in place since shortly after World War II. This precipitated a bitter struggle that dominated virtually the entire legislative session. Proponents of a return to an unregulated residential real estate market argued that regulation subsidized the rich and that deregulation was essential to the economic health of the city. Opponents argued that continued regulation was the only way to ensure that middle- and working-class people could continue to afford to live in the city. (The average income of families in rent-stabilized apartments was $30,000; 27 percent lived below the poverty level.)

More than two-thirds of the residents of New York City are renters, and in 1997, 61 percent of the rental apartments in Manhattan, 54 percent in the Bronx, 43 percent in Brooklyn and Queens, and 19 percent in Staten Island were rent stabilized. Almost 3 million city dwellers were affected by this debate; in the end their organized resistance ensured that regulation continued under relatively unchanged conditions. But the crucial point for this analysis is that a fundamental question of social policy—equity between classes in the city with respect to the availability of housing, one of the necessities of life—was decided by the state legislature meeting in Albany, not by the city council meeting at city hall. In this example, as in those concerning education, transportation, taxation, and other key policy areas discussed throughout this volume, the metropolitan government could not effectively pursue social equity, a prime goal of modern metropolitanists, because the power to do so lay not with it, but with the state.[6]

Efficiency versus Equity: Great Expectations, Limited Resources

In the late 1980s, well after the 1970s fiscal crisis that led to a contraction of New York City government, James Musselwhite examined the relationships between the twenty biggest cities in the United States and their state governments, with special attention to New York. Musselwhite's analysis considered socioeconomic characteristics, political and institutional relations, and fiscal relationships. He concluded that

> New York City is unique among big cities in the enormous scope of its activities. The City is responsible for the full range of activities carried out by a combination of local governments in most communities and also carries out and finances activities that are normally the responsibility of state government elsewhere. For this reason, New York City government is qualitatively different from big-city government nationally. . . . No other city is in the same class with New York in absolute size or relative importance to its state.[7]

There are two major reasons for the size and scope of government in Greater New York, one general, the other specific. Generally in New York State, where governance is highly decentralized, most public service delivery is through local governments. In most areas there are several local governments—counties, towns, school districts, and special districts—through which the gamut of services is delivered. By contrast, in New York City there is "one big government" through which virtually all these services are provided.

More specifically, Greater New York does more because the metropolis was long regarded as rich and strong enough to have its local government function uniquely as an agent of social mobility and provider for the less advantaged. For example, the city for decades maintained a free system of higher education, developed an extraordinarily extensive network of public hospitals, and invested massively in public housing.

Through the end of World War II and for a decade after, the metropolis continued to contain most of the people and enterprise in the region, and these assumptions about its economic strength—and therefore its capacity for redistribution—proved more or less correct. But then, as Charles Morris noted in 1980, a convergence of factors radically and irreversibly altered the environment: "racial shifts, an aggressive civil rights movement, a revolution in citizens' expectations, newly muscular unions, a collapse of basic managerial capacity, [and] steep and seemingly permanent economic recession."[8]

Nevertheless, captive to its metropolitan heritage and bolstered by state and federal aid, the city continued to spend—and at an accelerated rate. The result was nearly fiscal collapse. According to Morris,

> The city could have afforded service expansion had it resisted the national inflation for common functions and public education. Or if the state had absorbed a much larger share of local welfare or

> Medicaid costs, the new taxes enacted during [Mayor John] Lindsay's term of office would have been enough to finance the increased commitment to hospitals and higher education and to pay for increases in employee compensation. But there was not enough money to pay for cost inflation in the common services, support the disproportionate share for welfare and Medicaid, and increase the commitments to higher education and hospitals all at the same time.[9]

Fifteen years later, in 1996 the Citizens Budget Commission (CBC) compared total local spending in New York City with local government spending in the rest of the nation. It found that the city's spending was higher for all major functional areas except educational services. Overall, local spending for social services and income maintenance absorbed four times the proportion of personal income in the city as elsewhere in the country, and for housing and community development, almost five times as much (table 5-1).

After its creation the Greater City government was viewed as an engine of equity not only in its role as service provider but also as an employer. Upwardly mobile men and women from a succession of ethnic and racial migrations settled in the metropolis and found city employment a stable and secure path into the middle class. In recent decades an added dimension has been aggressive advocacy by public employee unions for advances in wages, benefits, and working conditions and for greater job security.

In the minds of some union leaders and their political allies, the city's role as job provider is primary, its role as service provider being distinctly secondary. In April 1998 Mayor Giuliani proposed laying off 900 hospital workers (most of them lower-income minority group members) for reasons of efficiency. A union leader described this action as "unconscionable" at a time when the city had a $2 billion surplus. The underlying assumption was that it was the job of the city to provide employment when it could afford to do so, efficiency notwithstanding.[10]

Even with costs for education, public welfare, and interest removed, the CBC's research showed that dollars spent by the city as a proportion of personal income exceeded spending by the same measure in other localities by more than two to one.[11] (See table 5-1.) This means that when the city's economic development efforts are deleted from the equation (in the form of interest on debt), when a large portion of the effect of New York State's decentralized service delivery system is removed (welfare),

Table 5-1. *Local Spending in New York City versus Rest of Nation, 1991–92*

Units as indicated

	Expenditures (millions of dollars)		*Expenditures (percent of personal income)*		*Ratio of NYC to other local governments*
	NYC	*Other local governments*[a]	*NYC*	*Other local governments*	
Education services	8,235	220,401	4.29	4.70	0.91
Elementary and secondary education	7,392	204,289	3.85	4.35	0.88
Higher education, libraries, other	843	16,112	0.44	0.34	1.28
Social services and income maintenance	10,486	61,873	5.46	1.32	4.14
Public welfare	6,840	20,668	3.56	0.44	8.09
Health, hospitals, other	3,646	41,205	1.90	0.88	2.16
Transportation and transit	4,575	47,695	2.38	1.02	2.34
Public safety	3,741	49,752	1.95	1.06	1.84
Environmental services	2,008	40,761	1.05	0.87	1.20
Housing and community development	2,445	12,671	1.27	0.27	4.71
Government administration, miscellaneous	4,379	50,714	2.28	1.08	2.11
Interest on general debt	1,697	27,367	0.88	0.58	1.51
Total	37,566	511,234	19.56	10.90	1.80
Total without public welfare and interest	29,029	463,199	15.12	9.87	1.53
Total without elementary and secondary education, public welfare and interest	21,637	258,910	11.27	5.52	2.04
As a percent of total spending	57.6	50.6			

Source: Citizens Budget Commission, *Budget 2000 Project: Restructuring Government Services* (New York: 1966), p. 44. Based on data from Bureau of Census, *Government Finances 1992*, and *Finances of Individual City Governments Having 300,000 Population or More, 1991–92*.

a. Does not include other New York local governments.

and when one of the effects of consolidation is also partly removed (education), the metropolis is still a big spender.

As we have seen, this is partly because the city government does more to meet the goal of equity. However, the metropolis is also a big spender because it costs more for New York City to do the same things that other cities do. One reason is that some things in New York City—energy and rents, for example—are generally more expensive than elsewhere. According to a recent study by Regional Financial Associates, the New York region "had the highest business costs of the hundred largest regions, with a weighted average cost of doing business that was twenty-nine percent above the national average in 1996."[12] Another reason is that the performance of tasks common to all cities—such as repaving roads and maintaining water and sewer systems—is more expensive in New York because of the greater density and sheer complexity of the city's layered infrastructure. However, a third reason is that the political and governmental dynamics of the city and state often increase the cost for labor and for other things the city buys to deliver municipal services.

When the high levels of spending by New York City are looked at over time and compared to spending by other local governments in the tri-state region, the most interesting finding is its *persistence*, even when social and economic change, population shifts, and reallocation of functions are taken into consideration. Data drawn from the U.S. *Census of Governments* show that New York City's share of direct local government spending in the region, with the effects of inflation removed, actually *increased* between 1962 and 1992 (table 5-2). In 1962 New York City accounted for 50.4 percent of all local government spending in the region. In 1992 the city was responsible for 52.5 percent of all local government spending, despite the city's intervening fiscal crisis, with its attendant austerity and downsizing. This is especially significant because the population of the core area (New York City and Hudson County, New Jersey), unlike that of the region as a whole, actually declined during these three decades.

Over a thirty-year period the rate of spending in the metropolis outpaced that of surrounding areas, even with all the growth-induced demand in the suburbs for additional roads, water and sewer systems, and new schools and more teachers. True, the departure from the city of more affluent, educated, mostly white middle-class people and their partial replacement by people who were poorer, less educated, and mostly minority group members significantly increased the demand for local government

Table 5-2. *Direct Local Government Spending, Tri-State Region, 1962 and 1992*

Units as indicated

	1962		*1992*	
	Billions of dollars	*Percent of total*	*Billions of dollars*	*Percent of total*
Core	14.7	53.4	42.3	54.1
NYC	13.9	50.4	41.1	52.5
Suburban rings				
Inner[a]	6.5	23.6	14.5	18.6
Intermediate[b]	5.1	18.5	16.5	21.0
Outer[c]	1.2	4.5	4.9	6.3
Total[d]	27.6[e]	100.0	78.3[e]	100.0

Source: Bureau of the Census, *Census of Governments: Government Finances,* 1962 and 1992.

a. Nassau and Westchester Counties, New York; Bergen, Essex, and Union Counties, New Jersey.

b. Rockland and Suffolk Counties, New York; Mercer, Middlesex, Monmouth, Morris, Passaic, and Somerset Counties, New Jersey; Fairfield and New Haven Counties, Connecticut.

c. Dutchess, Orange, Putnam, Sullivan, and Ulster Counties, New York; Hunterdon, Ocean, Sussex, and Warren Counties, New Jersey; Litchfield County, Connecticut.

d. NYC value added as part of the core.

e. Values greater or less than the sum due to rounding error.

services. But it appears from the New York experience that once created, big metropolitan government sustains itself and makes itself even bigger. As conditions change, it is more likely to seek additional resources than find ways to spend less by either doing less or becoming more efficient.

A look at real per capita spending growth in local government for the region during this period reinforces this point since this is a statistic that is adjusted both for inflation and for population change. Table 5-3 shows spending up 152 percent for the entire region between 1962 and 1992, while in New York City it was up 214 percent. Thus during this period government in the tri-state region's metropolis not only sustained itself relatively well under adverse circumstances but grew faster than all of the surrounding local governments.

Drawing upon personal experience that resonates with that of many New Yorkers, noted urbanologist Jane Jacobs remarked that "anyone who has had to deal with a big-city bureaucracy knows that the idea that bigger is more efficient is laughable."[13] Impressions aside, the question of whether the creation of metropolitan government brings efficiency remains hotly debated among academics. A number of comparative studies suggest that there is no economy of scale with respect to most core municipal services and that governmental consolidation actually may

Table 5-3. *Per Capita Direct General Expenditures by Local Governments, Tri-State Region, 1962 and 1992*
Constant 1992 dollars

	1962	*1992*	*Percent increase*
Core	1755.06	5374.28	206.2
NYC	1788.24	5611.17	213.8
Suburban rings[a]			
Inner	1509.27	3413.79	126.2
Intermediate	1287.52	3460.88	168.9
Outer	1299.62	2702.39	107.9
Mean[b]	1565.14	3944.04	152.0

Source: Bureau of the Census, *Census of Governments: Government Finances,* 1962 and 1992.
a. See the notes to table 5-2 for a list of counties that constitute each of the three suburban rings.
b. Mean for NYC and 26 counties.

lead to increased spending.[14] At the largest scale, at least, the New York experience suggests that "one big government" almost certainly means more expensive government.

Metropolitan New York, long the nation's wealthiest locality, for decades pursued the nation's most redistributive local government policies. But the experience of the past quarter century proved this approach untenable. In the wake of the New York City fiscal crisis of the 1970s, urbanologist Paul Peterson concluded that even in New York, city limits had to be acknowledged and accepted.[15] Although New York City government still remains functionally broad gauged, over time it has become less so as responsibilities have been off-loaded. The subways, for example, were turned over to a public authority (see chapter 7). The state assumed responsibility for a number of city governmental functions, including higher education and operation of the courts, after the city's fiscal crisis in the mid-1970s. Mayor Giuliani's effort to privatize the city hospital system, already turned over to a public corporation, was another attempt to narrow the functional scope of city government.

Metropolitanists forget that even the biggest, most unusual local governments have only local powers and resources and thus have very limited capacity to advance redistributive goals in society. As a local government, New York City relies on authority from the state to generate almost all the revenue it collects. It levies only property tax as a matter of right—and even the level of property taxation is limited by the state constitution. The sales tax, the city personal income tax, and a range of business and transaction taxes are all generally or specifically authorized by state law, often for limited periods of time. And as the repeal in 1999 of the tax on commuters' income earned in New York City illustrates, what the state government gives, the state government can take away.[16]

Historically, the state has used four means to provide New York City with help: direct financial aid, assumption of costs, eased property tax limits, and new authorized taxing authority. However, it has preferred to use the last.[17] New York State's level of local, not state, taxation is the reason that it ranks among the highest states in the nation in combined tax burden. And within the state, the burden of New York City's local taxes is, in the aggregate, the highest; their level and diversity are often cited as one reason for the economic "waning of New York."[18]

Economic Development and Borrowing Limitations

Supporters of the creation of Greater New York intended to use the property wealth of Manhattan to back the borrowing needed to develop the roads, bridges, sewer and water systems, and mass transit that would bring people to the outer boroughs, where property was for sale in abundance. In other words, metropolitanists then wanted to generate economic growth—the same goal that metropolitanists today pursue in the name of competitiveness. However, previous binges of local borrowing had led to inclusion of borrowing limits (linked to total property tax values) in the New York State Constitution. As a general-purpose local government, Greater New York was covered by these limits—in place when it came into being—and ran head-on into them.

As a result of the borrowing frenzy that ensued in anticipation of consolidation, and because pre-existing county debts were counted as obligations of Greater New York after consolidation, the new metropolis found itself extended beyond its constitutional borrowing limits on the day it came into existence. As is frequently the case in New York, a legal fiction was created to remedy this situation. A state constitutional change was adopted in 1899 that allowed the Greater City to exclude county debt from its limit, although existing county liabilities that predated consolidation still had to be honored by the city. Note again that state—not city—action was required to fix the problem.

State constitutional amendments also were needed regularly in the early twentieth century to allow borrowing for major city infrastructure projects, especially the construction of the subways. According to Peter Galie, New York's leading constitutional historian, "Between 1905 and

1908 the city reached its debt limit two or three times, causing suspension of the . . . [subway construction] project."[19] A 1909 amendment allowed exemption of subway and port construction bonds from the limit, but only if they were payable from revenues generated when these projects began to provide services. (As it turned out, this condition could not be met for the level of borrowing needed.) Additional changes were passed in 1927 and 1938 to exempt hundreds of millions in borrowing for subway building from the city's debt limit.

As New York City's population increased, the pressure to build infrastructure to support its growth expanded correspondingly. Because it was a general-purpose local government subject to the state's constitutional borrowing limits, the city could not raise enough money to respond to the range of public infrastructure demands it faced. One response was the creation of a number of special-purpose local authorities to build roads, tunnels, and bridges.[20] More recently, special entities have been created in the city to allow borrowing outside constitutional limits to improve the city's water system and to enable school construction.

The linking of constitutional borrowing limits to average aggregate property tax values became a major concern in New York City in 1997. When property values throughout the city dropped during the recession of the late 1980s and early 1990s, a dramatic reduction in the cap on borrowing followed. Calculated from the average of real property values in the city in the previous five years, the cap went from $55 billion to $32 billion. This drop threatened the city's capacity to obtain the funds needed for its $14 billion capital plan.

Experts agreed that the constitutional limit was unrealistic; its calculation on the basis of property values was based on the outdated, nineteenth-century assumption that the property tax was the city's sole source of discretionary revenue. Consensus on this point provided a supportive context for Mayor Rudolph Giuliani's proposed remedy: the creation of a public authority under his control to borrow for the city in a way that bypassed the constitutional limit. Legislation was passed in February 1997 creating the New York City Transitional Finance Authority under mayoral control, with a life of four years and $7.5 billion in temporary borrowing capacity.[21]

The important general lesson is that though metropolitan governments may be created to advance economic development (that is, competitiveness), the capital financing constraints on all local governments apply to them and limit their capacity to fulfill this goal. New York City's general debt service expenditures doubled between 1984 and 1995.[22] According to New York State Comptroller Carl McCall, by the year 2002 nearly one of every five dollars spent by New York City will go for debt service; yet studies show that many capital needs in the city go unmet.[23] Designed as a general-purpose regional government, the consolidated City of New York has lacked the wherewithal, from the day it took its first breath and ever since, to pay for the sort of major capital items necessary for economic development within its boundaries.

Localities are not sovereign: state constitutions and legislatures limit them, and their governmental powers and fiscal resources are constrained. Thus they are redistributive at their peril. Creation of a metropolis brings with it great expectations; however, as the New York experience shows, these cannot be met by what is, after all, merely a local government. And as the New York experience also demonstrates, trying to fulfill these expectations is very likely to get metropolitan government into big trouble. Ironically, as the Greater City surpasses its 100-year anniversary, both the city and the state continue to struggle together to make New York in fact what it is in law: not some broad-reaching entity but a local government—a city—with a more narrowly defined and affordable range of functions.

Rigidity of Newly Created Metropolitan Boundaries

The New York experience suggests that successful metropolitan reform may generate obstacles to future change. Establishment of the Greater City actually provoked a political backlash that froze the city's boundaries. In 1927 Assemblyman Edwin Wallace and State Senator George Thompson, both Republicans from Nassau County (that eastern portion of Queens not included in the Greater City at consolidation), and State Senator Walter Westall, a Republican from Westchester County (a northern neighbor that lost some of its territory to consolidation), proposed a change in the state constitution to bar a city from annexing any territory without the majority consent of that area's residents. These suburban legislators sought "to prevent the encroachment of New York City on their counties"; they feared that otherwise they would someday be "gobbled up" by the city.[24]

During a year in which the state was considering such major constitutional changes as the adoption of the executive budget and lengthened terms for legislators and statewide officials, this proposal to constrain the growth of Greater New York attracted little attention. Even within the city, what notice it got was favorable. The *New York Times*, applying a then-current concept borrowed from Wilsonian foreign policy, described the change as "an entirely reasonable exercise in the right of self-determination."[25]

The amendment passed both houses of the legislature, and voters adopted it by a more than two-to-one margin. Initially it applied only to annexation by cities. Further refinements in subsequent years produced the current constitutional language preventing annexation of any local government or part of its territory by another without approval of both a majority of the people in the place to be annexed and the governing bodies of the affected local governments.[26]

In his book *Cities without Suburbs*, David Rusk elegantly demonstrated the consequences of frozen municipal boundaries:

—growing social, economic, and racial differences between central city and suburb as the poor, who are often minorities, move into older housing stock while the white middle class departs;

—tax hikes as the city tries to handle the growing burden of providing expected, traditional services while meeting the service demands of an increasingly needy population;

—a declining city tax base as economic activity and new growth shift from the city to suburban locations, often with the help of government subsidies.[27]

The final effect is a cycle of urban decay and decline. Rusk's answer is, where possible, to create "cities without suburbs": general-purpose metropolitan jurisdictions that can at once provide competitiveness, efficiency, and a measure of social justice.

Acknowledging its impossibility, Rusk does not advocate a single metropolitan government for large complex regions like that of New York. The New York experience suggests that uniting city and suburbs into a metropolis is not a permanent solution, even where it is possible. After all, this is what the creators of Greater New York achieved. However, social, economic, and political environments are dynamic, and growth, development, and change continued after the consolidation of Greater New York. Linked by ever-expanding transportation and communication networks, the region continued to redefine itself. Soon the boundaries of the metropolis were again no longer coterminous with the "real region," and the same logic that drove the original creation of the metropolis suggested the need for further boundary adjustments.

Table 5-4. *Population of Greater New York as a Percentage of Tri-State Regional Population, Selected Years, 1890–1990*[a]

	1890	*1910*	*1930*	*1950*	*1970*	*1990*
Core (region in 1890)	**90**[b]	90	90	92	93	92
+ Inner ring	84	73	70	68	60	60
+ Intermediate ring	67	61	58	55	43	41
+ Outer ring (region now)	54	57	55	52	40	**37**[b]

Source: Authors' calculations based on data from *Census of the Population* for the selected years.

a. Each percentage in this table is calculated on a cumulative base. For example, in 1990 New York City had 92 percent of the population of the region's core; 60 percent of the population of the region's core plus the inner ring; 41 percent of the population of the core plus the inner and intermediate rings; and 37 percent of the population of the core plus the inner and intermediate and outer rings, or the entire region now. See the notes to table 5-2 for a list of counties that constitute each of the three suburban rings.

b. Boldface values show the decline in the city's share of regional population as both the territorial extent of the region and its population moved outward.

Table 5-4, which only looks at population growth, illustrates the dynamic nature of this region. When metropolitan New York was created, what is now the urban core—consolidated New York City and Hudson County, New Jersey—constituted the entire metropolitan region. Over time, the region was redefined, acquiring additional "rings" of suburban counties. For its second plan in 1961, the Regional Plan Association counted twenty-six counties in the core and two suburban rings; for its third plan, the RPA counted thirty-one counties in the region, spread in three rings around the core.[28] (See chapter 1, figure 1-1.)

The table shows that Greater New York had 90 percent of the population of the region as it was defined in 1890, just before creation of the metropolitan government. The governmental boundaries of the metropolis remained unchanged over time, but the "real" region took in more and more territory, stretching further north up the Hudson, east into Connecticut, and south and west into New Jersey. Even though a large amount of then-unsettled territory was included in the consolidated city of 1898, by 1990 the old metropolis contained only 37 percent of the region's population. At first the population in counties immediately outside the city's boundaries grew faster than the city's population did; later, rapid growth shifted to the intermediate and outer rings. The modern city's population peaked in 1970; after that, in a slow-growth period for the region, the city's share declined even faster because it lost population while intermediate and outer ring counties continued to gain.

Studies relying on economic data from far back in the region's history document the same phenomenon: economic growth has been faster and greater outside than within the metropolis. This was the message of analyses done in connection with RPA's second regional plan in 1961.[29] Almost twenty years later, a report by the Twentieth Century Fund observed that "since the late nineteenth century, the suburbs accounted for a disproportional share of metropolitan growth."[30] A decade and a half beyond that, Bruce Berg and Paul Kantor demonstrated "steady, if not rapid, economic growth in the suburbs and declining or stagnant growth in the CBD (Central Business District) and its inner ring. . . . As a result the CBD's share of the metropolitan economy is declining while the suburban share grows."[31]

The boundaries of the "real" region are tough to pin down; they keep shifting as the economy and society change. Inevitably growth and change suggest the need for further boundary adjustments. Therefore, metropolitanization is not achievable by a single action at a single moment in time but instead requires reconfiguration and redrawing of boundaries again and again. Yet repeated successes at expanding metropolitan boundaries are politically unimaginable.

Indeed, the New York experience shows that in reaction to the initial successes of metropolitanists, surrounding jurisdictions try to create political conditions that foreclose subsequent expansion. In New York State this effort was successful: now the elasticity of local government boundaries may be regained only through state constitutional change. The state constitution may be amended through the state legislature, but a body dominated by suburban and rural interests is unlikely to make changes that would allow border suburbs to be more easily included within city limits.

Interstate Metropolitan Government: An Orphan in the Federal System

By removing restrictions on interstate commerce, the U.S. Constitution in Article I, Section 8, encouraged the kind of economic integration of regions across state political boundaries that the tri-state region has achieved, even as disputes over those boundaries raged.[32] Indeed, creating a common market in the former British colonies was one of the Constitution's primary purposes. But simultaneously, by inventing and entrenching modern American federalism, that same Constitution effectively blocked *political* integration of those same regions across those same state lines.

Apart from the role of the federal courts in settling territorial disputes that states agree to bring to them (over Ellis Island, for example), the national government may not alter states' boundaries without their consent. Structuring local government is left by the Constitution to the states and therefore occurs *within* states. With the singular exception of the District of Columbia, no provision was made for any general-purpose local government to exist outside the jurisdiction of state governments.

It is theoretically possible for two states to create by interstate compact a single general-purpose locality across state lines. In fact, there is a bit of tantalizing evidence that Andrew Haswell Green actually gave serious consideration to the creation of a bi-state metropolis. In 1894 he received a letter from Calvert Vaux, the prominent landscape architect, discussing a "radius of consolidation" that included "Jersey City and a portion of the State of New Jersey." Vaux envisioned a process in which the Greater City's charter would be adopted by both state legislatures, with any later change "initiated either at Trenton or Albany but approved by both legislatures before it became a law controlling of the Greater New York City Government."[33] But as a practical matter, state boundaries limited the creation of a single government at the mouth of the Hudson River, a region acknowledged for centuries as an economic unit.

Although the New York region is unique because of its size and economic complexity, its multistate character is far from exceptional. In fact, economically defined metropolitan areas extending into more than one state abound in the United States. According to a study published in 1979 by the U.S. Advisory Commission on Intergovernmental Relations, "close to half of the Nation's metropolitan problem is an interstate problem as well, and . . . well over half of the States are affected by Interstate Metropolitan areas."[34] Today, 38 of the 277 metropolitan areas in the United States cross state boundaries. Collectively these contain more than a third of the nation's metropolitan population and over a fourth of its total population. Fifteen multistate metropolitan areas have populations that exceed 600,000; of these, seven are in three or more states.[35]

Metropolitanists look to state governments as the key actors in extending metropolitan boundaries. However, they give little consideration to the limits embedded in the federal system itself that constrain creation of metropolitan governments in many regions of the country, including half of those that are most populous. The manner in which the American governmental system is structured virtually assures that general-purpose regional governments will not be created across state lines in the United States.

Rivalries within and among States

Experience shows that where regional economic and social development *crosses* state lines—and where, therefore, no single state can play an integrative role—change tends both to divide states internally and to intensify the competition between or among them. Well-known fault lines within New York, New Jersey, and Connecticut illustrate both the intra- and interstate impacts of the economic and social unity of the tri-state region.

Intrastate Friction

In New York the up- and downstate economies are conventionally regarded as distinct, and politically, the upstate-downstate split is a fundamental starting point for any analysis. In 1994 New York State Assemblyman Don Davidson of Geneva (who later became agriculture commissioner) offered a constitutional amendment splitting the Empire State in two. "New York" would be made up of New York City, Long Island, and Westchester and Rockland Counties; the rest of the state would become "West New York." T-shirts featuring a map of the new states were available in Davidson's offices in his district and at the state capitol.

The *Elmira Star-Gazette* in Davidson's district invited its readers to call in with reactions to this idea. Five thousand did so, far more than for any other question the paper ever raised; most liked the idea. When the *Corning Leader* editorialized that the Empire State ought to remain intact, a flood of protest followed.[36]

The division of New York was not a new idea. During the past century, there were regular attempts by New York City partisans to separate and create "the State of Manhattan" to protect the city from exploitation by upstate Republicans.[37] Jimmy Breslin and Norman Mailer advocated making New York City a fifty-first state in their 1969 mayoral campaign. The idea of creating the state of "New Amsterdam" out of the city was resurrected in 1996, in reaction to a proposal by the state senate majority leader, Republican Joe Bruno of Rensselaer County, to let rent control lapse within the five boroughs.[38]

In New Jersey, originally two separate colonies, the division is north and south. According to James Hughes, a professor of public policy at Rutgers, the two parts of the state were not unified by the economic growth of the 1980s. "It only confirmed their separateness from each other," Hughes observed.[39] The north is richer (outside its cities), more industrial and commercial, faster paced, and more urbane. It also holds the political power. With more limited economic opportunities, south Jerseyans resent environmental constraints—imposed upon them by North Jersey majorities—that limit pineland and coastal development.

With regard to Connecticut, a group of community leaders interviewed for this study commented that their state's New York City suburban counties are "not part of New England," unlike the rest of the state. People in Litchfield and Fairfield Counties, they said, read the *New York Times* and "think that their state capital is in Albany." In fact, one group member remarked that the Litchfield market was so New York–oriented that the cable company offered no access at all to Connecticut television stations!

Reinforcing these perceptions, Connecticut Governor John G. Rowland joked at a press conference in the spring of 1996 that one barrier to selling enough season tickets to keep the Whalers hockey team in Hartford was that fans in adjacent Fairfield County rooted for the wrong team—the New York Rangers.[40] (The Whalers ultimately left.) At the same time, Southern New England Telephone was running radio ads giving Fairfield County residents special discount rates for calls to all of New York State—but not to the rest of Connecticut.

The fault lines that delineate the tri-state region within New York, New Jersey, and Connecticut demarcate an area in which not only the economic and social life but the "political culture" is shared and distinctive. Political scientist Daniel Elazar has written that downstate New York, eastern Connecticut, and northern New Jersey have more in common with each other in their "pattern of orientation to political action" than they do with the portions of those states that lie outside the region.[41] They are united in an "individualistic" approach that views government as "a marketplace" in which self-interest might be profitably pursued. Elazar suggests that like the boundaries that British colonial governors drew in Africa, sundering tribes and throwing together peoples of vastly different backgrounds and cultures (often with tragic effect), state lines in the tri-state region split areas with common political cultures and unite places with dramatically different orientations toward government and politics.[42]

Interstate Rivalry

The informal "capital" of the tri-state region, Manhattan, is not a state capital at all; it is not even a municipality. Trenton is the only state capital that lies within the region, and it is at the edge. It is fair to say that all

the state governments making critical decisions that affect the region are on the outside, looking in. Connecticut and New Jersey have always resisted New York State's overwhelming presence. And within New York, as noted earlier, upstate-downstate differences have been a stubborn barrier to regional action. For state political leaders in all three states, there is potential value in using the region and its problems as a political foil.

It is rarely rewarding for federal or state political leaders from the region's three states to act or think across state lines. Governors are naturally motivated by the parochial desire to attract jobs and tax base to their own state, especially in a difficult economy—and are quick to take credit if they succeed, or appear to. Although regional "nonaggression" pacts have occasionally been negotiated and announced, the state governments of both New Jersey and Connecticut nevertheless offer inducements to New York companies to move into their states while staying within the region. New York has responded with raids of its own, complete with costly retention strategies to preserve *its* job base.

One example of such competitive conflict arose when Connecticut provided benefits worth $120 million ($60,000 a job over ten years) and changed state law to encourage the Swiss Bank to move most of its operations from Manhattan to Stamford. In ads placed in southern Connecticut newspapers, New York City condemned this as "a blatant and unneighborly raid" and promised retaliation. Then-governor Lowell Weicker responded, "I don't think anything is achieved by either state yelling words across its line."[43]

On those rare occasions when state interests converge, cooperation does occur. This was the case, for instance, when New York and New Jersey joined in 1996 to provide some of the funds needed to purchase 15,000 acres in Sterling Forest and to lobby the federal government to provide the rest. This tract of land, previously slated for commercial and residential development, is part of the tri-state region's outer ring—mostly in Orange County, New York, about an hour's drive from New York City. Environmentalists pressed for the preservation of this open space, which was also vital to New Jersey as the source of drinking water for a fourth of the state's population.

The outcome achieved in the Sterling Forest case was the result of an unusual convergence of political interests—those of governors Christine Whitman of New Jersey and George Pataki of New York, both Republicans; then Republican presidential candidate Bob Dole, former U.S. Senate majority leader, who supported federal participation; and influential Republican members of the northern New Jersey congressional delegation who were up for reelection.[44] The cooperation it evidenced, however, was the exception, not the rule.

Goals versus Reality

New metropolitanists seek to extend city boundaries in the belief that this will effect greater social and economic equity between city and suburb by overcoming racial differences while simultaneously achieving efficiency and advancing the prospects for regional competitiveness. A century of experience in Greater New York brings into question their strategy for achieving all of these goals.

First, this approach simply does not work in multistate regions—like New York—where a large proportion of Americans live. No general-purpose metropolitan government has ever been created in a multistate region. In fact, evidence from the tri-state area demonstrates that a single economy reaching across state lines divides rather than unites a region's states.

Second, facilitating economic development requires the ability to finance major capital projects that support growth. The New York experience shows that general-purpose local governments lack this ability. As a local government with both legal and practical borrowing limits, Greater New York City has always lacked the capacity to finance the massive investments necessary to support economic development.

Third, metropolitan governments encounter severe limits as promoters of equity. Equity between classes and races, as we have seen, was not a goal when Greater New York was created. As it developed, however, the consolidated city sought to do more things to help more people than any other local government in America. But in recent years, even this enormously rich locality has had to retreat from much of its long-established social agenda. It proved to have insufficient power and resources to persist in the pursuit of equity. In fact, the modern history of the city can be seen as a struggle to transform it from a metropolis, presumed to have extraordinary power and capacity, to a mere city like other cities, with limited powers and fewer functions.

Fourth, Greater New York has not been a model of governmental efficiency. Compared with city governments elsewhere, metropolitan government in New York has been more, not less, costly. New York has persisted in maintaining big, expensive government even as its resource base has contracted. And this is not just because the Greater City tried to do more than other localities. It is also because New York has paid more than the others to deliver traditional municipal services.

Finally, the New York experience brings into question the presumption, implicit in new metropolitanists' thinking, that there can be a once-and-for-all answer to the size question in regional government. While technological advances continue to push regional boundaries outward, the successful creation of a metropolis is as likely as not to produce political conditions resistant to the further extension of its boundaries. This is what happened in the case of New York. Thus as time passes, the boundaries of the new metropolis may well become the same kind of barriers to action in the expanded region that the old city's boundaries were in the old region.

PART THREE

Functional Regionalism

CHAPTER SIX

Across State Lines: The Port Authority

As the inherent limits of Greater New York City as a regional government became evident, economic development pressures proved a persistent force for other, partial attempts at regionalism. Especially in the area of transportation—crucial for economic development—technological advances both generated economic growth and required massive public investment to sustain it. Local government was expected to provide new highways, bridges, tunnels, and port facilities to integrate the economic region and keep it competitive. Airports required hundreds of acres and hundreds of millions of dollars in new investment. Additional demands on government arose as private market failure transformed bus systems, subways, and commuter rail systems into public services.

Pressing out from the center, the region grew without regard for state and local governmental boundaries. The investment necessary to sustain this growth was beyond the jurisdiction and fiscal capacity of Greater New York, let alone of the other counties, cities, towns, and villages in the region, beleaguered as they continually were by demands for spending on a great range of pressing needs that outstripped available resources.

Research by Anita Summers of the University of Pennsylvania shows that "the delivery of transportation services is clearly the dominant catalyzing agent for regional cooperation" in major American metropolitan areas.[1] But regional approaches to transportation in the tri-state area have not been cooperative—nor planned or comprehensive. Rather, transportation policy has been incremental and crisis driven, with key decisions regularly reached at the state, not the local, level. Continued economic viability, not economic development, was most often the compelling consideration. With survival at stake, efficiency was a secondary concern.

Each new crisis brought forth a new organizational solution. All took the form of public authorities: the bi-state Port Authority of New York and New Jersey (PANYNJ) in the 1920s, the Metropolitan Transportation Authority (MTA) within New York in the 1960s, and New Jersey Transit (NJT) in New Jersey in the 1970s. These three agencies, discussed in this chapter and the next, performed partially overlapping functions in partially overlapping geographical areas.

As the twentieth century drew to a close, the Port Authority was responsible for all highway links between New York and New Jersey: the George Washington Bridge, the Bayonne Bridge, the Goethals Bridge, the Outerbridge Crossing, the Holland Tunnel, and the Lincoln Tunnel. In 1997 these six facilities together carried almost 325,000 vehicles into New York City each working day.[2] The Port Authority also operated most (but not all) of the region's airport and port facilities, ran a commuter railroad that served 70 percent of the passengers entering New York by rail from New Jersey, and had for twenty years been the region's statutorily designated economic development agency.

For its part, the MTA served one-third of the mass transit users in the nation. Its operating arms ran New York City's subways and buses, were responsible for two major commuter rail lines to the east and north—the Long Island Rail Road and Metro North—and provided mass transit services on Staten Island and in suburban Nassau County. Also, through the Triborough Bridge and Tunnel Authority, the MTA administered nine toll-producing facilities: seven bridges and two tunnels. Across the Hudson River, New Jersey Transit, organized not just in the region but statewide, operated the fourth largest commuter rail system in the country. (See chapter 7 for a fuller discussion of these agencies.)

Awareness of the tri-state character of the New York–New Jersey–Connecticut area is as important for understanding its experience with functionally focused regionalism as it is for comprehending the region's experiment with metropolitanism. Again the states were the key players. When existing localities (including the New York metropolis) could not or would not meet critical regional needs, the *state* governments responded with regional agencies for transportation. Whether acting together or alone, New York and New Jersey organized the new entities they created, defined their powers and duties, and delineated the boundaries within which they operated. When it suited the states—as it did in the late 1970s, when an explicit economic development function was added to the Port Authority's mission—they altered basic agency priorities. Equity considerations were geographically, not socially, based and focused on distribution of services and benefits between or within states, not among classes or races. Furthermore, concerns for this sort of equity often militated against efficiency.

These new, functionally focused public authorities were far less constrained by law and regulation in their daily operation than were general-purpose local governments or more conventional state agencies, and in differing degrees they had independent revenue bases that enhanced their autonomy and allowed for longer-term planning. But unlike New York City, these regional authorities enjoyed neither the legitimacy of being headed by local elected officials nor the home rule protections (limited as they are) provided in state constitutions for general-purpose governments. Governors in capitals outside the region or at its edge controlled their boards and oversaw their actions. If organized and operating within a single state, like the MTA and NJT, these entities are better described as state agencies functioning within the region than as regional local governments. If operating in more than one state, like PANYNJ, they appear at least as preoccupied with demonstrating balance in allocating resources between or among states—that is, with state government priorities—as with fulfilling overarching regional goals (that is, with regional priorities).

As Anita Summers documented, functionally focused regional entities have been created throughout the United States to deal with transportation problems. But the experience of the New York–New Jersey–Connecticut region has been different. Aside from its scale and tri-state character, this region already had a vast general-purpose metropolitan government—New York City—subsidizing, building, or operating large transportation systems when the area's regional transportation agencies were created. Frozen within its original borders, New York City could never extend transit services outward to serve the entire tri-state area as the region grew. Within its borders the city did the best it could for decades, but its fiscal limits ultimately caused it to relinquish control of mass transit. The well-being of the Greater City nevertheless depended upon an effectively functioning mass transportation system and thus upon the agencies created by the states to overcome the city's geographical and fiscal limits as a general-purpose (local) metropolitan government. Continuing conflict between the city and these agencies was therefore inevitable.

Reports in the 1990s on the battles between New York City and the Port Authority, or between the city and the MTA, treat the city as a local government within the larger region and the Port Authority and the MTA as regional entities. This is a misconception. In fact, all three are regional governments but with regions defined at different moments in history and under different political conditions. With this acknowledged, the intergovernmental relationships among them are better understood. The conflicts that arise reflect competition between differently conceived, structured, and financed regional governments, each trying to control vital regional functions and assets within overlapping territorial jurisdictions. Only when this is fully appreciated can new approaches to functional regionalism in transportation in the tri-state region be conceived.

A Regional or Two-State Agency?

In his State of the City address in January 1997, New York City mayor Rudolph Giuliani called for a rail freight tunnel under the Hudson as the keystone of a plan to revive Brooklyn's deepwater port as a center of international shipping. Because the city was surrounded by water and lacked a direct rail link to the mainland, the mayor said, its roads were congested with trucks, its air was unnecessarily polluted by their exhaust, and its port facilities were noncompetitive with those across the harbor in Newark and Elizabeth. If such a tunnel were built, Giuliani argued, both economic development and environmental goals would be served in one stroke.[3]

Ironically, it was the same agency that developed the ports of Elizabeth and Newark (and did not invest on the New York side of the harbor because the city would not relinquish control of its docks in the 1940s) that failed to build a rail freight tunnel under the Hudson when it was proposed two-thirds of a century ago. The Port of New York Authority (later the Port Authority of New York and New Jersey) was created in 1921, over the objections of New York City, to cure "destructive competition" among railroads at the New York harbor and to prepare and implement a plan for the orderly development of the greatest commercial port in the United States. Established to solve a rail transportation problem with an integrated regional approach, the authority evolved instead into a bridge, tunnel, airport, and latter-day economic development agency, torn between two states' distinct priorities.

Origins and Mission

It was Republicans at the state level who created the Port Authority, as they did Greater New York—only this time its jurisdiction was in two states, not one. After a failed attempt to gain an advantage in freight rates for New Jersey destinations from the Interstate Commerce Commission, Republican governor Walter Edge (later a U.S. senator) pushed for an interstate solution to rationalize the chaotic commercial shipping situation in New York's harbor. An unprecedented plan for an interstate operating agency, formed under the Compact Clause of the U.S. Constitution, was conceived by Julius Henry Cohen, working at the time as counsel to the Harbor Development Commission created by New York and New Jersey in 1917.[4] In addition to Edge, the idea was supported by New York's Republican governor, Charles S. Whitman, and by Republican legislatures in both states.

Democratic opposition in cities on both sides of the Hudson has been attributed to "unenlightened, short-sighted and machine-controlled" politics, that is, to fears of loss of control over the jobs and other patronage opportunities on the waterfront.[5] But at least for Greater New York City, there was also an economic rationale. Leaders in the metropolis reasoned that without the creation of the new interstate agency, which would have to invest in facilities in both states, only the city, of all the municipalities on the harbor, might command sufficient capital to further develop piers and terminals and thus maintain a comparative advantage for attracting shippers. (Even after the Port Authority was created, the Greater City pursued [regional] port development schemes independent of the authority's plans.)[6]

Edge's Democratic successor as governor was Edward I. Edwards, a former state senator from Hudson, the county in which Jersey City is located. Strongly influenced (some said bossed) by Mayor Frank Hague of Jersey City, Edwards twice vetoed his state's legislation creating the Port Authority. (His actions were reminiscent of the suspensive vetoes cast by Mayors William Strong and Frederick Wurster of New York and Brooklyn, respectively, to block the creation of Greater New York.) An override of Edwards' second veto by the Republican state legislature was necessary to bring the agency to life.

Unlike Edwards, Democratic governor Alfred E. Smith of New York was not resistant. Smith was a Lower-East-Side product of Tammany but was nevertheless the twentieth-century New York governor most devoted to the progressive reform agenda; he believed deeply in regionalism and in rationalizing government structures.[7] Nor did Smith's defeat by Nathan Miller in 1920 stand in the way: the resulting fully Republican New York State government adopted the Port Authority legislation in 1921.

The boundaries defined for the Port Authority might have been those used for Greater New York City a quarter century earlier if the logic of economic reasoning had held sway and if state lines had not interfered. The territory within the authority's jurisdiction—all within a twenty-five-mile radius of the Statue of Liberty at the harbor's center—included 1,500 square miles, an area almost four times the size of Greater New York. (About one-third of this was water; the rest, land.) Within the circle defined by this radius was all of consolidated New York, the City of Newark, parts of Westchester and Nassau Counties (expected in 1898 to eventually become part of Greater New York), a small piece of Rockland County, and all or parts of eight counties in New Jersey (figure 6-1). Interestingly, territory in Connecticut was quite explicitly excluded; the region's boundaries came up to and ran along the New York–Connecticut line. This was because the federal government had authorized a *bi-state* compact.

The Port Authority was first governed by six commissioners serving five-year overlapping terms, three each appointed by the governors of New York and New Jersey. There was then and is now no role for the preexisting regional government—Greater New York City—in the governance of this new regional agency. An early attempt by the city to gain control over appointment to two of the state's three board seats failed.[8] In 1930, concomitant with the transfer to the Port Authority of control over the Holland Tunnel, the term of commissioners was changed to six years and their number to twelve, six from each state.

Localism was not completely vanquished. Opponents were able to deny the new Port Authority the overarching regulatory power in the port area that it initially sought. Additionally, existing localities still had the right to develop their own waterfronts, and their agreement was required before the authority could take control of their assets. Thus the powers of the Port Authority, even within its primary functional spheres, were neither plenary nor exclusive. Nevertheless, the agency was broadly

Figure 6-1. *Counties All or Partially in the Port Authority Region*

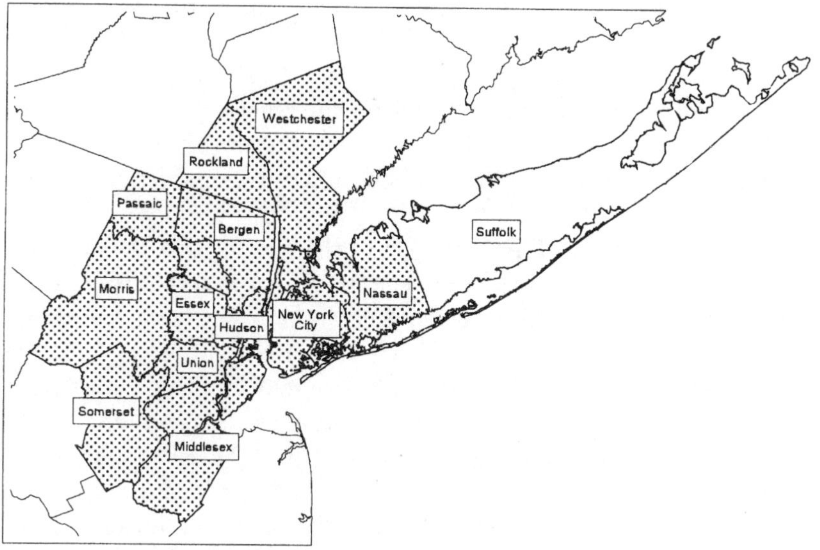

Source: Hugh O'Neil and Mitch Moss, *Reinventing New York* (Urban Research Center, Wagner School, New York University, 1993).

charged with developing and running "terminals, transportation and other facilities of commerce" and appeared to have a good deal of discretion in defining its own focus.[9]

However, the protection of *state* interests, built into the initial operating rules of the authority, reveals where the real power was retained. The interstate compact provided that no action could be taken without half of the commissioners present and without the agreement of at least two of those present from each state. States also reserved the right to veto authority actions. Pursuant to this provision, the governors in 1927 gained approval power over agency minutes and therefore could block its actions.[10]

The Port Authority's early "efforts to introduce joint use of yards, stations, engines and rights of way; to construct a union beltline railroad in Manhattan; and to secure reciprocal switching, sharing car floats, and other cooperative practices—all came to naught," one definitive account noted.[11] The fiercely competitive railroads resisted, in part because collaboration was foreign to them and in part because they did not want to provide the capital needed to build the tunnels linking the Hudson's two sides.

Unsuccessful at its primary mission in the port, the agency evolved into a builder and operator of bridges and tunnels connecting New York City and New Jersey: the Outerbridge Crossing, the George Washington

Bridge, and the Holland and Lincoln Tunnels.[12] Port Authority facilities were built with borrowed funds, which were repaid from tolls or fees charged for their use. As the region grew, this revenue stream proved mighty. Under the leadership of the legendary August Tobin and backed by a powerful coalition of road builders, investment bankers, and highway users that he assembled, the agency invested the excess revenues in expanding and improving these facilities and into ports, terminals, and airports.

The clout of this coalition was one of the reasons that the Port Authority was able, for a time, to control its own agenda. Unlike Greater New York, it was not a beleaguered general-purpose government facing unmeetable demands upon its resource base from all quarters. People wanted cars and good road systems on which to drive them, and governors were happy to leave discretionary power with an agency that could respond to these demands without tax increases. The cash (and power) that August Tobin's strategy and political acumen generated made the agency a darling of elected leaders and Wall Street and a major force in the region's economy.

Ultimately, however, the Port Authority's successes—making long-distance automobile travel from the metropolitan center easier—generated growth beyond the limits of its own jurisdiction. This growth shifted the region's economic center away from its original locus when the authority was created and thereby, ironically, diminished the agency's capacity to function as a regional institution. Its boundaries, like Greater New York's, remained the same while the region expanded, so it could no longer expand into the entire region. The authority also stubbornly resisted taking on responsibility for money-losing mass transit, even though its legislative authority and geographical reach allowed it to enter this field.

When Greater New York City was created, dozens of other local governments were abolished. However, the Port Authority was a special-purpose government: it replaced nothing but rather was added to the hundreds of local governments already in the region. Later, the MTA and New Jersey Transit became still other additions. Now even regional governments with overlapping boundaries within and across state lines were being layered one upon another.

The Authority versus the City: Airports and Marine Terminals

In the mid-1940s planners who had been in touch with the Port Authority behind the scenes told the government of Newark, New Jersey, that revitalization of its airport and marine terminals was essential for future economic growth. They recommended that these facilities be leased to and operated by the Port Authority to enable them to become a part of an "integrated regional system." After some hesitation, the Newark city government agreed to ask the authority to study the idea.

Once this process had begun, Executive Director August Tobin of the Port Authority focused on the other elements of the regional picture—New York City's LaGuardia and Idlewild (later Kennedy) Airports, both in Queens. The city's new mayor, William O'Dwyer, wanted to spend his limited capital funds on schools, hospitals, and other infrastructure needs, not on the development of these airports—projects dear not to his heart but to that of his predecessor, Mayor Fiorello LaGuardia. Robert Moses, head of the newly assembled Triborough Bridge and Tunnel Authority and the city's acknowledged master builder, convinced O'Dwyer to support the creation of a New York City airport authority, with a board appointed by the mayor, to run the airports and borrow money for their further development. Such an agency, though never brought to life, was actually created by the New York State legislature in 1946.[13]

O'Dwyer first thought that turning over control of the city's airports to the Port Authority, with its directors chosen by the governors of New York and New Jersey, would be "an abject surrender of the city's planning powers."[14] But August Tobin convinced media outlets, investment bankers, and airline executives interested in the question that O'Dwyer's (and Moses's) approach, using a new agency without a record in the credit markets or experience running big operations, was both risky and expensive, especially when compared to turning control over to his tested, respected bi-state agency.

Tobin had the money: revenues from his bridges and tunnels were growing dramatically in the postwar years. He had been given broadly defined power to develop and run "terminals, transportation and other facilities of commerce" under both the federal interstate compact authorizing the authority and the laws of the two states that created it.[15] He had the discretion to choose his opportunities, based upon past success, careful management of his board, and years of cultivating support in the region. And he had the leverage of Newark, with a plan to spend $55 million to build it into "one of the greatest airports in the world." If New York floundered or made a misstep, it might be left at a permanent disadvantage in the region as air travel burgeoned. Mayor O'Dwyer reconsidered and asked the Port Authority for a study. In short order it produced a $197 million proposal for the development of New York City's two airports. Then a media campaign was cranked up, and Tobin sweetened his profit-sharing proposal to the city. On April 17, 1947, New York City agreed to a fifty-year lease (Tobin wanted ninety-nine) under which the Port Authority would develop and run New York City's airports.

While New York City was being successfully romanced, Newark's elected officials were getting cold feet. But now the threat arose of authority resources being used to develop New York City's airports, to Newark's disadvantage. New Jersey's newly elected Democratic governor, Alfred Driscoll, publicly endorsed the authority's plan and leaned on Newark officials, his copartisans. On October 22, 1947, they capitulated, signing over control not only of Newark's airport but also of its marine facilities.[16]

New York City, however, held on to its piers. Although designed like the Port Authority to be a regional government, the Greater City was also a general-purpose local government with a strong political party system. Is port was still the locus of hundreds of patronage jobs and a potential source of additional political money when dollars for reconstruction contracts began to flow. Mayor O'Dwyer, ever sensitive to the scarcity of municipal capital funds, was receptive when the Port Authority offered a $114 million rehabilitation plan. But the Board of Estimate, dominated by county political organizations and influenced by labor unions on the docks that preferred the status quo, failed to act positively on the authority's offer.[17]

The law creating the Port Authority permitted it to take control of local government assets within its territory only with the locality's consent. Thus New York City chose for political reasons to retain its primacy in the specific policy area that this functionally focused regional government was created to handle. The seaport, however, was already a resource of diminishing economic importance, and as O'Dwyer feared, there was not sufficient city money to invest in it. The Port Authority later purchased facilities in Brooklyn, but the bulk of its investment went into the ports of Newark and Elizabeth, where the space was available to develop containerized facilities.

Thus New York City lost twice. It gave up control of an asset with enormous future value, its airports, while retaining control of one of diminishing value, its ports. And by doing so it lost the opportunity to keep the ports modern and competitive within and outside the region.

As the twentieth century drew to a close, the ghost of Robert Moses seemed to be rising again in the person of New York City mayor Rudolph Giuliani. The mayor had been firing salvos at the Port Authority on every possible occasion since his initial election in 1993. He demanded increased rents for the two authority-run airports in New York and proposed that their management be contracted out to other operators (when the current lease runs out in 2015).[18] He sought increased charges for disposal of wastes from authority facilities in city landfills. He denounced the degree to which the authority subsidized the Port Authority Trans-Hudson (PATH) train commuter fares, charging that suburbanites were favored over city subway riders, and challenged the use of authority money to cover PATH deficits instead of paying the city for rents and services.[19]

Mayor Giuliani also commissioned studies that showed the Port Authority was a sinkhole of inefficiency and waste (not surprising in light of its sponsor's views).[20] Joining in, Public Advocate Mark Green (another citywide elected official and then an aspirant for a U.S. senate seat) released a report in 1996 that analyzed fifteen years of Port Authority operations. It found that the agency used money made in New York to subsidize operations in New Jersey and favored New Jersey over New York in its capital spending.[21]

More concretely, in May of 1996 the mayor proposed the purchase of the two giant airports in Queens (for $1.9 billion) by a newly created New York airport authority (just like Moses's 1946 creation), which would turn them over to a private operator to run. Under this proposal the Port Authority of New York and New Jersey would be abolished, PATH commuter trains between New and New Jersey would be taken over by the Metropolitan Transit Authority (a New York State entity), the Port Authority police would be absorbed into the New York City force, and the agency's World Trade Center would be sold.[22]

In earlier years it was New Jersey leaders who argued that the Port Authority's priorities were skewed—against them.[23] Now they spoke up in the agency's defense. Through her press secretary, Becky Taylor, Governor Christine Todd Whitman defended the agency for delivering "valuable services to people in the region" and being "a very powerful tool of the economic development of both states."[24] Robert Janiszewski, the elected Hudson County executive and an authority board member, argued that subsidies to PATH "benefited the entire New York Metropolitan Region."[25] Regionalists joined in. "We are one region, one economy," said H. Claude Shostal, president of the Regional Plan Association.[26]

But unlike the mayor with respect to the city, there is no single, acknowledged, legitimate *elected* advocate for regionwide interests. The city may be geographically and fiscally limited (and less of a regional government since the time of its creation), but it has a clear voice. The Port Authority has a broader geographical reach but is a creature of the states that dominate it, with no single elected leader to speak for it; therefore it has no such voice.

Assertion of State Power

According to Alan Finder, "One of the prime tasks of the executive director and board chairman . . . [of the Port Authority], who reign from offices high in the World Trade Center, is to maintain a deliberate balance between the states, with each reaping equal awards from the agency's activities."[27] It is no accident that the Port Authority's executive director is regularly a New Yorker, while the board chairman is regularly from New Jersey. The need for balance has always been present, but interstate pressures were mitigated as long as Executive Director Tobin could influence gubernatorial board appointments from both states, induce board members to follow his lead in establishing agency priorities, and produce powerful support for the agency from Wall Street and the highway lobby.

In 1931 New York and New Jersey agreed to use Port Authority surpluses to build a general reserve fund equal to 10 percent of the value of the agency's outstanding bonds.[28] Beginning in 1952 the Port Authority began to secure its borrowing not by using the revenue flowing from specific projects but by a pledge of money from this general reserve fund. This gave it great power in the credit markets, allowed tunnel and bridge revenues to be invested in airports, and offered a defense against political leaders who sought the authority's involvement in money-losing mass transit efforts.

Since its earliest days, the New Jersey legislature was interested in having the Port Authority take responsibility for "the problem of passenger traffic." In 1927 it passed an act directing the agency to add "interstate and suburban transportation facilities for passengers" to its comprehensive plan. The legislature in New York was supportive, but not the governor: after a similar bill was passed in New York, Governor Alfred E. Smith vetoed it. Taking up "an entirely new line of problem connected with . . . suburban transportation," Smith said, would distract the authority from its primary mission, "the solution of the great freight distribution problem."[29]

The issue returned as the commuter railroads neared collapse in the 1950s. When a bill was introduced in New Jersey that directed the Port Authority to take over and run the bankrupt Hudson and Manhattan Line (the rail system between Newark and Jersey City and lower Manhattan, first put into service in 1908), the agency responded with a new provision in its contract with bondholders. This clause barred the issuance of new bonds secured by the authority's general reserve funds without its certification that these would not negatively impact its credit rating. Port Authority bonds were issued in 1962 for a mass transit purpose—to buy $100 million in passenger cars and locomotives for the Penn Central and Long Island rail lines—but these carried the guarantee of New York State, not of the agency.

Under pressure from his brother David—who as president of the Chase Manhattan Bank in 1962 was leading the effort to revitalize lower Manhattan—New York governor Nelson Rockefeller sought to construct the World Trade Center in New York City. Governor Richard Hughes of New Jersey agreed, but only after the authority moved the planned project to the West Side of Manhattan and committed to take over the Hudson and Manhattan Rail Road (subsequently the PATH line), whose terminal and office building were already located on the West Side.[30] The Port Authority has run this railroad at a loss ever since.[31] However, in assuming this responsibility, it extracted assurances—later enshrined in covenants with its bondholders—that no additional assistance for rail commuter transport would be demanded of it.

These decisions of the early 1960s were watershed events for the Port Authority. Caveats and limits notwithstanding, taking on the PATH project was a precedent-setting departure from its highway focus and its carefully crafted fiscal criteria for its projects. Moreover, building the Trade Center—a facility in a place rather than between places (and not an air, sea, or bus terminal)—endangered the agency's capacity to pursue a self-defined regional agenda. The door was opened wider to distributive pressures from elected state leaders who demanded balance—geographical equity—in the treatment of New York and New Jersey with respect to the location of facilities and agency investments.

In the later 1960s and early 1970s, in response to the collapse of commuter rail and mass transit systems, governors increasingly challenged the Port Authority's autonomy. They no longer supported the agency's definition of its own agenda. As August Tobin's control over the authority weakened, the carefully nurtured board selection and socialization processes that dampened interstate competition began to slip.

Elected in 1969, Democratic governor William Cahill of New Jersey pressed the Port Authority hard for additional involvement in mass transit. It was upon Cahill's insistence that "and New Jersey" was added to the agency's name. The governor's attacks on Executive Director Tobin were direct, public, and continuous. He used his veto power over agency minutes to block routine action and directed board members from his state to caucus before meetings to develop a "New Jersey point of view," threatening to not reappoint them if they failed to follow his lead. Under this unrelenting pressure to depart from all the strategies upon which he had built the agency, Tobin resigned in December of 1971, as did his vice chairman, Hoyt Ammidon.[32]

Legislation passed in 1972 in both New York and New Jersey provided for Port Authority expenditures of almost $300 million to improve the PATH system, provide a direct rail link from Manhattan to Kennedy Airport in Queens, and construct a rail line to Plainfield, New Jersey, by way of Newark Airport. This, in effect, overrode the bond covenant restricting further agency investment in mass transit. Project costs escalated, and federal aid diminished. Concurrently, a national energy crisis developed. To generate further resources for mass transit, both New York and New Jersey passed laws in 1974 retroactively repealing the 1962 bond covenants. However, the United States Supreme Court said these statutes violated the contract clause of the U.S. Constitution and overturned them.[33]

Sponsored by Nelson Rockefeller, William Ronan became the Port Authority board chairman in 1972. But Ronan—a strong mass transit proponent (see chapter 7) and a New York partisan—could not get support for his own appointment as executive director. Instead, a succession of agency careerists filled the post. Ronan became disengaged, and scandals damaged the authority's reputation. Using the power to veto minutes to disrupt routine operations (as had his predecessor), New Jersey governor Brendan Byrne kept up the pressure for added PANYNJ involvement in mass transit.[34]

PORT AUTHORITY AS BI-STATE ECONOMIC DEVELOPMENT AGENCY. After this period of drift, Peter Goldmark took the agency's helm as executive director in 1977. The board chairmanship was assumed by Alan

Sagner, Governor Byrne's transportation commissioner. Under Goldmark, who as state budget director steered New York through its worst fiscal crisis in modern history, the Port Authority became much more responsive to demands that it provide resources for mass transit. An early step was finding alternative means, in the wake of the aforementioned Supreme Court decision, to pay for $240 million in new commuter buses and mass transit improvements.

In its biggest change, the agency sought and gained from New York, New Jersey, and the federal government an economic development role that went far beyond the transportation function.[35] "We are behind the rest of the country in regionalism," Goldmark told the *New York Times* in 1977. "The Port Authority incarnates a multi-state approach. The time is ripe politically and intellectually. Can the Port Authority do something about it? Yes."[36]

The agency was still constrained, however, by Tobin's 1962 bond covenants. A bold attempt to free resources for transit by refinancing $1.9 billion in outstanding debt seemed promising but ran afoul of new federal regulations blocking advance refunding. A few years later, Goldmark advanced an alternative plan that sought to generate and leverage funds for transit capital spending (but not money-losing operations) by dedicating to it World Trade Center rents.

WORLD TRADE CENTER AND DISTRIBUTIVE POLITICS. When the World Trade Center was first completed, it seemed to be a white elephant; in 1975 New York State had to rent space in it equivalent to the square footage of the entire Pan Am Building (now the Metropolitan Life building) to keep it afloat. Then the real estate market in the city improved. By 1980, backed by a study they commissioned that demonstrated the viability of the idea, Governors Carey and Byrne pressured the Port Authority to sell the Trade Center in order to free agency resources for other purposes.

Mayor Ed Koch of New York City liked this idea. The PANYNJ was making $10 million in payments to New York City in lieu of taxes, but city officials estimated that a privately owned trade center would produce $100 million in real estate taxes.[37] These revenues would enter the city's general fund and be used to meet its needs, with priorities established by city-elected officials.[38]

With the Port Authority in control, however, priorities were set by the two governors and their appointees. All Koch could do was "criticize and embarrass and castigate" to get his way.[39] Michael Del Giudice, a top aide to Governors Carey and Cuomo, contrasted the city's "local" perspective on the World Trade Center with the state's "regional" outlook. "This is not just a New York City asset," Del Giudice insisted. "It is an asset of two states and the region."[40] But what really was at stake was *which* regional government would benefit from an asset located in an area where their territories overlapped: the Port Authority with regional boundaries defined across state lines in 1921, or the Greater City, with boundaries defined within state lines in 1898.

BANK FOR REGIONAL DEVELOPMENT. In 1982 Peter Goldmark pointed out that if New York State were to move out of the Trade Center and the space it was in was rented at market rates, the resulting revenue could support $150 million in borrowing by a newly created bank for regional development—which, he suggested, could be *controlled by the two state Governors.*[41] Because the new bank would not be constrained by bond covenants, the proceeds of borrowing could be used for mass transit. And, Goldmark added, an additional $300 million in capital could be provided to the new bank if tolls on the Hudson River crossing were raised by a third to $1.00—less than what was already being charged by the Triborough Bridge and Tunnel Authority (which used tolls to generate the surplus that covered the operating deficits of the MTA-run city subways and the commuter railroads).

The new governors of New Jersey and New York—Tom Kean, a Republican, and Mario Cuomo, a Democrat—both embraced the idea, which, not incidentally, allowed the Port Authority to keep control of the increasingly profitable Trade Center. In June of 1983, they announced a "new relationship" between the states and the Port Authority that, in Cuomo's words, would allow them to "do more with this money, *our* way."[42]

Three bills were introduced in each state to, respectively, establish a bank for regional development, empower the Port Authority to extend its economic development activities, and allow the authority to create an export trading company. These were needed to help advance a $1.1 billion infrastructure renewal plan, carefully balanced to benefit both states relatively equally. It included rehabilitation of the Port Authority Trans-Hudson Corporation (PATH) train system, construction of a new office building in Newark, and waterfront redevelopment. (Major industrial development efforts were later sited at Hunters Point in Queens and in Hoboken, New Jersey.) Investments were also slated for Brooklyn: a container port in Red Hook and a "fishport" in Erie Basin. For balance, $27 million was reserved for related projects in New Jersey. New York State was also to receive $95 million from the Port Authority to cover both the expenses of moving out of the World Trade Center and the increased rents it would pay elsewhere.[43]

In addition to the trade center rents, financing for this plan was to be provided by raising the PATH fare and increasing the toll on the Hudson River crossings to $1.50. This doubling of the tolls went far beyond the one-third increase Goldmark had proposed. (As noted, both governors had just been elected: Kean in 1981, Cuomo in 1982. But to ease the political pain of the toll increases, they were not to apply to motorists using commuter books or to commuter buses.)

This time the barriers were political, not legal. The necessary legislation passed and was signed in New Jersey in 1983, and it cleared the Democratic New York Assembly. But the three bills got hung up in the Republican New York State Senate, even though the development bank proposal had actually passed there in the previous year. The senate did not want to put these resources into a Democratic governor's hands. Moreover, the local interests of the key senate Republican from New York City, Finance Committee chairman John Marchi of Staten Island, were not being addressed in announced development plans. Although some projects—those that did not need new legislative authorization—moved forward, the development bank idea died.[44]

THE CUOMO TURNABOUT. Although state political leaders run the Port Authority, it sometimes serves their political purposes to suggest that they do not. Consider Mario Cuomo's turnabout. In 1983, his first year as New York's governor, Cuomo identified the Port Authority as a virtual cornucopia of capital funds. With great fanfare he took as his own Peter Goldmark's idea for a regional infrastructure bank financed from World Trade Center rents, and he announced a major multiyear capital program. Again in 1987 he joined with Governor Kean in announcing a massive Port Authority capital program, this one more than five times bigger ($5.8 billion) than that of four years earlier. Cuomo's press release was a model of regionalism. "Our states are not competing with each other," it said, "but with other domestic and foreign metropolitan areas." But in the materials he handed out, the governor listed only New York projects, including $1.5 billion for the JFK Airport 2000 project and $500 million for improvements at LaGuardia.[45]

Then things soured. Stories on wastefulness in the Port Authority's efforts to redevelop Kennedy Airport broke in Long Island's *Newsday*. In reaction, the governor—who for years had been taking credit for its capital plans and projects and shared ultimate authority over the agency—condemned the authority as "a kind of government of its own" and called for an independent review panel to propose reforms that would bring greater accountability.[46]

A Bi-State, Not a Regional, Agency

In 1994 PATH, a rail subsidiary of the Port Authority, told the United States Supreme Court that the authority was a state agency. This was a bit curious, since the PANYNJ usually insists (for example, when it enters the bond market) that it is autonomous. But in this case the agency was seeking sovereign immunity (under the Eleventh Amendment to the U.S. Constitution) from two civil suits brought against it.[47]

Writing for a bare majority, Associate Justice Ruth Bader Ginsberg concluded that the Eleventh Amendment to the United States Constitution was designed to protect the states' "solvency and dignity" and that neither were compromised if the Court allowed the suits against the Port Authority to proceed. The Port Authority, Ginsberg wrote, was "a discrete entity created by constitutional compact among three sovereigns [New York, New Jersey, and the United States] . . . [and] . . . financially independent."[48]

The four dissenters used a different standard: political control. "The proper question," Associate Justice Sandra Day O'Connor wrote, "is whether the state possesses sufficient control over an entity performing governmental functions that the entity might be called an extension of the state itself." Under this standard, these justices concluded that the Port Authority was indeed a state agency and entitled to sovereign immunity.[49]

In the real world of tri-state regional governance, it was the Supreme Court minority, not the majority, that was right. Although the Port Authority may look like an independent regional authority and even may have acted like one in the past, in recent years real power over its operations has shifted to where it was always formally located: the two state capitals. Regionalism, even by bi-state compact, could not overcome the fundamental fact of transcendent state power.

With economic development more broadly defined in the 1970s and 1980s, Port Authority projects had to reflect careful consideration of geographical equity. It added an incinerator and legal office building in Newark (nicely nicknamed the "tort port").[50] Industrial parks were built in the South Bronx and Yonkers, New York, and in Elizabeth, New Jersey; the fishport was built in Brooklyn. Housing and office space was planned in Hoboken, New Jersey, and in Brooklyn Heights and Hunters Point, New York. In retrospect, balance in the location of what the Port Authority built seemed as important—or more important—than what it built. Efficiency in pursuit of regional interests had given way to equity in pursuit of state interests.

Ultimate authority over the agency was with the state's governors, and their bottom line was state, not regional, interests. The measure of success for each was benefits to state residents resulting from Port Authority projects or something visible built in the state with agency money—and the avoidance of blame when something went wrong.

Thus the agency had been rendered vulnerable by the politics of the very states that created it. By the early 1990s, George Sternleib, a leading urban planner at Rutgers University, described the Port Authority as "an old-fashioned steam engine that for the moment . . . [was] . . . just lying on the scrap heap."[51] Others agreed. Three-quarters of a century earlier, Republicans had brought the agency to life; now, as the twentieth century drew to a close, the election of Republican governors Christine Todd Whitman in New Jersey and George Pataki in New York brought major downsizing and refocusing.

Explicitly abandoned, the Port Authority's economic development function, enshrined in law in 1978, was not mentioned in the new mission statement developed for the authority by appointees of the new governors.[52] "The determination has been made," said Lewis Eisenstein, Whitman's choice for new board chairman, "that we are not a real estate development agency and that our core mission is transportation infrastructure."[53] In pursuit of this new philosophy, the agency cut and privatized functions, divested assets, and reduced staffing by almost 20 percent in two years. The Vista Hotel was sold, as were portions of the Yonkers, New York, and Elizabeth, New Jersey, industrial parks and the Brooklyn grain terminal, a facility that had been closed for thirty years. Discussions were reopened, too, on the sale or lease of the World Trade Center.[54]

It was one thing for the mayor of New York City, a rival entity with overlapping jurisdiction in the region, to question the need for the Port Authority. It was quite another for the governor of New York, with real power over the agency, to ask the same question. "In my mind," Governor George Pataki told *Crain's New York Business* in March of 1997, "it is still an open question whether the Port Authority is salvageable."[55]

For former Port Authority board chairman Richard Leone, still a great champion of the agency, Pataki's and Whitman's policies were the problem. These governors and their appointees were, he said, creating an agency more like the MTA and New Jersey Transit, "living day to day, putting off maintenance."[56] In truth, however, state dominance of the Port Authority—as of these single-state agencies—was ensured by the agency's original design. At a conference in 1993, far before Pataki's and Whitman's policies took hold, Leone himself observed that "the two states benefit from their share of Port Authority revenues . . . while they require the agency to invest in projects that will not generate future revenue," that is, they elevated priorities devised in state capitals over those defined by the Port Authority for the region it supposedly served.

Leone attributed part of the problem to a loss of support for the Port Authority among decisionmakers in the region. "The previous consensus and support of elites and the media for the Port Authority," he said, "has been replaced by criticism and apathy."[57] But the Tobin era, the period of greatest agency autonomy (and public support), was one in which its goals were aligned with those of the states. For reasons embedded in state and interstate politics, the Port Authority that was originally designed to be a "regional government" now functioned regionally only when the governors of New York and New Jersey permitted it to do so.

CHAPTER SEVEN

Single-State Agencies: The Metropolitan Transportation Authority and New Jersey Transit

In the 1950s, as in the 1920s, the tri-state region's railroads were again a cause for concern, but the problem this time was mass transit, not freight. Bankruptcy faced the Hudson and Manhattan Railroad, which since 1908 had been the commuter link by tunnel under the Hudson between Manhattan and New Jersey's river-port population centers—Jersey City, Hoboken, and Newark. Other commuter railroads in the region were also operating in the red, and separate attempts by New York and New Jersey to find solutions were stalled.

The process used to approach the problem in the 1950s was the same as the one employed decades earlier to create the Port Authority. The governors of the two states—Alfred E. Driscoll in New Jersey and Thomas E. Dewey in New York, both Republicans—appointed a joint commission, the Metropolitan Rapid Transit Commission, to look into the problem and find solutions.[1] After several years of study and constituency building, this commission proposed a bi-state agency—the Metropolitan Region Transit District—to finance, build, and operate a regional rail transit system. The proposed Metropolitan Region Transit District would initially encompass thirteen counties, three in New York and ten in New Jersey. (Provision was made, if they later opted in, to extend the agency's jurisdiction over those New York and Connecticut suburban counties to the north and east served by commuter rail systems.) The agency's capital and operating expenses would be met from fare box revenues; the deficits, regarded as inevitable, would be apportioned for mandatory payment by participating counties from their own resources.[2] Finally, governance was to be by a thirty-two-member board appointed by participating county governing bodies, that is, it was to be locally based.

In 1958, four years after the commission that proposed it was established, the Metropolitan Region Transit District came tantalizingly close to being created.[3] Even though the gubernatorial successors to Driscoll and Dewey—Robert Meyner and Averell Harriman—were both Democrats, they endorsed the transit district idea. Regional reformers liked it, and business interests in Manhattan and Rockland County, New York, and in Bergen County, New Jersey, mobilized behind it. There was even some backing from railroads.

Elsewhere in the New Jersey suburbs, however, such an agency was seen as potential drain on the state's work force and retail sales. New Jersey mayors in the region mistrusted its county-based governance, and some New Jersey counties feared that a Manhattan-dominated coalition might develop, leaving them with little real power on the board of the new agency.[4]

The two existing regional governments—Greater New York City and the Port Authority—were divided on the issue. The Greater City had just turned its subway system over to a newly created public authority. While other localities feared New York City's dominance in a new regional transit agency, Mayor Robert Wagner, just starting his second term, was concerned about the metropolis assuming the burden of new rail subsidies of unknown magnitude. For its part the Port Authority happily endorsed the transit district idea: such an agency would provide an alternative that would relieve pressure on the authority to provide a mass transit solution for the region. In fact, the Port Authority, hoping for an outcome that would serve its interests, provided most of the money for the transit commission's research (after carefully setting parameters for the study).

With crises and commuter fare increases making daily headlines, the transit district bill passed in the New York State Legislature with strong bipartisan support. It was signed by Governor Harriman, despite Mayor Wagner's opposition. After a tough fight, passage was narrowly gained in the Republican New Jersey Senate as well, but only after Thorn Lord, a Port Authority board member, convinced Sido L. Ridolphi, the Democratic state senator from Mercer County, to provide the decisive vote. (Six of ten state senators from the region were opposed, two of them Republicans.)

However, in the Republican New Jersey Assembly, members from counties within the proposed transit district region constituted the majority, and local opponents prevailed. An alternative plan was offered by opponents of the district, one that would give responsibility for commuter rail to the Port Authority. That agency, of course, violently opposed this idea. As the debate proceeded, changes in federal law went into effect that allowed railroads to cut back commuter services. They did so, and to sustain remaining lines and schedules, they pressed their demands for tax relief and public subsidies. Still another legislative alternative was developed; it offered a transit district with lesser powers. But in the end, time ran out before a majority in the New Jersey Assembly could be found for any plan.

Local opposition killed the Metropolitan Region Transit District, but this local opposition operated in the state political arena. As with the creation of the two already existing regional entities—Greater New York and the Port Authority—it was state, not local, priorities and state, not local, politics that were crucial.

The distinction between regional entities that are locally governed and those that are governed from state capitals is important. The political and fiscal calculations of statewide elected leaders on regional questions—concerned as they are with the entire state budget and responsive as they must be to voters and interests outside the region—are necessarily different from those of leaders chosen within a region and accountable to its citizens. Moreover, in state legislatures decisionmakers from outside the region have a say in crucial regional questions but little political stake in the outcomes. The potential mischief that can arise in such circumstances was a key reason for the centuries-long fight for local home rule in the United States.

Had proponents succeeded in establishing the Metropolitan Regional Transit District, they would have created a bi-state agency that, like Greater New York City but unlike the Port Authority, would have been locally governed. Once in place this agency might have expanded as the commuter crisis deepened, ultimately becoming an integrated mass transit system for the New York–New Jersey–Connecticut region, one responsive to intraregional, not bi- and intrastate, priorities. But a locally governed regional transit district was *not* created, and all subsequent organizational responses were delimited by state boundaries and constrained by state-level political realities.

Governmentalization of Mass Transit

In an era of privatization, the Metropolitan Transportation Authority (MTA) in New York and New Jersey Transit (NJT) across the Hudson are primary examples of the opposite: "governmentalization." Commuter railroads, bus lines, and even most subways in the tri-state region started as profit-seeking private businesses. Government ownership and operation of mass transit arose from a century-long sequence of market failures. Today, massive public subsidies are required to keep mass transit systems equipped and operating.

For many political leaders, choices about mass transit policy were not driven by regionalism's values. They reluctantly took over businesses proven to be economically inefficient, with no thought of expanding them to facilitate economic development or of altering service levels in a quest for social equity. Their primary motivations were not those of today's regionalists: equity, efficiency, competitiveness. For these governmental guarantors of last resort, the choices were simple: governmental service or no service. Regionalism was not a reformer's goal but a pragmatic way to meet a need essential to local economic viability and therefore, to preserving local communities.

In addition, when the MTA and NJT assumed responsibility for New York City's subways and buses and for commuter railroads, suburban bus lines, and the Triborough Bridge and Tunnel Authority's bridges and tunnels, this marked the culmination of a basic shift in governmental responsibility for these crucial services: from general-purpose governments serving localities or a small "region" (Greater New York) to larger, functionally focused regional governments, still within states but serving much larger areas. In fact, the emergence of a broader region was the result of, and synergistic with, the development of the very transportation systems that the MTA and NJT were created to rescue and run.

The MTA and NJT came into existence because of what one previously created regional government—the Greater City—*could not* do and what another—the Port Authority—*would not* do. New Jersey Transit was created out of a group of failed commuter bus lines and began operating railroads when more private companies failed and the national government walked away from the job. The MTA was hailed at its establishment by the *New York Times* as a "tremendous forward step" and "the greatest advance in the metropolitan transportation system in at least half a century," but it was also described by its first chairman, William Ronan, as "the biggest collection of losers ever assembled under one roof."[5]

Today the MTA oversees the largest mass transportation system in North America; in 1998 its operating budget was $6.4 billion. It transports 1.7 billion passengers a year on 343 rail lines, subway lines, and bus routes.[6] New Jersey Transit is the third largest public transit agency in the United States and the only one organized statewide; its operating budget in 1998 was $854.8 million. NJT carries 357,900 daily passengers on 12 rail lines concentrated in the tri-state region, on the Newark subway system, and on 178 bus routes that serve every one of the state's counties.[7] Under the terms of a contract with the MTA, rail service extends into New York on the Port Jervis and Pascack Valley lines. Special programs provide intrasuburban mass transit in parts of the state and mobility for the disabled as mandated by the Americans with Disabilities Act.

Market Failure and the Evolution of Regional Mass Transit

In his economic and political history of urban transportation in the United States, David Jones demonstrates that the financial difficulties of mass transit and its demands for government assistance long antecede competition from automobiles and the development of the national highway system.[8] Certainly this is true in the tri-state region, where it is reflected in the long evolution of public arrangements for transit governance and service delivery.

New York

From their creation in the 1940s to the time they were absorbed in the MTA, both the New York City Transit Authority and the Triborough Bridge and Tunnel Authority operated only within the city. The first of these public authorities was jointly controlled by New York State and New York City. The second, in form if not in fact, was entirely controlled by the city.

SUBWAYS: THE NEW YORK CITY TRANSIT AUTHORITY. Initially, the subways were built with New York City money but were leased to private subway operating companies. To get these lucrative leases in the early twentieth century, the private companies contractually limited themselves to a five-cent fare. In the 1920s this limitation undid them, and they went into receivership. The city assumed the subways' outstanding debt. Then, in 1940 it took over the two bankrupt, privately owned subway lines—the BMT and IRT—and operated them under the aegis of a city board of transportation, in tandem with the Independent Line (IND) that the city had just completed building.

Subway ridership peaked in 1947. During the post–World War II period, deficits mounted as suburbanization—encouraged by various federal policies—proceeded. City officials raised the fare to a dime, politically a very difficult action, and then sought new taxing authority from the state to subsidize transit. (The city had not even requested subsidies from the state; that came later.) However, the Republicans who controlled state government had long advocated the creation of a public authority "to lift the fare and other financial decisions out of the city administration."[9] They believed that mass transit operations should be financed from the fare box. Moreover, along with their reform allies, they sought to deny the Democrats—who usually held sway in city government—control of the jobs and contracts that the subway system generated.

Over the objections of the mayor and other city leaders, the state responded not with taxing authority but with creation of the New York City Transit Authority (NYCTA) to take over operation of the subways and "pay operating expenses from operating revenues."[10] Unlike the subsequent MTA board, the three-person NYCTA board (which was full time and had operational control) was not entirely controlled by Albany. The governor and the mayor each appointed one member, with a third chosen by these two appointees.[11] The NYCTA was denied borrowing authority; therefore, capital projects for the subways still had to be financed by the city itself, although state constitutional borrowing limits were eased occasionally to provide some leeway.

TRIBOROUGH BRIDGE AND TUNNEL AUTHORITY. Assembled in 1946 from a number of smaller authorities created to build specific projects, the Triborough Bridge and Tunnel Authority (TBTA) was "given exclusive power to construct bridges and tunnels connecting boroughs of the city."[12] The authorizing legislation permitted the refinancing of original debt at the agency's convenience. This allowed it to avoid going out of existence when its bonds were paid off—by the simple expedient of never paying them off.

Under the nominal control of a three-member board appointed by the mayor, the TBTA was actually dominated by the man who drafted the 1946 legislation, Robert Moses. Moses selected and nominated board prospects, who then were almost always appointed by the mayor.[13]

The TBTA used an ever increasing stream of bridge and tunnel tolls to build new bridges, tunnels, and other facilities. Like the Port Authority, it was supported by a daunting political coalition of highway users and construction and banking interests, was defended as an agency that "got things done" when others couldn't, and used the need to "protect access to the capital markets" to shield itself from political accountability and guard its independence. Thus, like the authority, it achieved relative autonomy from elected officials, until it finally ran afoul of a governor it could not dominate.

METROPOLITAN COMMUTER TRANSPORTATION AUTHORITY. In 1965 an ad hoc committee headed by William Ronan, then secretary to New York governor Nelson Rockefeller, recommended that the Long Island Rail Road (LIRR) be purchased by the state. Then serving 80,000 commuters, the LIRR was on the brink of bankruptcy. After the state's purchase, it was turned over for operation to the newly created Metropolitan Commuter Transportation Authority (MCTA), which was authorized to coordinate or operate all rail, bus, air, and ferry services in New York City and in the state's counties within commuting distance of the city to the east and north (Nassau, Suffolk, Westchester, Putnam, Rockland, Orange, and Dutchess). Although Nelson Rockefeller said he would never allow it, the new agency soon assumed operating responsibility for the region's two remaining commuter railroads, which reached into the Hudson Valley and suburban Connecticut.

METROPOLITAN TRANSPORTATION AUTHORITY. Two years later crippling mass transit strikes in New York City led Governor Rockefeller to propose integrating the New York City subway and bus lines (then run by the New York City Transit Authority and Staten Island Rapid Transit) with the commuter railroads to form a single entity, the Metropolitan Transportation Authority. The MTA also took over the Triborough Bridge and Tunnel Authority, and in 1973 it assumed responsibility for the Metropolitan Suburban Bus Authority in Nassau County. Metro-North was formed as an operating division of the MTA in 1982 in response to the federally ordered divestiture of commuter lines by Conrail, the federal agency handling the national rail crisis (see below). Currently, Metro-North operates the former Harlem River, Hudson, and New Haven commuter lines. (The Connecticut portion of the last is operated under contract with the Connecticut Department of Transportation.) In addition, it supervises the New York State portions of NJT's Hoboken–Port Jervis and Pascack lines.

From the first the MTA board included representatives *nominated* by the mayor of New York City and elected leaders in each of the suburban counties; but board members were all *appointed* by the governor, and the chairman was the governor's choice alone.[14] Thus, although the MTA took the form of a public authority, the agency was, in the words of one of its later chief executives, "ultimately a gubernatorial responsibility."[15]

Surplus revenues from Robert Moses's Triborough Bridge and Tunnel Authority were to be used to meet mass transit deficits. Interestingly, the law creating the MTA provided that this TBTA money, generated entirely within the city, would be applied equally to operating deficits of the subways and the commuter railroads.

Moses's support for these changes was won by promising him a place on the MTA board, continued control of the TBTA, and authority for the TBTA to build two bridges across the Long Island Sound to Connecticut. None of these promises was ever fulfilled. TBTA bondholders sued to block this deal on the grounds that the bond covenants were being violated (the same argument that would be used by Port Authority bondholders years later). Governor Rockefeller offered a deal to their representative—his brother David, president of the Chase Manhattan Bank—that gave them a greater return on their investment and added security; they settled. Moses was marginalized in the new agency—and then forced out.[16]

New Jersey

Like the MTA New Jersey Transit arose out of market failure. The immediate problems were rapidly escalating subsidies required by commuter bus lines and a ten-year-old subsidy program tinged with scandal. Moreover, the program, based upon recovery of operating deficits, offered private operators no incentives for improving performance; annual costs in 1978 exceeded $50 million and were rising rapidly. The preamble of the bill creating NJT in 1979 noted: "Major public investment in capital and operating assistance to New Jersey's network of predominantly privately owned and operated public transportation services has failed to increase ridership, stabilize fares, or substantially rationalize or improve services."[17]

Battling for governmentalization, State Commissioner of Transportation Louis Gambiccini (Governor Byrne's appointee) argued that the state government was already supporting mass transit and was blamed for its problems but had no direct control over fares or the level or quality of service provided. Gambiccini later recalled that bus and rail lines were "in chaos," on-time performance was "in the cellar," militant commuter groups were in "open revolt," and "passengers were leaving the system in droves."[18] But there was opposition from the private carriers, and committee chairs in both legislative houses strongly opposed the creation of a new public agency. The Byrne administration's bill finally passed in the assembly with a one-vote margin. In the state senate, Republicans Thomas Gagliano of Monmouth County and Corey Edwards of Bergen County crossed over in support. (Interestingly, in 1989 Tom Kean, a Republican governor, appointed Gagliano head of NJT.)

Commuter rail had been in continuous crisis in New Jersey since the 1950s. Federal efforts to rescue the nation's railroads such as the Transportation Act of 1958 focused on freight service. Provisions of that law that hit the tri-state region particularly hard allowed railroads to more easily eliminate interstate commuter service.

Thus on the day the act was signed, New York Central Railroad announced abandonment of rail ferry service across the Hudson; this immediately made the railroad's West Shore rail line useless for commuters to Manhattan. New York Central then could demonstrate to the Interstate Commerce Commission that no one was using the line, and on this basis gain permission to end service—which it did. Announcements of cutbacks or abandonment of service by the Erie, Lehigh Valley, Delaware, Lackawanna and Western, and Pennsylvania Railroads soon followed. The shoring up of money-losing commuter rail was left to the states and localities.[19]

New Jersey's first response (like that of New York) was to subsidize private carriers, in part from a "commuter benefit tax" on New Yorkers working in New Jersey. In addition, the Port Authority was strong-armed into taking over the old Hudson Tubes, now the PATH system (see chapter 6). When Penn Central went bankrupt in 1970, followed soon by eight other companies in the Northeast and Midwest, federal legislators created Conrail in1973. However, 193.8 miles of commuter rail in New Jersey were deemed unprofitable and therefore were not conveyed to Conrail. With tens of thousands of daily commuters dependent on them, the state had little choice but to assume ownership of these lines. It first contracted with Conrail to provide service over much of this network; but as with the bus lines, this resulted in subsidization without control.

With federal assistance there was some investment in capital improvements for rail transportation. However, New Jersey had the most heavily used highway system in the nation, and thus it was no surprise that most available state transportation bond issue monies continued to go to highways. While poor performance drained riders from the system, and road improvements reinforced their predisposition to commute by car, the massive capital needs for modernization, new equipment, rail bed improvement, and station rehabilitation that might have attracted new train riders or retained old ones went largely unmet. NJT's first executive director, Jerome C. Premo, recalled a rush hour trip on the New Jersey Coast Line that left him "red-faced and embarrassed" six weeks after he started in his job. He was, he recalled, with a state senator on a "hot and humid July day." The train's air conditioning malfunctioned, and a drawbridge stuck, requiring three and a half hours to fix and leaving 10,000 commuters delayed and enraged.[20]

Like the MTA, NJT went from owner to owner-operator of the state's commuter rail system in the early 1980s, when Conrail was ordered by Congress to cease passenger rail service. As it assumed operating responsibility for commuter rail, the agency found "remnants of a system built a century ago by private interests. An initially strong and large market for both passenger and freight service resulted in numerous private operators competing for a share of the market. The independent rail systems that emerged . . . were not necessarily interconnected and/or used non-compatible power sources in the case of electrified routes."[21]

Although it is organized as a public authority with independent power to borrow and to set fares, New Jersey Transit—again like the MTA—is firmly under the control of the governor. He or she appoints the entire seven-member board: three members are drawn from state government and four from the general public. By provision of state law, the board chair is the state transportation commissioner, who like the state treasurer, serves ex officio.

DEALING WITH PERMANENT DEFICITS. In 1995 New Jersey Transit showed $429.8 million in subsidies in its operating budget. In 1996 the operating deficit of the New York City Transit Authority was $1.046 billion, and that of the MTA's commuter railroads was $764 million. Mass transit operations everywhere in the United States receive public subsidies for both capital and operating purposes. In the tri-state region these are provided by governments at all levels: federal, state, and local.

After the federal government preempted state regulation and allowed railroads to more easily opt out of interstate commuter service in 1958, Senator Harrison Williams, a Democrat from New Jersey, took the lead in seeking federal involvement in mass transit.[22] Federal programs passed in 1962 and immediately thereafter focused on capital for infrastructure needs. The energy crisis and the burgeoning environmental movement brought about the first operating subsidies, adopted in 1974 and extended later in the decade.[23] Mass transit access to highway trust funds, long a goal of urban advocates, was achieved in 1982. Today, however, federal support for operating costs is "small and declining."[24] Federal mass transit aid remains far more important in the region for capital than for operating purposes.

State aid is both direct, from general tax levy funds, and available in the form of dedicated regional or statewide taxes. States also mandate local government support.

Developed in an ad hoc manner over decades in response to a series of crises, contingent on the expected level of fare box revenue and revenue from other sources, and subject to the vagaries of state budgeting, the mix of aid for mass transit is complex and unpredictable. Most significantly, it is decided in state capitals, not in pursuance of regional priorities or regionalists' values, but rather in accord with the overall taxing (or tax cutting) priorities of state leaders.

FARE-INCREASE POLITICS. The early years of New Jersey Transit were tumultuous. Initial attempts to control labor costs and insert productivity standards in union contracts resulted in a month-long strike in the spring of 1983. Repeated increases in fares and state subsidies were necessary to put the agency's operating budget on a sound footing. However, federal and state aid allowed the launching of a major capital plan: the purchase of new cars, electrification of several lines or reelectrification to put all service on the same standard, station rehabilitation, and the modernization of service facilities. Through the mid-1980s, service improved and ridership rose. Then came the 1987 downturn in the regional economy. Fuel and other operating costs increased. The destructive cycle of fare increases and loss in ridership resumed, with declines especially heavy in bus ridership.[25] Financial irregularities caused Jerome Premo to leave the agency under a cloud, and NJT drifted under temporary leadership and turmoil at the top resulting from changes in partisan control of state government.

Both Democratic and Republican legislators from northern New Jersey argue that transit policymaking is not partisan inside the legislature. This is partly because the state legislative districts are organized to ensure that both Democrats and Republicans represent constituencies in which NJT services are important. Furthermore, fare-increase politics dominates the mass transit debate in a way that puts the focus on choices made by the executive branch, not on those made by the majority in the legislature.

With federal operating aid for mass transit diminishing through the 1980s and 1990s, state aid became the key revenue source used to offset potential fare increases for NJT riders. Fare increases not only angered commuter voters but also diminished ridership, increasing the need for subsidies or requiring service cutbacks—a vicious spiral. As noted, the NJT board is controlled by the governor, so whether the chief executive is Republican or Democrat, mass transit subsidies are an annual executive budget issue. Under these circumstances the mass transit financing debate becomes one element in the general executive-legislative struggle over the budget, heating up especially in gubernatorial election years.

The three-way politics—among the governor, the legislature, and NJT—can become quite intricate.[26] In April 1992, for example, Governor Jim Florio sought a $67.4 million increase in the NJT subsidy, saying it was necessary to avoid a 34 percent fare hike for 1993 (not incidentally, a gubernatorial election year). Operating costs were up, and cuts in federal aid were being threatened. Citing tentative plans prepared by NJT, Florio argued that without such an increase, massive service reductions would be necessary on two of NJT's rail lines and almost half of its bus lines. Interestingly, NJT's plans were made public only after its board—acting on the urging of Carl Van Horn, the governor's representative—"required" their disclosure.

The Republican-controlled legislature was trying to cut the governor's budget by the $1 billion it said relied on nonrecurring revenues. Mass transportation aid was one target. A study by the respected Office of Legislative Services suggested that a fare increase to cover inflation might produce $16 million to reduce the required subsidy from the general fund. In angry response to NJT's adherence to the governor's $67.4 million request, the chairman of the Senate Budget Committee, Robert E. Littel (R, Sussex-Morris), put in a bill to abolish New Jersey Transit as an independent agency.[27] Assemblyman Rodney Freylinghausen (R, Morris) of the Assembly Transportation Committee said the subsidy estimate was designed to produce "political turmoil." With the governor her boss yet ever mindful of the importance of the legislative relationship, NJT Executive Director Shirley DeLibero took offense: "As a professional, that's not the way I do business."[28] Ultimately the legislature appropriated an additional $32.5 million to the NJT, with the caveat that there be no fare increases or service cuts. The board reluctantly agreed.

MTA and the Politics of Geographical Equity

As Robert Moses predicted, the Metropolitan Transit Authority was fiscally problematic from the first.[29] A financial cushion was initially available from a 1967 state transportation bond issue and surpluses from the Triborough Bridge and Tunnel Authority, but operating deficits grew and with them subway and commuter fares and dedicated taxes.[30] The consequences of deferred maintenance and employee attrition—to cut costs—and of regular fare increases—to add revenues—were reduced ridership and declining revenue at the fare box. It was a downward spiral.[31]

The statistics became alarming: subway derailments in 1983 numbered twenty, and extra caution due to poor roadbed conditions contributed to an all-time low 68.9 percent on-time performance record for the transit authority.[32] Proposed fare and toll increases and service disruptions due to labor unrest were make-or-break political issues for state leaders and produced headlines almost every year. Finding ways to pay for both operating and capital costs of mass transit—and be reelected—was a major preoccupation of New York's state and local government leaders throughout the 1970s and 1980s. In 1985 Felix Rohatyn, who had played a major role in resolving New York City's 1975 fiscal crisis, reported to the governor that "the projections [of MTA deficits] . . . portend a fiscal crisis at least as severe and perhaps worse than the great fiscal crisis of 1975."[33]

In response to these persistent crisis conditions, increasing state subsidies were required. In addition to gubernatorial dominance of its governance, this need for annual legislative enactment of subsidies ensured that the MTA is substantially controlled from Albany. Virtually every year the legislative politics of passing the MTA operating aid package requires a careful balancing of city and suburban interests. Payments from the state's general fund are made—either according to a complex statutory formula or through direct *separate* local assistance appropriations—to the NYCTA (for subways) *or* the MTA (for commuter rail). Aid levels are adjusted according to revenues expected from fares, dedicated taxes, and transfers from the TBTA. A prime consideration is the overall state budgetary objectives of the governor and the legislative majorities—for example, to avoid tax increases or achieve tax cuts. In 1996 the general fund appropriation to the NYCTA was $159 million, and to the MTA for commuter rail operations, $29 million. As required by law, these amounts were matched by local governments: New York City for the NYCTA, the suburban counties for commuter rail.[34]

Balancing Regional Interests

In addition to aid from the general fund, the MTA also receives operating funds from the Metropolitan Mass Transit Operating Account.

Money flows into this account from two statewide taxes and from a number of taxes levied only in the Metropolitan Transportation District.[35] The fact that there are regional taxes supporting regionwide service delivery is not widely recognized in New York. However, the managers or board of the MTA may not direct these resources as they please; their distribution, for either the subways or the commuter lines, is specified in law by the state legislature. Moreover, the state's decision to use revenues from some dedicated taxes to back bonds to pay for the agency's capital program has preempted their use for operating purposes. The key points here are that the state government controls the most important decisions and operators of regional rail lack the power to deploy their resources for optimal efficiency, even though achieving efficiency is a supposed benefit of a regional approach.

Fair Treatment: Suburban Counties

To justify the regional taxes levied to support it in its service area, the MTA in 1983 produced a study that sought to demonstrate equity in the geographical distribution of its services and revenues—between the city and suburbs, within the city, and among the suburban counties. It found that "most of the jurisdictions within the MTA region . . . [were] . . . receiving net benefits from the current service and financing structure of the MTA [due to] . . . its position as a regional entity."[36] This study also showed, however, that residents in three Hudson Valley counties in the intermediate and outer rings of the region—Dutchess, Orange, and Rockland—got less than they paid for. The inner suburban counties of Westchester and Nassau, along with Putnam in the outer ring, were the big winners.

Responding to the discontent that this imbalance caused, in 1986 (not insignificantly, a statewide election year) Governor Cuomo proposed and the state legislature passed a bill that allowed these three counties to opt out of the MTA region effective January 1, 1989. But two years later, before any of the counties acted, a second bill was passed that allowed each of them, if they stayed in the region, to recover part of the revenue collected from a mortgage recording transfer tax (passed in 1986 as part of an MTA rescue package) to use on transportation within their borders.[37]

The MTA wanted to protect its revenue stream: residents were already paying the tax. The new law meant $1.5 million each for Orange and Dutchess and $2 million for Rockland. The interests of the county governments prevailed over those of the county sales-tax payers, and the counties gave up the chance to opt out of the MTA region.[38] The MTA effectively bought back, in a nongubernatorial election year, for $5 million *a year* in forgone revenues—what it had been required to give away in a single year in which the incumbent governor was running for reelection.

Geographical Balance in Capital Spending

Capital spending is another area in which the operating definition of equity is place based. As noted, the New York State Legislature authorized $25.9 billion in capital spending by the MTA during the fifteen years between 1981 and 1996. As with labor settlements and fare increases, the agency's five-year capital plans were the product of state politics.[39] A rigid formula in the 1981 legislation adopting the first capital plan ensured that capital expenditures would be distributed consistently: 77 percent within the city and 23 percent outside. The bill also created the MTA Capital Program Review Board, with voting members selected by the governor, the speaker of the assembly, the majority leader of the senate, and the mayor of New York City (for New York City Transit Authority projects only).

To proceed with any capital and borrowing plan, the MTA needs the unanimous approval of this board.[40] Because the state senate has been consistently Republican and the assembly has been Democratic, this means bipartisan balance, regardless of the party holding the governorship. Because most of the assembly majority has been from the city, and the state senate majority's base has been strongly suburban, this ensures intraregional balance between commuter and subway rider interests and between the suburbs and the city.

Balance in Subway and Commuter Rail Fare Increases

The idea of intraregional geographical equity also extended for years to the proportion of operating costs for the city's subways and suburban commuter railroads met from the fare box, and to the rate of fare increases for both. During the turbulent decade between 1980 and 1990, there were five fare increases for subways and commuter rail, all by roughly similar proportions. This, former MTA chairman Robert T. Kiley said, gave city and suburban legislators an identity of interests: they had to "hang together, or hang separately."[41]

The pattern was broken in 1991, when subway fares were raised but commuter line fares were not, and again in 1995, when the 20 percent increase for mass transit was more than twice the 9 percent increase for commuter rail. These subway and commuter fare increases adopted by the MTA were clearly the result of shifts in state policy. As has been the case for half a century or more, Albany-based Republicans wanted more of the costs of both the subways and the commuter lines to be met by those who used them. Moreover, implementation of a commitment by newly elected Governor George Pataki to cut state taxes forced spending cuts across the state government, including capital and operating aid for mass transit. In defending their fare increases in federal court, the MTA's board and management argued that both the level of state support for the agency and its distribution between the subways and the commuter lines were entirely outside their control.[42]

Regionalism, its advocates argue, enhances fairness in the distribution of governmental resources among people of different races and across social classes. The 1995 MTA fare increases led to an evaluation of the extent to which the agency could or should be expected to achieve social equity. Advocates for mass transit within the city argued that because more subway and bus riders were poor and members of minority groups, the failure of the MTA to persist in a policy of geographical equity was *socially* inequitable. Claiming that civil rights laws were violated when commuter transportation services for more affluent, whiter suburban areas were more heavily subsidized than city buses and subways, the Urban League and the Straphangers Campaign sued in federal court to block the fare increase.[43]

District Court Judge Robert Patterson accepted this argument. He concluded that subsidies of commuter rail by New York State and the MTA were indeed disproportionate and that therefore the MTA's proposed fare increases, though not intentionally discriminatory, were likely to have "a racially disproportionate effect or impact."[44] This expected impact caused Judge Patterson to issue an injunction blocking the fare increases.

However, Patterson was reversed a month later by the United States Court of Appeals for the Second Circuit.[45] It regarded the Metropolitan Transit Authority's NYCTA and commuter rail operations as two separate, noncomparable systems. In addition, the court said that subsidizing commuter rail brought indirect benefits to city residents: less pollution, less congestion, and support for the city's economy. At this level the social equity argument as a standard for allocation of resources to mass transit within a regional agency did not prevail.

A careful study of the MTA's financing by Columbia Law School's Legislative Drafting Research Fund was undertaken as part of the settlement of this Urban League–Straphanger Campaign lawsuit. Released in 1998 the study found that state transportation subsidies had shifted substantially in favor of commuter rail in the 1990s, that is, in the direction opposite that which would be expected if a regional approach was actually advancing social equity. Law school researchers could find neither an equity- nor efficiency-based rationale for this shift.[46] However, the report stopped short of pointing out that the absence of such a rationale stems from the primacy of state budgetary and political considerations over regionalist values in agency decisionmaking.

Introduction of the Metrocard for mass transit riders in New York City in 1997 partially redressed the subsidy imbalance caused by the 1991 and 1995 fare increases and attendant decisions. Discounted fares and free transfers between subways and buses were introduced, and two-fare zones were eliminated for many riders.[47] These initiatives were Governor George Pataki's choices, and he was out-front, making the announcement and taking the credit.[48] Later, when the governor announced his plan for unlimited-ride monthly and weekly subway passes, there were no MTA officials at the press conference—only mass transit advocates.[49]

Whether it is good news or bad for social equity proponents, the core point is the same: the MTA is a state agency in the region, responsive primarily to state priorities—not to priorities defined in the region, by leaders accountable to the region. When it comes to major mass transit policy affecting the tri-state area, intraregional interests are balanced by the decisionmaking processes of the state government, not those of a regional institution. Thus regional issues become state issues, which gives legislators from outside the region—all the way north to Plattsburgh and west to Jamestown—a vote on their settlement.

The Metropolitan Transit Authority was designed to "operate free from control of local governments," but it is clearly a creature of New York State politics. Although exercising varying degrees of independence, the agency's leaders—most recently its president, Virgil Conway—have publicly acknowledged the governor as their boss.[50] Crucial financial decisions affecting both its operating and capital budgets are made in Albany. The political agendas of the governor and legislature are carefully considered in the decisions the MTA board controls—on fare increases or cuts, for example—and such decisions are often contingent on prior choices made in Albany. The distributive politics that thus constrain the

MTA's operation are similar to those operative in school aid politics, where there is no regionwide structure operating at all.[51] In 1978 Annmarie Hauck Walsh remarked that "the arrangement of the MTA in New York is the product of a more than half-century search, without success, for a responsive and financially viable structure for providing mass transit services."[52] This was still true at the turn of the twenty-first century.

A Single Transportation Agency for the Tri-State Region?

A Region at Risk, the Third Regional Plan published by the Regional Plan Association (RPA), argued that an integrated, upgraded network of subways, buses, and commuter railroads would not only better link the suburbs to the center in the tri-state region but would tie them to each other as well. Such a "metamorphosis," the RPA contended, "would create a transit system that can help strengthen [the region's] threatened core, repair the torn urban fabric, connect multiple centers of activity, preserve communities and open spaces, and offer equality of access for citizens in an economically efficient and environmentally sensitive manner."[53]

The RPA suggests that the foremost obstacle to realizing this vision is the current organizational structure for governing regional mass transit. Major regional transportation agencies often do not work together, nor do they proceed on the same planning premises. Even within agencies, operating units act without considering their impact on other units (for example, the subways and the Long Island Rail Road within the MTA) or fight over priorities and the use of facilities (for example, the Long Island Rail Road and Metro-North, also within the MTA). "No one has a mandate or a mechanism," the planning group says, "to focus on either long-term or *regional* perspectives."[54]

To remedy this situation, the RPA proposed a "re-formation" of two existing regional institutions—the PANYNJ and the MTA—to give each a distinctive functional focus. For the PANYNJ the focus would be on the air- and seaport functions. (As we have seen, this proposal for the PANYNJ conforms with the objectives of current agency leadership.) In addition, the RPA called for rail and bus transit to be consolidated in a regional transit agency.[55]

Is a Single Agency Necessary?

Even without such reorganization, it is generally acknowledged that the two great mass transit agencies in the tri-state region have made significant progress. Since the early 1980s, service has dramatically improved at the MTA and NJT as a result of extensive capital investments (with state, local, and even private money used to leverage federal aid); state, local, and federal operating subsidies; management improvements; reduction of subway crime; and fare structure stabilization. During the decade and a half between 1981 and 1996, there were three massive capital spending plans: $7.2 billion authorized in 1981, later expanded to $8.5 billion; $7.8 billion in 1986; and $9.6 billion in 1992. These funds transformed the stations, equipment, and facilities of the MTA's operating companies. "By the end of 1995," the new MTA chairman, Virgil Conway, wrote, "the [capital] program had succeeded in rehabilitating 177 subway and rail stations; air conditioning all buses, trains and subway cars; and overhauling or replacing all rolling stock."[56]

As a result of these investments, subway operating costs per passenger mile dropped, and subway and commuter rail on-time performance improved dramatically. In 1995, 95.4 percent of Metro-North and 90.9 percent of Long Island Rail Road trains ran on time. Twice in the early 1990s—the second time on March 20, 1993—Metro-North ran every one of its trains on time, all day![57] As noted earlier, on-time performance on the subways reached a low of 68.9 percent in 1983; by 1995 the comparable figure was 90 percent. In addition, time between train breakdowns lengthened: subway cars in 1995 traveled an average of 58,622 miles between breakdowns, about seven times the distance between breakdowns in 1992.

Responding to these changes, riders returned to commuter rail and the subways in the 1990s. Although Long Island Rail Road ridership remained flat between 1986 and 1996, demand for service on Metro-North was up 21 percent. There were 1.1 billion customers for rail mass transit in New York City in 1996, the highest number in almost a quarter of a century. And though bus ridership was down again in that year, the introduction of free transfers in 1997 reversed this trend, and dramatic increases followed.[58]

New Jersey Transit invested $4.1 billion in its rail and bus systems between 1983 (when it took operating responsibility for rail transit) and 1996. Important infusions of capital funds from the 1991 federal Intermodal Surface Transportation Efficiency Act permitted such major service improvements as direct access to Manhattan on the Morris and Essex Lines and completion of the rail link between Hoboken and Newark. The Secaucus transfer station now being built in the New Jersey Meadowlands (with some assistance from the MTA, whose customers will benefit, too) will further speed the connection to Manhattan and link northern New Jersey by rail to other parts of the state when it is completed in 2002. And when the Hudson-Bergen Light Rail System between Bayonne and Ridgefield Park is completed, it will tie together established waterfront communities in the New Jersey portion of the tri-state region.[59]

Between 1990, when Shirley DeLibero took the top management post at NJT under Democratic governor James Florio, and 1998, fares were continuously held in check and ridership climbed, especially on commuter rail.[60] The agency has received national recognition for being well managed, but budgetary balance has also been helped by a change in state law in 1990 that permitted the use of tens of millions of dollars from state transit trust funds for expenses formerly met from the NJT operating budget.[61] For NJT, as for the MTA, the use of capital resources for operating expenses remains a serious management issue.

Integration at the Customer Level

Perhaps a better approach is to allow structural reorganization of government in the region to follow, not lead, service integration at the customer level. The experience with the E-ZPass for the payment of bridge and tunnel tolls offers a potential model. The pass works on facilities run by multiple agencies, creating a seamless process for service delivery that makes the question of who runs a particular facility—and who receives the toll—irrelevant to the customer. And ultimately, the very high levels of interagency collaboration needed to ensure the effectiveness of this single system may produce a compelling case for their consolidation into a single entity.

The MTA had projected that in all of 1997, 170,000 E-ZPass vehicle identification tags would be installed by its bridge and tunnel customers to allow electronic payment of tolls; in fact, 570,000 of these tags were distributed in *the first three months* of that year. The Port Authority's experience was similar; it distributed 218,000 tags to drivers in 1997.

There were glitches, but a mere eighteen months after the introduction of the new technology, traffic moved far more speedily through most toll plazas of both agencies, as the proportion of vehicles using the E-ZPass approached two in five. Agency officials were delighted. "If this were a private company," declared Vice President for Operations Harris M. Schechtman of the TBTA, "we'd probably be the hottest stock on Wall Street."[62]

This common, customer-focused technology was the result of collective effort over almost a decade by the E-ZPass Interagency Group, which comprised seven public authorities, four of which operated in the tri-state region. Its vision was a "seamless system from Buffalo to Baltimore": the traveler would need only one tag. Meanwhile, operating costs could be lowered, both because fewer toll takers would be needed and because new back-office functions could be shared or privatized.

The introduction of the E-ZPass was not without problems. For example, as late as mid-1998, litigation over the massive contract to be awarded for its installation—valued at almost $500 million—continued to block the installation of the E-ZPass, first scheduled for 1995, by several agencies operating the New Jersey portion of the system.[63] Moreover, as the Metrocard experience thus far illustrates, generalization of a single-card technology across agencies is more difficult for mass transit and commuter rail than for vehicular traffic. Even more fundamentally, this kind of operational bottom-up integration does not ensure that state agencies, or those serving parts of the region, will concur on the prioritization of major capital projects. Nevertheless, a customer-based approach may offer some of the efficiency regionalists seek and hold out hope for further functional consolidation without creating a new, geographically bounded agency that itself would be transcended by later technological advances.[64]

Framework for a Single Regional Agency

Now, as before, we can outsmart or outmaneuver the governmental systems we have created; technology can help overcome barriers raised by entrenched structures. This is the incremental, customer-centered, bottom-up approach. Yet creation of a single, locally governed agency that is truly regional in its approach and priorities might be worth considering as a way to eliminate the obstacles thrown up by existing organizations serving parts of the tri-state region—especially in the case of mass transit.

However, such restructuring would have to be undertaken with eyes wide open. Experience tells us that those who operate such an agency must be able to control its allocation of resources if the range of possible efficiencies is to be achieved. (And even then there are limits to the efficiency regionalism can allow; a single, regionwide transportation agency would continue to require heavy subsidies to function effectively.) Experience also tells us that in delivering its services, such an agency is more likely to be concerned with measurable geographical equity (fairness in serving different places) than with less quantifiable social equity (fairness in serving people of different classes or ethnic groups). Finally, experience suggests that an agency governed by state appointees and subsidized from state coffers would be driven not by regionalists' values—efficiency, equity, competitiveness—but by the fiscal and political requirements of state policymakers.

To advance a truly regional agenda, an integrated tri-state transportation agency would have to be a regionwide government, with regionally based operational and fiscal autonomy. Only regionwide elected leadership—either a single executive or a governing board—can provide operational autonomy for a regional transportation agency. Our earlier discussion of Greater New York City provided a prime example: however limited New York City has become as a regional government, its consolidation did produce a strong advocate for the "region" that is the Greater City—its citywide elected mayor.

It is not uncommon for states to have separately elected statewide officials for functions regarded as especially important. The *Book of the States* offers various examples for education, higher education, utilities regulation, and agriculture, to name just a few.[65] They provide a precedent for having a regionwide elected official or board for a single important function in a region with a population and an economy bigger than most states.

The Third Regional Plan suggests that a regional agency created for mass transit be subsidized from tolls now collected or newly imposed on all the major bridges and tunnels in the region.[66] Both the MTA and the Port Authority provide models for this approach. But this probably would not be enough. A locally governed regional agency, run by popularly elected officials, would need dedicated regional taxes unconstrained by allocation formulas set in state capitals. Regional taxes now dedicated to the MTA within New York provide a model that might be extended throughout the region. The elected leadership of the new agency would also need the authority to raise specified taxes within the region, within limits prescribed in national or state law. This practice is, of course, common in other key functional areas: school districts, fire districts, and library districts come to mind. If state aid was still a requirement, it might be formula driven, based on service delivery and performance, with barriers to formula alteration if states got into fiscal trouble. And federal aid for operations and capital improvement, augmented if possible, would have to flow into the regional transportation agency directly, not through the state governments in the region. Whatever system is chosen for electing and financing a regional governing body, and however its functions are defined, creation of the resulting region would require special federal action, along with the consent of the affected states. Both are highly unlikely—impossible, many would say.

Perhaps this is true. But consider this: if the proposed Metropolitan Region Transit District had been approved by the New Jersey Assembly in 1958, this chapter might instead be a critique of its operation as a multistate, regionally governed, regional transportation agency.

PART FOUR

The Regional Idea in Subregional Settings

CHAPTER EIGHT

The Persistence of Suburban Localism

Princeton, New Jersey, is world renowned for its educational and research institutions. However, it is unlikely that many who know it as the home of Princeton University or the Institute for Advanced Study also realize that when it comes to local government, there are actually two Princetons—a township and a borough. The two Princetons are located in Mercer County, fifty miles from New York City, in the tri-state region's intermediate ring. Their combined population is about 25,000; a slightly larger number live in the 16.25-square-mile township than reside in the more densely settled 1.76-square-mile borough that it surrounds (figure 8-1).

Unlike most other urbanized areas in central New Jersey, the inner section of the Princeton area (the borough) is more affluent than the surrounding township. Overall, however, residents of both Princetons are similar in their demographic characteristics and in their expectations of local government. Perhaps this is why the two Princetons are able to share costs and responsibility for service delivery in seventeen functional areas, including education (but not for the two largest municipal functions, police and public works). Cooperation, however, has not led to consolidation. In 1996, as on several occasions dating back to 1952, an effort to consolidate the two municipalities failed.

Intermunicipal consolidation has been encouraged in New Jersey by statute since 1977 to achieve "more rational control of growth and development, more efficient provision of local services and more effective pub-

Figure 8-1. *Princeton Township Encircling the Borough*

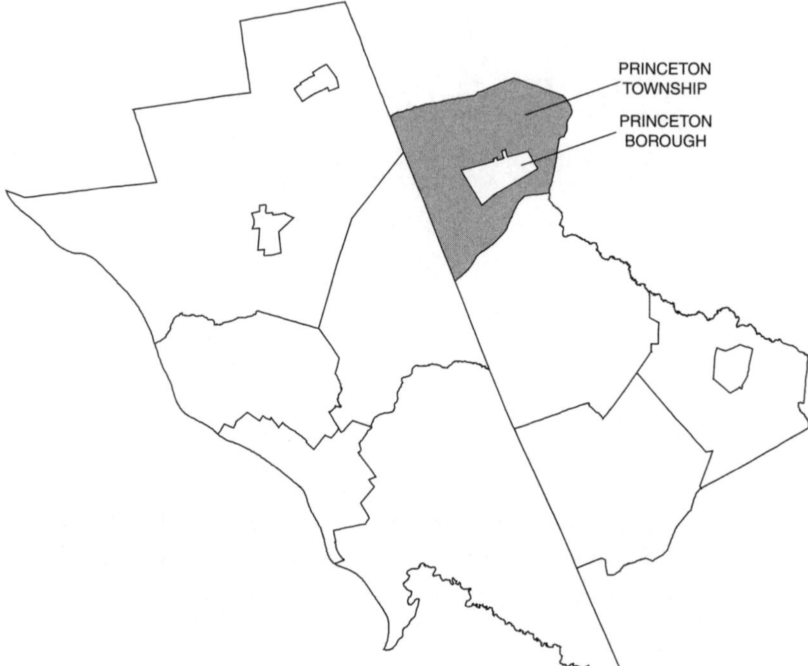

Source: Department of State, Mercer County, New Jersey (www.mercercounty.org/_private/our%20towns.htm [February 2001]).

lic administration."[1] Under the law a proposal to create a commission on the consolidation of two or more localities may be placed on the ballot by the board of an interested government or by citizen petition. In each potentially affected community, voters then decide simultaneously whether to create a commission and who shall serve on it. If this proposal passes, the commission, aided by an appointee of the state's Department of Community Affairs, is required to report its recommendations to the department and the potentially affected localities within six months.

Spurred on by the prospect of having to build an expensive new municipal building, these steps were taken by the governments of the two Princetons in 1995. The proposal passed by a wide margin in the township but by only twenty-four votes (936 to 912) in the borough. The 1995 commission studied "whether the two Princetons should consolidate or remain separate and, if they remained separate, whether they should consolidate additional services."[2] It received assistance from both a management consulting company and an architectural firm. Several commission members also presented briefs on key areas of concern. Commission meetings were open and public participation was encouraged; additional public input was obtained through focus groups. Local press coverage was extensive, and reports were made available.

In its preliminary report, supported by eight of its ten members, the 1995 commission recommended consolidation of Princeton into a single entity with a borough form of government. It further recommended that within seven years a charter commission should be established to review the effectiveness of this newly formed government and, if necessary, propose needed changes. This recommendation was affirmed in the final report of the commission.

In New Jersey, as in most states, consolidation of local governments occurs only if majorities in all (or both) the affected communities agree.[3] Therefore, the final step to consolidation of the two Princetons in 1996 was obtaining separate supportive majorities in the township and the borough. The mayors of both entities were, from the first, strong backers of consolidation. The debate was not organized around differences between the two governments; rather it was structured by community groups organized to affect the referendum's outcome. The result was a hot confrontation. Those in favor of "One Princeton" made what was largely an efficiency case; they argued that what was in reality one community could best be served, at lowest cost to taxpayers, through a single government. Those opposed—organized as "Save Our Historic Borough"—confronted what they characterized as this "stark economic reasoning" with a campaign focused on "cultural values." They argued that the borough was unique, "an older Princeton with its own traditions" worth preserving.[4]

A majority of all those in Princeton Township and Borough combined who voted on consolidation supported the idea, but not a majority in each of the Princetons as the law required. As in the past, backing in the township was solid; also as in the past, a majority of borough voters demurred. Opposition was strong among older residents, who were most attached to the place as it always was, and among public employees, who were most immediately threatened by change. Even sophisticated local residents—people who might otherwise have responded positively to reform appeals in this, the quintessential university town of the tri-state region—balked at changes in governmental structure that they saw as threatening their sense of community and diminishing local democracy.[5]

Our review of the Greater New York experience demonstrated that even as metropolitan government strives for ever greater centralization in its operations, citizens strive to retain or re-create their local government to protect those things they value most: their families and their neighborhoods. It is no accident that despite their limitations, the existing community-level entities in New York City—the community boards and community school boards—concern themselves with neighborhood conditions and children, with land use and schools. Concomitantly, with the negative example of the metropolitan experience before them, suburbanites also adhere to their local governments to protect what *they* value most: their families and their neighborhoods. Whether in borough, village, town, or school district, the local government entity and the community value become synonymous in citizens' minds. Attempts to consolidate or dissolve local governments or—as some reform-minded people occasionally suggest—to abolish entire classes of them (all villages, all towns, all counties) are inevitably seen as attacks on community.

This is why the Princeton outcome is so typical and why the failure rate for this type of reform is so high. The New Jersey Department of Community Affairs reports that despite "nine studies of potential consolidation and various calls for studies by a single willing party," the last successful joining of two municipalities in New Jersey occurred in 1954.[6]

Based in part on the experience of the two Princetons, the New Jersey Department of Community Affairs has proposed changes in law, regulation, and state practice to encourage consolidation. The agency urges early retirement incentives, funded by the state, to reduce local government employee opposition. It also recommends state aid incentives and statutory and regulatory changes to ensure that state fiscal and policy requirements do not place greater demands on residents of either participating locality after consolidation. In addition, the department has recommended changes in the consolidation process: easier ballot access for commission candidates; reduced size for the required study commission; a longer time period for study; and approval by a simple majority of all the members on the study commission to move the idea forward (rather than a separate majority of members from each community).[7]

Even with these changes, the procedures set out in New Jersey law for local government consolidation reflect the power of localism as much as they reflect any state commitment to the law's ostensible purpose. Like the proconsolidation Princetonians who failed in 1996, those who want to consolidate *today* still must achieve popular support in two successive referendums within a brief period of time—first to start the process, then to approve the result. The status quo is known and comfortable; therefore, mobilization of simultaneous majorities twice in two jurisdictions, with initial success likely to galvanize the opposition, is a high political hurdle.

Such state-imposed procedural barriers to structural change in local government are common and usually established in the name of local democracy. The New York state legislature's elimination of numerous local governments by fiat in order to create Greater New York City was the structural reformers' greatest success in the region. Yet this led to adoption of a state constitutional amendment blocking further consolidations without consent from those living in all affected jurisdictions.

There is one exception: under New York law villages may be dissolved by their residents entirely by local action. The participation and consent of residents of the town or towns within which they are located is not required. However, the steps involved still allow ample time for opposition within a village to mobilize. The elected village board of trustees may place the question of dissolution on the ballot at any time and *must* do so if a third of the electors in the village petition for it. But any call for a dissolution referendum by the village board must be preceded by a public hearing. If a majority of voters favor dissolution, it becomes effective on the last day of the year after that vote. This not only provides transition time but also time for opponents to press for reversal of the outcome.[8]

Using these procedures, and with state encouragement, some few villages in the tri-state region have been dissolved.[9] In Ulster County in the region's outer ring, the citizens of tiny Pine Hill voted it out of existence in 1986 after the mayor was implicated in a scandal. Ten years earlier the village of Rosendale was dissolved after a bitter fight; its board of trustees, which favored dissolution, forced three separate votes before a 179 to 87 majority to abolish the village was obtained. However, the outcome in the Village of New Paltz in 1993 was more typical: after a heated debate that divided the village board and anticipated in almost every detail what later occurred in the two Princetons, villagers in this university town rejected dissolution.[10]

Advocates have long pursued systematic reduction in the number of local governments in the tri-state region. Apart from the creation of Greater New York, their efforts have yielded only two major successes in the twentieth century. In Connecticut an entire class of local governments, the counties, was eliminated by state action; in New York the number of school districts was massively reduced with state encouragement. Achieved in the name of efficiency and equity, these two cases involving broad-scale reductions in the number of local governments reveal more about the limitations for future consolidationist approaches than about their prospects.

Eliminating an Entire Class of Local Governments

Counties in Connecticut go back to the early seventeenth century.[11] But there, as in much of New England, they were not embedded in communities, nor were they the principal general-purpose local governments; towns fulfilled this role. The only countywide elected officials were sheriffs. Early Connecticut counties had few functions beyond court administration, did not levy property taxes directly, and were run by officials appointed by the state legislature. In the mid-nineteenth century, political control of counties was given to the county delegations in the state legislature. Not surprisingly, counties subsequently became major sources of Republican patronage in that rock-ribbed Republican state.

By the early twentieth century, counties had lost control of court administration but were issuing liquor licenses (and collecting fees), running jails, administering aid to widows, running homes for neglected children, and taking responsibility for some bridge, highway, and other capital construction. When Prohibition came in 1919, it killed the liquor licensing function and cut off this source of revenue. (Liquor licensing returned as a state function with the repeal of Prohibition in 1933.) In Hartford, the state's largest city, an alternative approach was developed in 1929 for regional delivery of water and other services requiring major infrastructure investments: the metropolitan district. This entity superseded the county as a potential deliverer of regional service. Then the Depression brought federal and state programs to aid dependent children, and the county role withered in Connecticut.

During the 1930s and 1940s, problems with jail and foster home administration ensured regular studies of county performance and occasionally brought reform. In the 1950s scandals in jails and foster homes gave added ammunition to Democrats, who had long pledged to abolish counties—and the GOP patronage systems they supported—if they gained control of state government. Quite unexpectedly, they did gain control: in 1958, for the first time since 1876, Democrats swept the governorship, both houses of the state legislature, and all eight county sheriff races. Even though they now controlled all the patronage, they kept their word. In

1959 legislation was passed abolishing Connecticut's counties, effective October 1, 1960.

The demise of counties in Connecticut was not inevitable. They could have become units for regional delivery of services that clearly needed to be provided on a scale greater than local boundaries permitted. They could have retained a role in key social welfare functions and expanded with the growth of the welfare state. Their importance as a guarantor of public safety might have gained importance. All these things actually happened in New York, and many of them in New Jersey, though both of these states were heavily influenced by New England practices in their early governance patterns. What was different in Connecticut?

In New York, as in Connecticut, counties began as "branch offices" of the state government. However, in New York, county governance ultimately became more closely linked to local community governments, whereas in Connecticut, the *state* took over county functions. In New York, town supervisors served both as heads of town governments and as members of county boards of supervisors. They were human links between communities, towns, and counties. When town supervisors became *elected* officials in the early nineteenth century, New York counties automatically were headed by boards of these locally elected officials, and their governance became locally rooted.

Because they were run by state legislators, Connecticut counties never stopped being primarily state branch offices. Thus the transfer of their functions, one by one, to Hartford was simply a movement from the branch office to the head office, not from a community government to the state government. In New York, by contrast, the same or similar events (Prohibition, the Depression, occasional scandal, reform movements) left the counties, as local governments, with a large measure of responsibility for administering programs and paying the bills—even if they were heavily influenced or largely controlled by state law and policy.

For almost a century, Democrats never had a patronage base in Connecticut's counties. In this most partisan of states, they saw little need to protect counties as a resource for *their* party. But they did see a good issue, a good government issue, for statewide elections. By contrast, in New York and New Jersey, partisan control of state government shifted regularly, and there were always some local areas controlled by each party. Attacking the counties as unneeded was a cost-free strategy for Connecticut Democrats—until they won so sweepingly. And by then they were committed to abolishing them.

Opportunity and incentive converged, and Connecticut eliminated an entire class of local government, leaving its local government system among the least layered in the nation. Is all this replicable through some *specific* reform strategy in New York and New Jersey? The answer is probably not. Localism is very powerful, and there are state constitutional barriers. Furthermore, many of the conditions that permitted Connecticut's abolition of counties were serendipitous and idiosyncratic. The political conditions under which *state* level leadership is willing to make far-reaching and basic changes in the *local* governance system were rare half a century ago and are rarer still today.

State Incentives for Change: School Consolidation

Education is by far the biggest and most important service local government delivers. In 1992 almost 30 percent of total local government spending ($24.272 billion) in the tri-state region was for schools, far more than for any other function. In more than a third of the region's suburban counties, education costs accounted for well over half of all local government costs in that year.

Apart from being the place where the most local dollars are spent, schools are at the emotional center of their communities. Providing elementary and secondary education is an obligation of state government; making their children available for education is an obligation of families. It is little wonder, then, that over the past fifty years the schools have been the battleground of some of the most divisive social issues in contemporary American life. One of these, of course, is racial integration. A second is fairness in providing and paying for the education of poor (often minority) children living in property tax base–poor inner cities. In most places in the United States, Americans have purposely separated the delivery of education from the provision of other local government services. But those who provide education, like those who are interested in general-purpose local government, have long pursued governing arrangements that would optimally balance the desire for local democracy and control with the need to achieve greater competitiveness, efficiency, and equity.

Success and Resistance

Across the United States, school district consolidation was the most massive and successful effort at structural change in local government in this century. Between 1930 and 1992, the consolidation movement eliminated eight of every nine school districts in the country. From 1952 to 1972 alone, the number of school districts plummeted nationally from 67,355 to 15,781, a drop of more than three-fourths. As Professors E. J. Haller and David Monk of Cornell rightly observed: "These governments were not obscure entities performing some trivial task; they were governmental bodies that daily touched the lives of citizens in a critically sensitive area, the welfare of their children."[12]

The trend in New York paralleled that in the nation. Between 1952 and 1972 the number of school districts in all of New York State dropped by three-fourths (from 2,915 to 746). The 61.5 percent decline within the New York portion of the tri-state region during this period was dramatic but not quite as great as it was in the rest of New York State. It occurred almost entirely during the 1950s and, interestingly, was far smaller in the rapidly growing counties closest to New York City than in the, at that time, more rural intermediate and outer rings (more evidence of the strength of localism as a suburban defense mechanism against potential absorption by cities.) There were 635 school districts in the region's nine New York counties in 1952; 266 in 1962; and 244 in 1972. In Nassau County the number went from 66 in 1952 to 56 in 1972, a drop of about 15 percent. Westchester County also lost ten districts (from a base of 59), for a decline of 17 percent.

Then, over the next twenty years, school district consolidation in New York State virtually ceased. Between 1972 and 1992, the number of school districts in the state declined by only 33, and in the region, by 3. The Tuckahoe and Eastchester school districts in Westchester County recently considered combining, but Eastchester backed away. Earlier in this decade Rye and Rye Neck brought the matter to a vote, but it failed. Sharing services, not consolidating districts, has become the preferred approach.[13]

Interestingly, Connecticut and New Jersey resisted the national trend, even when it was at its height. In these two states, school consolidation never got started. In fact, the number of districts reported by the census in these states actually has gone up.[14] To be sure, this growth was something of a statistical artifact. As noted earlier, the Census Bureau does not regard most school districts in Connecticut as independent governments.[15] In New Jersey, though some new regional school districts were created, the increase was largely the result of local voters choosing to have their schools operate independently of general-purpose governments. But this statistical artifact notwithstanding, these states clearly resisted the national trend: while virtually everyone else was doing it, they did not reduce the number of school districts.

This was not because school consolidation was not an issue in these states. In New Jersey, pressed by the need to find money for schools while controlling property tax increases, both Democratic and Republican governors were drawn to the logic of reducing the number of school districts. In 1993 a commission appointed by Governor James Florio, a Democrat, recommended a nonpartisan, base-closing-type process to eliminate about 60 percent of the school districts in the state by the 1997–98 school year. The stated goal was to improve the quality of education while reducing costs.[16]

In her 1998 State of the State message, Governor Christine Todd Whitman, a Republican who had defeated Florio four years earlier, proposed to a skeptical legislature a statewide referendum on school regionalization. Whitman's speech addressed quite explicitly the tension between the values of community and efficiency in the school consolidation debate. The governor said that she remained opposed to "forced regionalization," but she nevertheless noted "the enormous potential [that] consolidation carries for reducing property taxes." "Our goal," she continued, "is not to end the cherished practice of neighborhood schools and local control. It's to give the people a say in how we get control of school spending, and how we make New Jersey a more affordable place in which to live, work and raise a family."[17]

Supportive evidence was at hand. A *Plan for School District Consolidation in New Jersey*, issued by the Center for Governmental Services at Rutgers in 1995, suggested a consolidation that would reduce the number of school districts in New Jersey by more than half (from 606 to 287), for a savings estimated at $200 million a year. But there had been lots of previous efforts, without success. A report advocating regionalization and consolidation published by the Public Affairs Research Institute of New Jersey in 1996 cited five major studies in the previous twenty-five years advancing this same point of view, none of which had been acted upon.[18]

A blue-ribbon commission report released in Connecticut in 1994 treaded more softly but sounded the same theme. It effectively proposed consolidation by endorsing the idea that all school districts in the state be organized to "span K thru 12." In their dissent from the majority, teacher union representatives on the commission took issue with the "dissolution of dozens of kindergarten through grade eight school districts in the state" that would flow from this recommendation. Ultimately, legislation effecting the commission's recommendations failed in the state legislature.[19]

Activists in New Jersey and Connecticut cite a fierce commitment to local control of education—and the identification of quality education with local control in suburbanites' minds—as the reason for the persistence of their local school districts. Yet these feelings were no less strong in New York when significant consolidation actually occurred. It seems two other factors may have been critical.

The first was the relative strength of the state education department in New York. According to David Strang, a leading student of the subject, "Where central actors play larger roles in the educational system, school districts are reorganized more quickly and extensively."[20] The New York State Education Department, an acknowledged national leader for much of the century, strongly promoted consolidation as the only way to ensure educational quality, and therefore opportunity, for the state's children living outside big cities. It paid for studies, produced a committed cadre of education professionals who advocated consolidation, enriched operating aid formulas, financed incentives for districts to merge, and withheld aid for new school buildings from districts that would not consolidate. When local residents resisted by voting against consolidation, the department got the state law altered so that a single majority overall, not a majority in each affected district, was enough to allow districts to merge.[21]

The second factor is structural. Unlike New York, both Connecticut and New Jersey took Horace Mann's advice: they based school district boundaries on those of local government entities. The resultant coterminality of school districts with towns and cities reinforced the link between the structure of the educational system and deeply held values of community. This made school consolidation more difficult.

Consolidation Ceases in New York

By the mid-1970s school district consolidation in New York had largely ground to a halt. This was the case even though the state, about midsized in geographical expanse, still had about twice the national average number of school districts. It was the case even though it continued to offer a rich package of incentives to merge. And it was the case even though many New York school districts—including 64 in the tristate region—were still proposed for consolidation under a state education department master plan.[22]

There still were powerful, well-placed advocates for school consolidation; one was the state commissioner of education, Thomas Sobol. In 1992 Sobol, articulating classic efficiency and equity goals, announced his intention to seek authority from the state legislature to impose consolidation. "The people of the state," Commissioner Sobol said, "have an interest in seeing that all children receive their constitutional right to an education and that the public's money is not squandered, *regardless of local wishes*."[23]

The commissioner had some allies in the field. Earlier in 1992 the Long Island Regional Planning Board had proposed a minimum district size of 4,000 students for Nassau and Suffolk Counties. Such a change would reduce the number of school districts there by almost half, from 127 to 66.[24] In the same year, the *Rockland Journal News* pointed out that reducing the number of school districts in that tri-state region suburban county from 8 to 3, with each serving about 12,000 students, "would save $500,000 per year in superintendents' salaries, plus perhaps an additional three-quarters of that amount in the salaries of business managers. And such totals were reached even prior to examining the salaries of assistant superintendents, clerical support staff, and office maintenance costs for each of these officials."[25]

Yet in the end nothing happened. Suzanne Spear, who has worked on consolidations for more than a decade for the New York State Education Department, says that to understand why consolidation ran out of steam it is important to understand what had earlier impelled it. There were three major factors: inadequate educational opportunities for children, especially at the high school level; property tax pressures; and a need for new school buildings. "At least two of the three have to be there," Spear insists, "if anything is to happen."[26]

In recent decades the argument that larger districts are needed to provide quality education has become less and less credible. In New York's tri-state region suburbs, most districts reached a size at which they could offer solid K–12 programs, or they were rich enough to pay a premium to do this at a smaller size. This left as candidates for consolidation the "hardest cases," those districts that for decades had resisted state pressures and inducements.[27] Moreover, creation of the Board of Cooperative Educational Services (BOCES) for regional delivery of education in New York (and other regional approaches in Connecticut and New Jersey) allowed small places to gain many of the benefits of larger size without consolidation.[28]

In addition, an important, countervailing "small is beautiful" paradigm developed that questioned the educational assumptions of the consolidation movement. "The basic thrust and objective has changed completely," according to Stanford University's Michael Kirst, a researcher in the field. "We've moved from bigger districts and a focus on consolidation to a focus on community identity."[29] Many suburban and rural places are literally organized around their school systems; the schools are both at the heart of their identities as communities and a vital economic presence. And though smaller schools cannot afford as deep and broad a range of high school offerings, the new reformers argued, they are likely to be more nurturing and supportive of each student and to educate better in the basics, too. From this perspective, consolidation irreparably harmed communities without necessarily enhancing the quality of education.[30]

To the degree that consolidation came to be seen as a trade-off rather than a win-win strategy—"lesser education for lower cost" rather than "better education *and* lower cost"—it became a much harder sell to localities. Finally, the idea that consolidation saved money was even challenged, although less vociferously and credibly than the educational aspect of the consolidationists' argument.[31]

The Issue of Race

The racial issue has been a critical factor in attempts to consolidate school districts. Gary Orfield has shown that schools in New York, New Jersey, and Connecticut are among the most racially segregated in the nation and that this segregation is directly related to the structure of service delivery. "The four states that have the most extreme segregation for African Americans—New York, Illinois, Michigan, and New Jersey," Orfield writes, "are all large states with fragmented school districts breaking metropolitan housing markets into many school districts."[32] In other parts of this volume we note that voluntary cooperation among local governments in the region is most likely to occur when they are demographically and socioeconomically similar. As racial differences between school-age populations grew over the last several decades, especially between cities and districts of the tri-state region's inner suburban ring, school consolidation came to be seen as a "forced" integration strategy—and was resisted accordingly.

Red Bank in Monmouth County, New Jersey, in the tri-state region's intermediate ring, runs a K–8 school district with 900 students enrolled, many of them poor and black. In 1995 it was scheduled for serious cuts in state funding because of its high administrative costs and the refocusing of state education aid on New Jersey's thirty poorest districts. In this same 1995 budget, Governor Whitman included $8 million in incentives to encourage smaller elementary and high school districts to merge. However, years of effort to join neighboring, more affluent white districts in a K–12 program taught Assistant Superintendent for Business Bruce Quinn that this was not an option. "It has a lot to do with the makeup of our schools," Quinn observed.[33]

In October 1998 John E. Rooney, an assemblyman from suburban Northvale in Bergen County, New Jersey, described as "not natural" the notion that a white child might attend school in a majority minority district.[34] Reflecting this sentiment, white county residents in Tenafly, Englewood Cliffs, and neighboring Livonia have spent millions in legal fees to resist the mandatory regionalization advanced by the City of Englewood—where the school enrollment is largely African American—as a way to desegregate its Dwight Morrow High School.[35] Arguing in 1997 (a gubernatorial election year) that mandatory regionalization would not result in desegregation but just cause white flight, Governor Whitman and her education commissioner, Leo F. Klagholz, supported the development of a voluntary plan. This position was later upheld by the New Jersey Board of Education.[36]

Reformers continue to argue for school consolidation as if race were not a factor. The 1996 study of the Public Affairs Research Institute of New Jersey, for example, suggests that consolidations might be achieved if the state were more assertive: funding incentives to promote consolidation; promoting regionalism through new school siting and construction; developing model proposals; aggressively educating the public on the fiscal advantages of consolidation; and easing statutory barriers to change.[37] But experience in New York, where very strong state incentives stopped working, challenges this conclusion.

As we noted, in her 1998 State of the State message, Whitman called for a statewide vote on school district regionalization. By attempting to shift the debate to a broader arena, the governor sought to alter its focus away from regionalism as a threat to community and onto regionalism as a mechanism for achieving efficiency.[38] But the cool legislative reception to Governor Whitman's 1998 proposals suggested the limits of this approach. In New Jersey, "regionalism" in education has become a code word for racial integration; thus the concept is endorsed by precious few state legislators from white suburban districts, which tend to dominate state politics.

Some experts continue to insist that school district consolidation is a good idea, using the same arguments that they have used for almost a century. They tell families who are paying some of the highest property taxes in the nation that consolidation is a holy grail, a way to make schools cheaper while also making them better. But this appeal to the pocketbook, usually so powerful, simply doesn't work when it comes to school consolidation. Even citizens who really hate the property tax just don't bite.

This is a very powerful fact. As we have seen, the reasons for it are complex—some compelling, some troubling. But it boils down to this: for those who are interested in achieving both equity and efficiency in education, consolidation is not a strategy that produces results. At the end of the day, citizens believe they are being asked to trade effectiveness (good schools) and democracy (local control) for equity (racial integration and equal spending for all children) and efficiency (lower costs)—and that is a trade they are not willing to make.

Structural Change Does Not Work

Writing in *The Regionalist*, the national journal of the regionalism movement, David Walker, a political scientist at the University of Connecticut, suggested recently that his state's abolition of counties was a mistake. "The absence of a middle tier of limited purpose but popularly elected governments," he maintained, was "part of the crisis confronting our localities."[39] The arguments were familiar. Counties, covering more territory and people than towns or cities, allow greater efficiency and equity in the delivery of local services, and—headed as they are by elected officials—are more accountable to the public than are other regional governing arrangements.

But in Connecticut today, the state government itself may be seen as a partial surrogate for regional government. When counties were abolished, most of their responsibilities were taken over by the state government. The relatively short travel time by car from the state's outermost limits to Hartford (about two hours) allowed Connecticut to eliminate the middleman, playing both the statewide and regional roles in financing and delivering services that are elsewhere performed by states and counties together. There are no local courts or jails in Connecticut, wel-

Table 8-1. *State Government Proportion of Combined State and Local General Spending and Revenue, Tri-State Region, 1995*

Units as indicated

	Spending		*Taxes*	
State	*Combined amount*[a]	*State share*[b]	*Combined amount*	*State share*
Connecticut	15,745	54.1	10,949	61.9
New Jersey	36,058	43.9	23,977	52.1
New York	107,025	36.3	66,347	48.1

Source: State and Local Sourcebook for 1999 (Washington: Governing Magazine, 1999), pp. 9, 29.
a. In millions of dollars.
b. Percent of combined amount.

fare is almost entirely a state function, and public health responsibilities are largely met at the state level as well. Perhaps this is why, of the three state governments that fall within the tri-state region, Connecticut's government has the largest share of total state and local taxes and general spending (table 8-1).

Counties are unlikely to come back in Connecticut. The state is widely admired for the simplicity of its local governing arrangements. Moreover, as other experience shows (see chapter 10, on solid waste), when there is a need for substate regional structures for particular functions, Connecticut devises them.

However, neither New Jersey nor New York is likely to eliminate an entire class of governments to simplify its local governance system. Some reformers in New York, for example, have advocated eliminating all villages, and as earlier noted some New York villages have been dissolved in recent years. Although the general abolition of villages in New York, like the elimination of counties in Connecticut, might reduce local government layering, it would also remove some units that are vital and needed. In Nassau County on Long Island, for example, where towns like Hempstead serve hundreds of thousands of people and spend hundreds of millions of dollars annually, eliminating all villages would be a step toward creating a local government vacuum similar to that now existing in New York City.

As explained in chapter 1 (see tables 1-1 and 1-2), each type of government in the region—counties, cities, towns, villages, boroughs—varies greatly in size and function. Moreover, unlike Connecticut counties, local governments of all types in New York and New Jersey are closely identified with the value of community. State political leaders count local copartisans among their core political supporters. (In New Jersey, in fact, state legislators often simultaneously hold local office.) State policies appear to support systematic reduction in the number of local governments, but in reality they remain very deferential to local preferences. For all these reasons, there is little hope for forceful state action to systematically restructure local government.

Despite this historical evidence, reformers continue to press for reduction in the number of general-purpose local governments and school districts through consolidation. In April of 1994—after two and a half years of study, discussions, and consultation—Westchester 2000, a public-private partnership, released an eighty-two page report on merging and consolidation of local governments in this inner-ring, suburban New York county. It attacked the "waste and complication" endemic in Westchester's more than 500 overlapping local governments and special districts, observing that this created "vast inefficiencies both in terms of monetary costs and the availability and quality of service delivery," and called for reducing the number of general-purpose governments from 44 to 24 and the number of school districts by more than half, from 40 to 19, at most.[40]

The reactions from the practical politicians in the trenches were predictable: it just would not work. Democrat Paul Feiner, supervisor of Greenburgh, the county's largest town (population 82,000—bigger than most cities in the tri-state region), insisted that there was no support for the merger of governments. Feiner defended "the smaller level of government" and suggested that maybe it was the county that ought to be abolished.[41] Republican Andrew O'Rourke, the county executive and a sponsor of the Westchester 2000 effort, agreed that there were "too many layers of governments" but also indicated that he was not ready to lead the charge for restructuring. "It has to be done somewhere along the line," the county executive remarked tepidly. According to Richard Lerer, superintendent of Southern Westchester BOCES, the answer was not consolidation but more sharing of services; that was doable.

He was right, or at least partly right, as we demonstrate in chapter 9.

CHAPTER NINE

Two Approaches: Bottom Up and Top Down

Some reforms of local governments proceed from the bottom up, that is, emanating from local demands, and some from the top down, that is, originating with or grounded in state and national policies. This chapter examines how these approaches come into play in the reform of local governance.

Bottom-up regionalism—voluntary, interlocal, functionally focused, cooperative action—is widespread, especially among smaller governments and in the suburbs. In the tri-state region, local governments frequently share equipment, make joint purchases, pool insurance costs, draw on each other's expertise, conduct joint studies, and sometimes combine facilities to deliver services on a larger scale. State governments may facilitate such cooperation, even offer inducements for it, but they are not the driving force for having localities act jointly in this way.

The top-down approach, on the other hand, involves actions by state governments to have local governments act together. State law or regulation may establish deadlines and redirect tasks from existing governments serving relatively small areas (towns or townships, for example) to those with a broader jurisdiction (for example, counties in New York and New Jersey). Sometimes state policy appears to offer choices, but local governments really do not have them; for example, when the state creates entirely new regional or subregional entities to provide services and requires localities to act with or through them in order to receive state aid.

These two approaches are distinctive but not mutually exclusive. Pressures for reform can come from both directions, with varying degrees of local and state support.

Bottom-Up Approach

Bottom-up reforms of local governance tend to involve relatively small changes, on the order of interlocal agreements and cooperative arrangements. These are more likely to occur for some particular types of functions and places. The three cases presented in this section exemplify the successes and failures of interlocal collaboration. The third case especially shows how race impinges so heavily on the way local governments do or do not work together.

Collaboration Succeeds: Cortlandt, Croton-on-Hudson, and Buchanan

One of the first things Linda Puglisi did when she was elected supervisor of the Town of Cortlandt in northern Westchester—the most rural portion of this inner-ring county—was to convene a tri-municipal task force (see figure 9-1).[1] Cortlandt has a population of 37,357. The task force included elected and appointed leaders from the town government and the governments of the two villages within it, Croton-on-Hudson (population 7,018) and Buchanan (population 1,970), which together contained about a quarter of the town's population. Puglisi had served for a long time on the town board before becoming supervisor. Her experience convinced her that she could use the idea of intergovernmental cooperation to "bring new programs to our community [and] keep costs as low as possible."[2]

A series of meetings was held to establish trust among participants and, Puglisi recalled, to get "a sense of what we really might be able to do." The first breakthrough was a collective purchasing agreement for the three governments; cooperative action followed on composting and equipment sharing. Also, to meet new environmental requirements regarding Freon disposal (from old air conditioners and refrigerators), the three jurisdictions collectively contracted with a private hauler.

Building on that experience, the town and the two villages joined four neighboring localities to create the Northern Tier Coalition Task Force. They all recycled separately, but they shared a transfer station in the City

Figure 9-1. *Weschester County Localities*

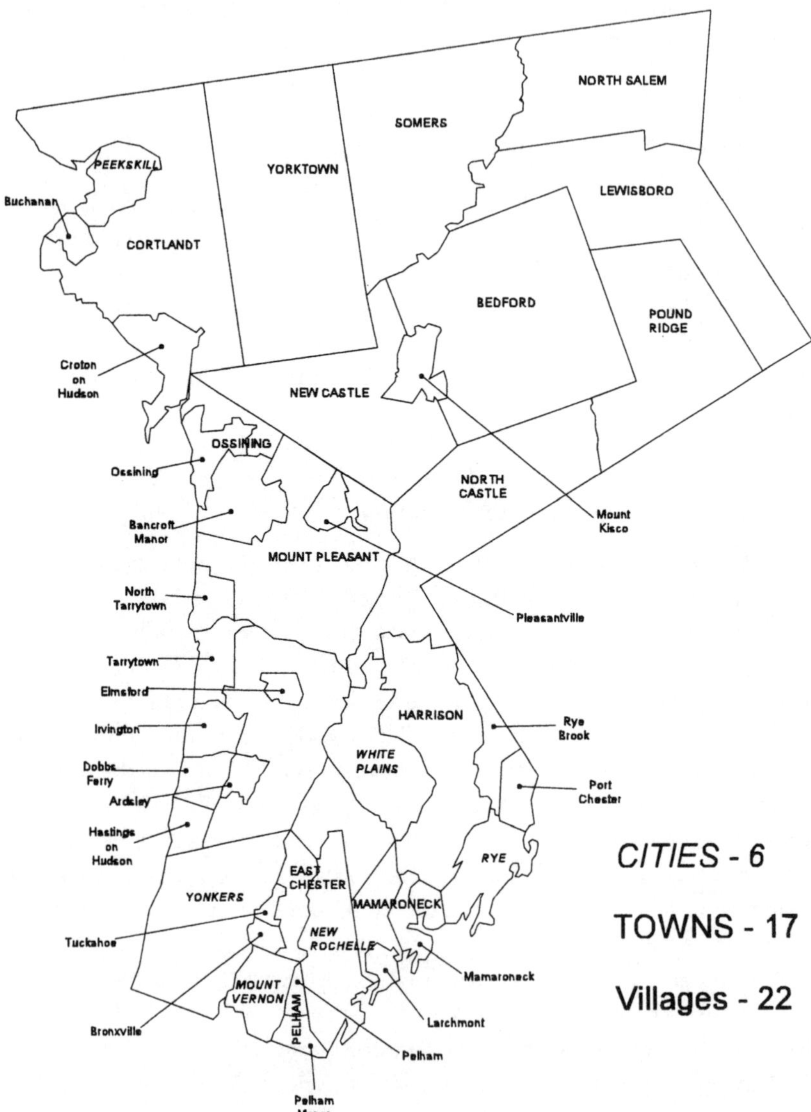

Source: Westchester 2000, *Government at the Crossroads* (1993), p. R2.

of Peekskill. This allowed Cortlandt to hold down operating costs and saved it the expense of constructing its own facility.

Perhaps all this seems prosaic, but Supervisor Puglisi estimated in 1995 that initiatives in intergovernmental cooperation had saved local taxpayers about $400,000. "Cortlandt has had two years of zero tax increases [and] no layoffs," she told the *New York Times*, "and we have still been able to provide our services." She planned to follow with other projects: one was a joint purchasing agreement with the local school district for buses; a second was cooperation with Yorktown and with the county's Montrose Improvement District for the construction of a water filtration plant.

In this instance one person's leadership provided the initiative for intergovernmental cooperation. A process was put in place to establish trust, familiarity, and a habit of working together. Those involved served the same constituents; their jurisdictions were layered and similar. They did not have to deal with major social or demographic differences among cooperating communities. Initial agreements involved only three jurisdictions, and the bargaining process was therefore not very complex. Efficiency could be achieved without sacrificing community. The decision to cooperate did not threaten the autonomy of the participating jurisdictions; each remained free to back out in the future or to go no further. Finally, cooperation occurred in easy areas first, where governments were not in direct touch with the public. Later cooperation measures built on early successes and were extended outward to neighboring, side-by-side communities.

Supervisor Puglisi was not unaware of the limits of intergovernmental action. For example, she regarded complete consolidation of governments to be outside the boundaries of what was feasible; this approach challenged the community's sense of itself. "Communities are very special to people," she observed. "People move to this area because they like their neighborhood boundaries."

Also, Puglisi noted, some services were especially difficult to consolidate. Discussions were initiated at one point with Yorktown and Putnam Valley (across the county line in neighboring Putnam) on consolidating police services, but this effort did not go forward. Puglisi concluded that this was an especially difficult function to consolidate because "people were afraid of losing their jobs. That is the number one fear." Her instincts were confirmed by the experience of two more southerly Westchester communities.

Collaboration Fails: Mount Pleasant and Pleasantville

In 1992 leaders of the Town of Mount Pleasant (population 25,452) and the Village of Pleasantville (population 6,592) within it approached Pace University's Michelian Institute with a request for a study of police services. What different models were there, the two jurisdictions wanted to know, for combining services? What legal issues might arise from such an attempt? Under each possible approach, how much money might be saved, and what would be the effect on service levels?[3]

The people of the town and village were alike demographically, although the Village of Pleasantville is, of course, more densely settled. The village maintained a twenty-one-person police department, thirteen of whom were line officers, at a cost to villagers of $1.4 million (in 1992). The Town of Mount Pleasant Police Department had a staff of sixty, about half of whom were line officers. The expense of the town force was just under $3 million. For each municipality, police spending was between a fifth and a fourth of the total budget.

The Michelian Institute outlined four options for consideration by the town and village boards, ranging from sharing selected elements of police services to abolition of the village police and full police merger at the town level. *Selective* sharing, they estimated, might produce a net gain of up to $80,000; a full merger could save as much as $570,000 if the staffing ratio in the town was used as the standard. Most of these savings would reduce village tax bills. However, jobs would have to be cut to attain the maximum savings; of the total projected savings, over 85 percent ($491,000) was in personnel costs, mostly for uniformed officers. The Michelian Institute concluded: "The Merged Police Force Model clearly provides the greatest cost savings potential. . . . However, it also creates the most radical change. It requires the Village to give up its authority over its own local police force . . . and would also result in a significant reduction in total uniformed personnel. Yet, the Village would gain much in cost savings."[4]

"Communities view basic police, public works and certain administrative services as the core of the local services structure and are reluctant to share these services," the Somerset Alliance concluded from its survey of collaborative ventures in their suburban New Jersey county in the region's intermediate ring.[5] Their observation proved right with respect to Westchester as well. Although some small steps were taken to gain some savings, police consolidation between Mount Pleasant and Pleasantville never happened. In a 1996 interview, Pleasantville mayor Gail Grimaldi stated that she rejected the police merger because town services were not at "the level of service the village is used to."[6] Pleasantville residents feared that a merger would mean loss of control over service levels and quality. But service consolidation would also mean the elimination of ten jobs: one police chief, two sergeants, two lieutenants, and five patrolmen. For some leaders in these small communities, the potential political battle would not be worth the half-million dollars that might be saved.

Many factors were right for collaboration between Pleasantville and Mount Pleasant. Leaders were willing to pay to explore the question. The communities were demographically similar, and the governments were layered, that is, they served the same people. There was a chance to save a substantial amount of money. There was even an advantage that Cortlandt did not have in undertaking its cooperative ventures: an institutional catalyst—a university think tank—was willing to help with research and advice at low cost and to put its imprimatur on a report about possible approaches for change. But the estimated financial savings for Pleasantville and Mount Pleasant, though substantial, were just not enough to lure them into a collaborative venture in a core area of service, especially if it meant taking on organized and locally popular police officers whose jobs were at stake in the process. In the end the value of community trumped the desire for greater efficiency.

Public Opinion about Bottom-Up Regionalism

The Newark *Star-Ledger* and the Eagleton Institute of Politics at Rutgers University conducted a poll in 1994 on attitudes about regionalizing government services in northern New Jersey. Regionalization was defined as a bottom-up effort: several towns combining services and sharing costs in order to bring property taxes under control. Although almost three in five respondents (58 percent) had not previously heard of the idea, most said they thought it would lower government costs. Two-fifths of the respondents said they favored regionalism as a method of holding down taxes, even at the expense of local control of services. Supporters of regionalism in the survey were more likely to be rural or suburban residents who felt their property taxes were too high. They hoped that interlocal cooperation would improve service efficiency. People in central cities or older suburbs tended to be more skeptical, expecting a decline in service quality if local control was diminished.

Respondents in the Rutgers survey varied in their views not only on the basis of where they lived and their perceptions of the property tax

Table 9-1. *Public Views of Regionalization of Services in New Jersey, 1994*[a]

Percent favoring regionalization of the specified service area

		Respondents[b]	
Service	*Total* (N = *801)*	*Pro-regionalism* (N = *362)*[c]	*Anti-regionalism* (N = *305)*[c]
Senior activities	83	92	78
Libraries	82	88	77
Road maintenance	69	82	59
Fire protection	61	75	45
Police	54	78	29
Schools	52	72	35

Source: Star-Ledger–Eagleton Poll (SL/EP 48-3 (EP 98-3)), July 10, 1994.

a. In response to the following statement: "I'm going to read you a list of different services that are provided by local property taxes. For each one I mention, please tell me whether you favor or oppose having your town share that item with a neighboring town if it held down your property taxes."

b. Pro- and antiregionalism respondents separately identified themselves in this manner on another survey question.

c. N = 801 for entire survey. However, the total of these two columns includes only those who answered both survey questions and thus does not equal the entire sample.

burden but also on the specific service considered for regionalization. As shown in table 9-1, those in favor of bottom-up regionalism liked it across the board, though somewhat less for fire, police, and especially schools. Those opposed were nevertheless willing to try regionalization for some services, such as those for seniors, libraries, and road maintenance. But they were even more uneasy about regionalizing fire services, and appeared especially to dislike the idea for police services and schools.

After the publication of the *Star-Ledger*–Eagleton poll, the graduate public administration department at Rutgers in Newark published a survey of local leaders on their experience with outsourcing and sharing services; it showed that they were most active in the areas in which citizen support was likely to be greatest.[7] Of the 567 municipalities in the state, officials from 97 responded with usable information. Perhaps reflecting the desire of local leaders to maintain control, this study found "a much greater willingness among municipalities for considering the sharing of services through interlocal or regional agreements than . . . for outsourcing, or privatizing services." Extensive sharing was reported in such areas as purchasing, provision of public health services, tax assessment and collection, insurance pooling, and senior citizen transportation. Cooperative action for core services such as police and fire was limited to linked dispatching systems. (See the discussion of the emergency 911 phone system.) "When compared to the other functional areas surveyed in this project," the authors wrote, "the outsourcing and joint service patterns of municipal governments in the area of educational functions are among the lowest reported."[8] Localities entered into shared service agreements, the Rutgers researchers reported, largely to save money. Additionally, some leaders reported that sharing was a way of improving the quality of services or maintaining a service in the face of growing resource scarcity. Loss of control, they said, was the fundamental barrier to sharing.

Although far from definitive, the *Star-Ledger*–Eagleton poll and the Rutgers-Newark survey, like our two examples from Westchester, indicate when bottom-up interlocal cooperation is likely to be considered, when it is likely to work, and when it is likely to encounter difficulties. In New Jersey, with its multiplicity of local governments, regionalism moved up on the agenda to stem rising property taxes. Citizens' views and their leaders' behavior appeared to depend on who would be their potential partners in regional efforts: people like them in adjacent jurisdictions or people unlike them. Leaders wished to retain local control of service delivery. New Jerseyans were less willing to experiment in policy areas in which the community value was strongest. In particular, for many in New Jersey, regionalism in education has been very controversial. Citizens were more willing to support regionalization for the back office activities of local government and for services that were used periodically and voluntarily.[9]

Patterns of Intergovernmental Collaboration in the Tri-State Region

To further examine the conditions that favor intergovernmental collaboration, we compiled and categorized published descriptions of bottom-up cooperative and collaborative efforts undertaken by localities in the three states. A total of 664 instances of intergovernmental cooperation were identified.[10]

MOST COLLABORATION INVOLVES TWO OR THREE JURISDICTIONS. Three-fourths of the instances of intergovernmental collaboration involved three or fewer jurisdictions, while only 4 percent involved more than ten jurisdictions (table 9-2). This suggests the commonsense conclusion that a high number of potential participants is itself a factor limiting the likelihood of cooperative action. As more jurisdictions are involved in negotiations, the process becomes more complex, and interlocal action becomes less likely.[11]

Table 9-2. *Numbers of Jurisdictions Cooperating in Intergovernmental Agreements, New York, New Jersey, and Connecticut, Selected Years, 1990–95*

State	*Number of agreements*	*Number of jurisdictions involved*			
		2–3	*4–6*	*7–10*	*10+*
Connecticut	54	19	10	12	13
New Jersey	396	319	49	20	8
New York	214	162	38	6	8
Total	664	500	97	38	29

Sources: Compiled by the authors from Connecticut Advisory Commission on Intergovernmental Relations, *Shared Services in Connecticut* (Hartford, Conn., 1990); New Jersey Department of Community Affairs, *Shared Service Directory* (Trenton, N.J., 1995); New York State Comptroller, *Special Report on Municipal Affairs* (Albany, N.Y., 1993).

Where relatively large numbers of jurisdictions were involved, this usually indicated that a county government was providing or administering a service in which the county's other local governments participated, for example, public health services for school districts in New Jersey and local government liability self-insurance pools. Multijurisdictional cooperation might so dramatically reduce local costs that a go-it-alone approach could not be publicly defended. Also, state subsidies might be contingent on cooperation.

In fact, large-scale, multijurisdictional collaborations were less likely to be pure cases of bottom-up action than those involving fewer localities. They tended to occur in relatively rare situations: when one larger government was given clear legal authority to act by the state but required the cooperation of others to act effectively, quickly, or with minimal political cost; or when the consequences of noncooperation in a larger effort, even for the most resistant jurisdictions, were fiscally or politically unacceptable.

COLLABORATION IS MORE LIKELY AMONG LOCAL GOVERNMENTS SERVING THE SAME CITIZENS. Our review of reported cases of collaboration (table 9-3) showed that in Connecticut, which has the least layering of local governments, there is far less opportunity for collaboration among two or more governments serving the same people—governments that are nested one within the other. However, as layering of local governments increases, there is more collaboration or cooperation among nested than side-by-side governments. This collaboration seems partly an adaptation to mitigate the adverse effects of layering. Among all the states, layering is greatest in New York and so is cooperation among governments serving the same citizens.

Table 9-3. *Frequency of Collaboration between or among Local Governments, Layered versus Side-by-Side, Selected Years, 1990–95*
Units as indicated

	Instances of collaboration[a]					
	Layered		*Side-by-side*		*Total*	
State	No.	*Percent*	No.	*Percent*	No.	*Percent*
Connecticut	5	7.8	59	92.2	64	100
New Jersey	110	26.7	302	73.3	412	100
New York	161	53.8	138	46.2	299	100

Sources: Compiled from Connecticut Advisory Commission, *Shared Services*; New Jersey Department of Community Affairs, *Shared Service Directory*; New York State Comptroller, *Special Report.*

a. Where a collaboration was among several governments, some layered and some side-by-side, it was counted twice.

FUNCTIONAL AREAS OF COLLABORATION. New Jersey poll results and the Rutgers survey of local government officials suggest that citizens are more accepting of intergovernmental collaboration in less visible or less traditional service areas, or in cases where direct contact between citizen taxpayers and local governments is discretionary and periodic. In short, collaboration is most common where it challenges the value of community the least. Our summary of reported local government experience in the three states (table 9-4) tends to confirm these findings. About two-thirds (64.5 percent) of the reported instances of collaboration are in four general areas of service: health and social services, general government, parks, and public works. General government involves administrative support activities for which other government officials and agencies, not citizens, are the primary clients. Public works are collectively (not individually) used. Parks are visited periodically and voluntarily and only by a portion of the citizenry. Health and human services are directly provided but mostly to clients or claimants who depend upon government for support rather than pay for government through property taxes. These citizens are least well situated to legitimately and effectively assert the community value in the face of efforts to increase efficiency through intergovernmental collaboration. Interestingly, intergovernmental collaboration among localities is least reported for an area that regionalists consider its most logical and important application: economic development. Localities' self-interest strongly impels them toward independent action in efforts to build their local property tax base—the fiscal basis for local autonomy.

CITIES RARELY ARE PARTNERS. The region's cities relatively rarely engage in voluntary side-by-side intergovernmental collaborative efforts.

Table 9-4. *Instances of Intergovernmental Collaboration by Functional Areas, Selected Years, 1990–95*

	Instances of intergovernmental collaboration							
	CT		*NJ*		*NY*		*Total*	
Function	*No.*	*Percent*	*No.*	*Percent*	*No.*	*Percent*	*No.*	*Percent*
Health, social services	11	20.4	88	22.2	35	16.3	134	20.2
General government	1	1.8	90	22.7	18	8.4	109	16.4
Parks	1	1.8	16	4.0	89	41.6	106	16.0
Public works	2	3.7	75	18.9	2	9.0	79	11.9
Police	5	9.3	46	11.6	6	2.8	57	8.6
Solid waste	3	5.5	25	6.3	14	6.5	42	6.3
Fire, emergency services	5	9.3	28	7.1	3	1.4	36	5.4
Water, sewer	5	9.3	0	0	28	13.1	33	5.0
Environmental protection	5	.3	2	.05	12	5.6	19	2.9
Courts, corrections	0	0	19	4.8	0	0	19	2.9
Transportation	2	3.7	6	1.5	4	1.9	12	1.8
Education	10	20.4	...[a]	...	...	...	11	1.7
Economic development	3	5.5	1	.02	3	1.4	7	1.0
Total	54		396		214		664	100.1

Sources: Compiled from Connecticut Advisory Commission, *Shared Services*; New Jersey Department of Community Affairs, *Shared Service;* New York State Comptroller, *Special Report.*

a. Because these sources concentrated on general-purpose governments, and lines of accountability and reporting are separate for education in New Jersey and New York, the number of reported cases of sharing in education is very small. Mechanisms especially developed for service sharing in education, but possibly applicable to general-purpose governments, are discussed in chapter 9.

In January 1995 Westchester 2000—the public-private planning group in that inner-ring suburban county—reported the preliminary results of its survey of service sharing by all the county's local governments. There are six cities in Westchester, more than in any other county in the state. Peekskill, the smallest, failed to respond. Yonkers, the largest, reported cooperation in a chlorination facility with Mount Vernon (another city) and in fire and emergency response with New York. All collaboration reported by Mount Vernon, Rye, and White Plains was with coterminous school districts. Only New Rochelle reported collaborative efforts with the county and with adjacent towns: on sewer district fees with Pelham and on cable TV contracts with Scarsdale, Pelham Manor, and Eastchester.[12]

Internal inconsistencies and other available evidence suggest that this compilation is not definitive. (The Yonkers–Mount Vernon collaboration, for example, was reported only by the former, and we know that Cortlandt and Peekskill have worked together.) But it does reveal that, in Westchester at least, side-by-side collaboration between cities and their neighbors is relatively uncommon.

Table 9-5. *Types of Jurisdictions Participating in Intergovernmental Agreements, Selected Years, 1990–95*

Number of jurisdictions

State	*Counties*	*Cities*	*Towns*	*Townships*	*Villages*	*Boroughs*	*School districts*	*State agencies*[a]
Connecticut	16	55	...	...	...	...	...	...
New Jersey	70	53	8	276	10	272	...	...
New York[b]	8	9	209	...	160	...	10	1
New York[c]	...	17	226	...	274	...	1	21

Sources: Compiled by the authors from Connecticut Advisory Commission, *Shared Services*; New Jersey Department of Community Affairs, *Shared Service Directory*; New York State Comptroller, *Special Report*; and New York State Conference of Mayors and Municipal Officials, *Municipal Consolidation and Privatization* (Albany, September, 1992).

a. State agencies sometimes were reported to collaborate with local governments.

b. Data from Comptroller's study (see *Sources*).

c. Data from New York State Conference of Mayors study (see *Sources*).

In general, other data confirm that cities in New York, New Jersey, and Connecticut collaborate relatively infrequently (table 9-5). The New York State Conference of Mayors is an organization in which only cities and villages are members; its 1992 report detailing 190 instances of intergovernmental collaboration found that only 13, or 6.9 percent, involved cities. Three more general, statewide compendia indicated that cities were involved in only about one in eight cases (12.2 percent) of collaboration, mostly as participants with other governments in county-based activities (see table 9-5).

Cities have fewer opportunities to collaborate because they are less numerous than other types of governments and less frequently overlap with other jurisdictions. In New York, for example, territory within cities has less intergovernmental layering than that outside cities, and therefore opportunities for collaborative effort are limited. But there is yet another reason: cities are different and thus are often viewed with mistrust by their suburban neighbors.

A useful but sad example of how hostility toward cities can be a barrier to intergovernmental cooperation is the case of the footbridge over the Hutchinson River Parkway connecting the Village of Pelham and the distressed City of Mount Vernon in Westchester County, New York. This footbridge was first built in the early 1960s as a walkway for schoolchildren; Mount Vernon residents now use it as a shortcut to Pelham's railroad station, which provides commuter service to Manhattan.

In 1995 Pelham mayor Joseph Durnin Jr. proposed that the footbridge be torn down, thus figuratively hauling up the drawbridge over the moat.[13] Based on complaints that village officials had been hearing for decades,

Durnin argued that the bridge provided easy access to Pelham and easy escape to Mount Vernon for criminals stealing from wealthy Pelham homes. (Three other bridges connect the two communities, but those are vehicle bridges and thus accessible to patrol cars.)

In response Mount Vernon mayor Ronald Blackwood, an African American, charged racism. Pelham is around 86 percent white; Mount Vernon is about 60 percent minority. The village and city also differ in size and in the wealth of their inhabitants. Pelham's population size (about 6,400) is approximately one-tenth that of Mt. Vernon and the average household income of its residents (about $63,500) is nearly double that of residents of the neighboring city.

Mayor Durnin of the village replied that his proposal had nothing to do with racism and everything to do with controlling crime. Mayor Blackwood did not deny that his city had problems with crime, but he argued that cutting one of its links with Mount Vernon would not solve Pelham's problem. Pelham would do better, he argued, to cooperate with Mount Vernon in its crime-fighting efforts.

Differences may block collaboration, but negative publicity also can have some effect. Time passed; the issue cooled, and new leaders were elected. As of 1999 the footbridge between Mount Vernon and Pelham was still open.

Race and space go together in American public affairs more than many people would like, and the successes of the civil rights movement have compounded, in an ironic way, the problem of small-city decline in the region. As more and more members of racial minority groups have taken advantage of the options they now have to live in better-off city and suburban neighborhoods, the problems of the worst-off areas of central cities have been exacerbated—thus limiting what might have been possible in an earlier day in the way of cooperative regional action.[14]

Suburbs surrounding cities do not cooperate more with them because cities are different—in their populations, fiscal capacity, mix of services they must provide, and needs they must meet. Long-time suburbanites have spent years defining themselves and their communities as entities apart from nearby cities. Newer residents have made affirmative decisions to leave the cities. All this makes joint action more difficult.

Summary and Analysis of Bottom-Up Regionalism

In examining when bottom-up subregionalism works and when it does not, we found that local governments are much more likely to work together voluntarily in some functional areas than in others: back-office and support service activities for which the government itself is the primary customer; public works, in which services are delivered to citizens collectively rather than individually; parks and libraries, used by citizens periodically and at times of their own choosing; and social services, where those being served are seen as clients or claimants rather than customers or taxpayers. In contrast, localities like to keep close control of the direct services that homeowner taxpayers care about most, consume personally, and see as defining their sense of community: for example, education, policing, and fire protection.

State governments in the region can generate more of this sort of bottom-up joint action by local governments without issuing mandates or sanctions. Aid formulas may be developed to reward collaboration or cooperation or to be less generous in its absence. State-financed teams of experts on collaborative or cooperative money-saving techniques might be organized to visit local governments at their invitation (an approach already employed by Governor Whitman in New Jersey and Comptroller H. Carl McCall in New York, both statewide elected officials). Seed money might be provided to each county or group of counties to establish centers for intergovernmental cooperation or collaboration at universities, chambers of commerce, or already operating public-private partnerships—with their continued funding linked to achieving quantifiable savings. After a demonstration period, they could be funded locally from a portion of the savings generated by cooperation or collaboration and matched by a state contribution.

As might be expected, there are far more instances of two or three governments working together than of cooperation or collaboration involving several jurisdictions. Moreover, governments of communities that are socially and economically similar are more likely to work together than those whose populations differ significantly. One important consequence of this reality is that cities, with high concentrations of minority groups and the poor, rarely engage in joint activities with adjoining suburbs.

Regionalists seek efficiency, competitiveness, and equity by combining cities with their suburbs, or at least inducing them to collaborate on a function-by-function basis. But experience shows that it is not only consolidation that is resisted; bottom-up collaboration between cities and suburbs is relatively rare for even the most mundane activities of day-to-day government.

Joint action by local governments is impelled by efforts to control costs and thereby hold down the real property tax levy. Business organizations and local media—those sensitive to economy, efficiency, and good government arguments—are likely to support collaboration. Agents for change—university research centers such as the Michelian Institute in Westchester County, New York, or regional public-private partnerships such as the Somerset Alliance in Somerset County, New Jersey—may also be critical in advancing new ideas for service delivery. But the key ingredient for success is committed, locally elected leadership.

Among the barriers to intergovernmental action, local employees' fear of job loss is most important, for it engenders organized opposition. Other major concerns of opponents include fears about reduction in service levels and, very importantly, perceived threats to the continued existence and viability of local communities. Thus incremental, functionally focused approaches work better than comprehensive efforts.

Intergovernmental activity appears to be a relatively spontaneous corrective to certain adverse effects of high local government density, like that previously identified in some inner- and intermediate-ring suburban counties in New York and New Jersey. The common sense of working together apparently becomes most compelling to localities when their governments are layered and thus serve the same citizens. This is demonstrated by the numerous examples of joint action among towns and villages in New York.

Those instances in which several governments cooperate, though uncommon, are particularly interesting. It usually occurs when an overarching government, most often a county, provides a service to all or most other governments in its territory or takes over a service from them. (See the discussion below on 911 service in Ulster County, New York, for an example.) Cities are regularly included in such multilateral cooperative or collaborative efforts led or facilitated by an overarching government, for the situation is very different from bilateral, side-by-side joint action. Here the equity argument is compelling: to exclude cities would make the overall effort less viable and also evoke objections from city representatives in the overarching government.

Thus the use of an overarching government to induce collaboration in a layered governmental system seems to offer a way of aiding cities when other approaches—through either consolidation or joint action with neighboring governments—have failed. In Connecticut, since there are no counties, the usual source of overarching authority efforts is absent; therefore, if this approach to helping cities is to be encouraged, it must be initiated by the state itself or through the creation or use of regional entities established for specific functional purposes. Moreover, if the goal is equal sharing of governmental resources with those who live in cities, other approaches that recognize the power of localism and accommodate it must also be found. One possibility could be vigorous state intervention to have an overarching entity—a county government or a private contractor—provide specific services under contract with all the other local governments "nested" within its geographical ambit. By doing this, cities are not singled out or treated specially but are aided on the same basis as other local governments by sharing with them the benefits of collaboration. We examine this approach in our discussion of top-down regionalism in the education section that follows.

Top-Down Approach

As we have demonstrated, the bottom-up approach is least likely to be applied to traditional local functions that most define community life. Generally leaders in state capitals respect localism in those policy areas in which community-based decisionmaking is most important to local citizens. But states do have the power to override local prerogatives and even force localities to act regionally.[15] Thus we are drawn to ask how state governments might advance regionalism's values. We found answers in both the successes and failures of state efforts to advance regional purposes in four areas of policy: housing and zoning, land use, public safety, and education.

The tri-state experience shows that when top-down regional reforms are compared to home-grown, bottom-up efforts, the former are much more likely to involve sensitive, important—even controversial—policy areas and initiatives. One such case focused on housing and race in New Jersey, where the courts played a large role. Another example entailed the reorganization of educational systems in New York State. Both cases were complicated. In the latter instance, progress was made; in the former, results have been minimal. Two other cases described in this section concern land use—protection of the Long Island Pine Barrens from developers—and public safety—setting up an emergency 911 phone system in Ulster County, New York.

Overview of Four Cases

The New Jersey Supreme Court's imposition of a fair-share regional approach to the provision of low- and moderate-income housing in all localities throughout the state provoked enormous opposition from local governments and the state's political branches. Ultimately, like parallel efforts in New York and Connecticut, this approach fell far short of its equity objectives for the distribution of affordable housing throughout the state's communities.

In contrast, New York's high court was mindful of legislative prerogatives and enlisted them in response to litigation on Long Island that pitted environmentalists, bent on protecting the Pine Barrens and the vital aquifer beneath it, against developers and their local government allies. State legislators from the region sought to create the conditions under which local leadership could negotiate a local solution, personally encouraged and advanced these negotiations, and then acted to ensure that the negotiated compromise, specific to one area of the state, was adopted in Albany.

With the emergence of new but costly communications technology, the New York legislature pursued a regional approach for enhancing 911 emergency communication systems, one within the existing framework of general-purpose local government. The state built local choice into the process but did so in a way that generated local political pressure for the choice the stated desired. Counties were not required to adopt the small surcharge on telephone bills that was passed by the state to finance installation of new emergency response technology, but once they were given the option to create an emergency-911 fund, local advocates pressured them to do so. Because they controlled the resulting resources, county government leaders gained the leverage to effectively regionalize emergency communications for numerous, highly autonomous local police departments, fire departments, and emergency ambulance corps, some with overlapping jurisdictions.

In another but much different statewide approach, New York State used regulations and financial incentives to induce school districts to create a collaborative, statewide yet regional system to increase equity in educational services in rural areas. Built into the authorizing legislation were provisions ensuring that regions would be redefined and that the number of regional entities in the system would diminish over time. The resultant regional system became enormously important, not only in rural areas, but in suburban New York (and more costly than some states' entire education budgets). But as economic and social conditions changed, critics challenged the system's efficiency. Calls for its reform and restructuring demonstrated that for functionally focused regional approaches, as for the creation of general-purpose metropolitan governments, implementation of regionalism's values is not about achieving an enduring outcome but about commitment to an ongoing process.

Limits of Forced Regionalism: Mt. Laurel

In 1971 the zoning board of the southern New Jersey township of Mount Laurel rejected a proposal to build the community's first moderate-income, multifamily housing—a modest-sized, thirty-six apartment complex. Low-income residents of the town's older Springville section, many of them African American, believed that the local government was using its land-use powers to block additional access to the community by minorities and those with lower incomes. They argued that the township's zoning requirements—large lot sizes and other devices associated with "exclusionary zoning"—ensured that only homes for the affluent would be built within the town. Backed by Camden Legal Services (a federal antipoverty group) and the National Association for the Advancement of Colored People (NAACP), the Springville residents and others challenged the town zoning decision in state court as being in violation of the New Jersey Constitution's "due process" and "general welfare" provisions.[16]

A New Jersey superior court agreed, and in 1972 it overturned Mt. Laurel's local zoning law. The town appealed. Three years later the New Jersey Supreme Court, in *Southern Burlington County NAACP* v. *Mount Laurel Township* (hereafter referred to as *Mount Laurel I*), sustained the lower court. In ruling against the township's zoning policies, the New Jersey high court said that each developing locality in the state was not only required to refrain from land-use regulations that denied housing to the less affluent, but had an affirmative obligation to "provide, through its zoning, a realistic opportunity for fulfilling its fair share of the region's present and prospective need for lower income housing."[17] This came to be known as the "Mt. Laurel doctrine."

Benjamin Franklin once likened New Jersey to a "barrel tapped at both ends" by cities outside it: New York to the north, Philadelphia to the south. Mount Laurel, a ten-minute drive from Philadelphia's edge, lies far outside the tri-state region, but this decision immediately reverberated up north throughout the New York metropolitan region's suburban rings. New Jersey judges with zoning cases already before them in Bergen, Middlesex, Somerset, and Morris Counties had been awaiting the state high court's ruling and were now governed by the precedent. Paul Davidoff, executive director of the Suburban Action Institute, said at once that he would seek to use the Mt. Laurel doctrine in litigation to open suburbs throughout the region to low- and moderate-income housing. Judges in New York and Connecticut with land-use cases pending in Oyster Bay and Brookhaven (on Long Island), New Castle (in Westchester), and New Canaan (in Fairfield County) were sure to hear *Mt. Laurel I* cited.[18]

Liberals praised the decision; conservatives condemned the high court's activist intrusion into local prerogatives. But the New Jersey Supreme Court decision did not specify standards and timetables for achieving fair-share housing goals in the growing suburbs—and achieving the court's equity goals was not going to be easy. "I don't think we need low-income housing everywhere," one Mount Laurel homeowner told a reporter. "We worked hard for what we have here," another said. "No way do I feel I should subsidize a home for them."[19] Local and state elected leaders got the message. Initial attempts by Democratic governor Brendan Byrne to develop a policy response acceptable to the legislature came to naught. Localities resisted in court, making the prime consequence of *Mt. Laurel I* a blizzard of lawsuits. Little changed on the ground.

Then, in 1982 the Mt. Laurel plaintiffs returned to court. In *Mount Laurel II* (1983), an angry and activist state supreme court—led by Chief Justice Robert Wilentz and with a majority appointed by Governor Byrne—detailed an elaborate plan for determining municipalities' fair shares in three regions of New Jersey, defined according to the state Development Guide Plan.[20] The New Jersey approach was explicitly regional (unlike that of Connecticut and New York, where affordable housing remedies—though acknowledging regional concerns—were sought within *municipal* boundaries).

The court's decision also allowed builders to exceed density limits set by local governments in order to build affordable housing ("the builder's remedy"). This was important, for it aligned the interests of builders with the court's regional approach and against local government. Usually market-like arguments are used to bolster localism; here market forces were to be released to advance regional interests. It worked: thenceforth almost all affordable housing lawsuits in New Jersey were initiated by builders, not by advocacy groups.

Finally, the New Jersey Supreme Court directed judges in three regions of the state to monitor progress in compliance with their decision. Thus it insisted on accountability for implementation at the state level and located it in the judiciary.

The uproar following *Mount Laurel II* was considerable. Republican governor Tom Kean, for example, called the court's decision "communistic."[21] But after passions cooled, and after one gubernatorial veto, the legislature passed and Kean signed the 1985 Fair Housing Act. This legislation calmed the suburban towns by reducing and shifting the impact of the court decision: fewer housing units were to be built; more middle-income people would be eligible for "affordable" housing; and many new units were to be reserved for established residents in communities rather than newcomers. In a 1986 decision, *Hills Development Co.* v. *Township of Bernards* (called, with some poetic license, *Mount Laurel III*), the state high court accepted this legislative outcome.[22]

The Fair Housing Act created the Council on Affordable Housing (COAH); it had the responsibility of identifying each jurisdiction's fair share of regional affordable housing. Following court guidelines, the agency developed a formula based upon growth rates and community income levels. As it turned out, the total number of units to be built or rehabilitated was far lower than that contemplated in *Mt. Laurel II*. Moreover, delays linked to agency start-up and formula development caused implementation of affordable housing policies to miss the mid-1980s construction boom in New Jersey, further dampening the effects of the new regulations.[23]

Localities were encouraged but not required to submit plans to the COAH detailing how they would comply with their fair-share requirement. Interestingly, the incentive that localities were offered was the return of local control over land use. Certification of a local fair-share plan by the COAH provided protection for six years against the "builder's remedy." That is, if an approved local plan was in place, there would be no court decisions to support a builder's proposal to increase project densities beyond locally permitted levels.

However, few towns with any significant fair-share obligation sought such certification.[24] They were not attracted to a compromise under which they would have to win back authority over land use, authority they were fighting to prove they already rightly had. Indeed, even though the COAH formula reduced the court-determined fair-share units required for most communities, some towns sought to further reduce their obligations through litigation.

In addition to lowering the required amount of fair-share housing, the COAH allowed towns to meet half their obligation under the Fair Housing Act by subsidizing units in other jurisdictions. This translated into

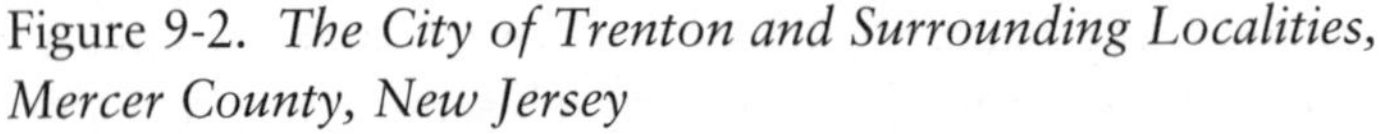

Figure 9-2. *The City of Trenton and Surrounding Localities, Mercer County, New Jersey*

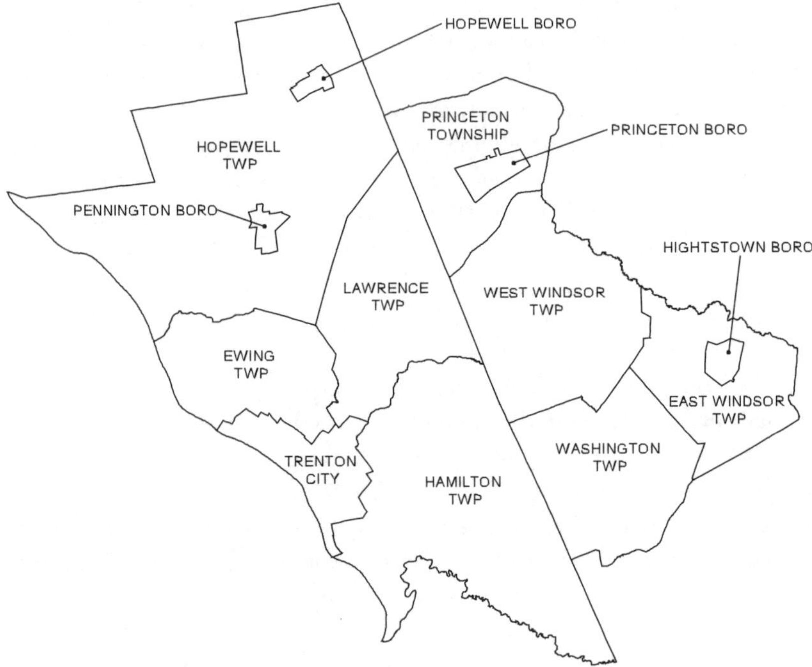

Source: Department of State, Mercer County, New Jersey (www.mercercounty.org/_private/our%20towns.htm [February 2001]).

affluent, white, middle-class suburbs paying poorer, predominantly black cities in order to relieve themselves of the need to build low-income housing. For example, in 1998 East Windsor township in Mercer County sought to pay the City of Trenton $940,000 to build 47 of the 345 low- and moderate-income housing units that it was required to provide under the Fair Housing Law. (See figure 9-2.) Previously in New Jersey, about $120 million in obligations to provide low- and middle-income housing was transferred under similar "regional contribution agreements." About 10 percent of this spending, for 576 units of housing, went to Trenton from Hopewell, Marlboro, East Windsor, West Windsor, Princeton, and other suburban townships.[25]

These deals made sense to struggling Trenton, Housing and Development Director Alan Mallach said, because "the single biggest problem we have is that there isn't enough money around to do what needs to be done." From East Windsor's perspective, Mayor Janice S. Mironov said, "We will get the credit. The City of Trenton will be responsible for actual construction. Our place is really to transfer the funds."[26]

What Mironov failed to note, however, was that a regional contribution agreement also allowed her township to meet its legal obligation under the Fair Housing Act at a bargain price. According to one authority, "Poorer urban towns bidding against each other for the housing funds the agreements provide have driven the price accepted per unit to about a quarter of the real cost of new units or half the price of rehabilitated units, although the suburbs get full credit against their quotas."[27] And fewer available funds meant that fewer units were built. Estimates of New Jersey's need for affordable housing over the last decade ranged from a low of 86,000 units to a high of 675,000.[28] Between 1983 and 1996, however, only about 21,000 units were built—and mostly in inner cities, not in the suburbs.[29]

A number of additional factors have militated against achieving the kinds of social change that equity-oriented regionalists hoped would arise from the Mount Laurel decision. Under the 1985 Fair Housing Act and its implementation by the COAH, half the affordable units built in a locality may be reserved for current residents and a fourth set aside for senior citizens. In East Windsor, for example, 110 units have been built for the elderly and another 85 are planned. In general, communities have been far more open to affordable housing programs intended for those of modest means already in their midst, some of them employees of local government upon whom they rely for local public services. Down-payment requirements, closing costs, and construction of smaller-sized units (typically with one or two bedrooms) are all factors that might limit the affordable housing pool to those who both have the means to buy such housing and find it desirable.

In New Jersey an activist high court seeking greater integration between races and classes mandated widespread change in local land-use regulations from the top down. The statutory response of the legislature and the governor—the 1985 Fair Housing Law—reflected both their electoral accountability to the state's suburban majority and their basic sympathy with localist values. The suburbs' defense is publicly presented in terms of avoiding rezoning battles and increases in population density, but it is, of course, substantially about race and class. Over time the social priorities of existing local communities—preservation of the community value as they define it—preempted those of the original advocates of affordable housing. Some additional money was provided for low- and moderate-income housing, and some affordable housing was built in more affluent suburbs, but it was largely on terms defined by these communities. There was, in the end, little real movement toward the equity goals—racially, socially, and economically integrated communities—sought by those who initially challenged New Jersey's local land-use controls.

The Mount Laurel battles occurred in a state that historically has been among those most hostile to any public control over land use. Municipalities in New Jersey gained the power to zone in 1927 and have been the locus of land-use decisionmaking ever since. Efforts at coastal zone management pitted the state government and its agencies against local government and developers and were largely undone by intense local opposition.[30] More recent efforts at state planning did produce a result after five years of review and revision, but one entirely dependent on local cooperation for its effectiveness.[31]

In reviewing local planning and zoning practices, New York's courts, like those of New Jersey, have called repeatedly for consideration of regional needs.[32] But as an exhaustive survey by Patricia Salkin of the Albany Law School confirmed, regionalism has made little headway in New York; land-use decisionmaking remains one of the strongest bastions of local power in the state.[33]

In Connecticut the courts long presumed the validity of local zoning decisions when these were under challenge, placing the burden of proof on those who opposed local land-use policy. A state law passed in 1984 urged localities to "encourage the development of housing opportunities," but little changed. Following a report by a blue-ribbon commission appointed by Governor William O'Neill to study the state's housing crisis, the legislature adopted the Affordable Housing Land Use Procedure Appeals Act of 1990. Its centerpiece was an appeals procedure for potential builders of affordable housing that reversed the traditional presumption of validity, placing the burden of proof on local governments to defend their land-use regulations.

Legislative action in Connecticut was not, as in New Jersey, directly compelled by a state supreme court decision. There was, however, growing willingness on the part of some judges in the state to look more critically at local laws and regulations.[34] Indeed, a key argument of proponents of the 1990 bill was that its passage was necessary to avoid the "more catastrophic solution of the Supreme Court of the state or a federal district judge decid[ing] to take the bit between his teeth and do[ing] a Mount Laurel decision in this state."[35] Still, references to regionalism were specifically deleted from the act. According to University of Connecticut Law School Professor Terry Tondro, who helped write the 1990 law, only 1,600 units of affordable housing were approved for construction in his state between 1990 and 1996; these constituted less than 3 percent of all housing construction authorized statewide during the period.[36] Moreover, recent attempts in the Connecticut legislature to institute statewide land-use planning to be administered through existing regional entities have come to naught.[37]

Like advocates for reform of education finance, proponents of overturning local land-use policies and practices—voices advancing a minority view—have entered the courts precisely because they have been unable to succeed in legislatures—a majoritarian forum. It has been state *courts*, relying on federal and state constitutions, that have been the institutional base for top-down challenges to local powers. And local governments, *with support in state capitals*, have maintained substantial control over land use even in the face of these pressures. This record is the best evidence that workable regional approaches in the policy areas people care most about must incorporate localism, not confront it.

State as Facilitator in a Single Subregion: The Long Island Pine Barrens

On March 11, 1991, the Appellate Division of the New York State Supreme Court, sitting in Brooklyn, voted to reverse a decision of Suffolk County state supreme court judge Paul J. Baisley and block all development in the central Pine Barrens on Long Island. The fate of 224 projects valued at $11 billion—some already locally approved, others pending approval—was thrown into doubt. Michael Gerrard, the attorney for the Pine Barrens Society, the environmental advocacy organization that had brought the original suit and followed up with the appeal, called the appellate division outcome "one of the most important environmental decisions handed down by the state courts in the past decade." But for Edwin M. Schwenk of the Long Island Builders Institute, it was a mortal blow to the recession-mired Long Island economy and the undoing of "the right of towns to effectively plan their own destiny."[38]

The largest remaining undeveloped area on Long Island still substantially in private hands, the 100,000-acre Central Pine Barrens comprises

17 percent of Suffolk County's land area but was home to only about 4 percent (56,000) of its people in the early 1990s. Thousands of plant, animal, and insect species are found there—many of them rare, some faced with extinction. The pygmy pine forest that gives the place its name is itself 12,000 years old.

Most important, the Pine Barrens provides a deep, natural, permeable cover and filter for a massive aquifer, the sole natural source of drinking water for the 2.5 million people living in suburban Nassau and Suffolk Counties. But the sandy soil that caused early settlers to describe the area as "barren" and that so effectively filtered the rain that recharged the aquifer was an insufficient barrier to the pollutants generated by modern, industrial society. Studies showed that once it was contaminated, the natural aquifer beneath the Pine Barrens would take centuries to clean itself.

This potential threat to the drinking water supply on Long Island attracted the attention of national and state regulatory agencies during the 1970s and 1980s. In 1974 New York State passed a law requiring more demanding state environmental quality review of proposed business, commercial, and industrial uses in the Pine Barrens. Four years later the federal Environmental Protection Agency designated the area a sole source aquifer. That same year, after studying and mapping the area, the Long Island Regional Planning Board (LIRPB) called for development restrictions. In 1984, when issuing its statewide framework for water resource planning, the state Department of Environmental Conservation singled out the Pine Barrens as in need of special protection.[39]

Then in 1987 the state legislature passed the Sole Source Aquifer Special Groundwater Protection Law. It called for comprehensive management plans to govern development in the state's nine federally designated sole source aquifer areas. In addition, for what it described as a demonstration project, the legislature provided $300,000 in funding, to be matched by $100,000 raised locally, so that the Long Island Regional Planning Board could develop a model management plan for the Central Pine Barrens. In taking this approach, the state remained most respectful of local land-use powers. Although entirely within New York's (easternmost) Suffolk County, more than half of the Pine Barrens is in the town of Brookhaven, about a third in Riverhead, and the remaining tenth in Southampton (figure 9-3.). This is important because, as we have seen, it is the towns in New York State that largely control land use. Thus, any systematic land-use policy concerning the Pine Barrens required either

Figure 9-3. *The Long Island Pine Barrens in the Towns of Brookhaven, Riverhead, and Southampton, Suffolk County, New York*

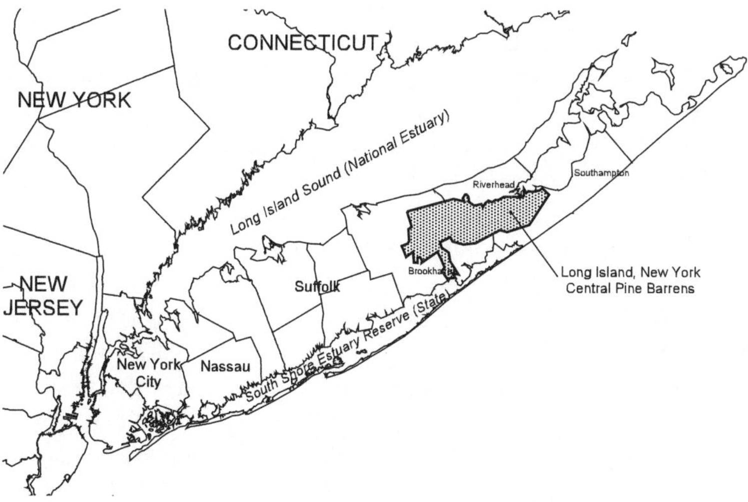

Source: Central Pine Barrens Joint Planning and Policy Commission, "Long Island, New York Central Pine Barrens: Locator Map" (www.pb.state.ny.us/chart_site_map.htm [February 2001]).

substantial intertown collaboration or state action—legislative or judicial—to provide an alternative to town-level decisionmaking in the region.

The 1987 state law, however, did not create a new regional agency with control over land use nor did it shift authority over land use in this especially sensitive geographical area to the existing overarching (but still local) county government. It did not even mandate that the three towns in which the Central Pine Barrens were located be bound by the results of the planning process. Instead it attempted to be a catalyst by providing state resources to ensure that a comprehensive plan would be placed on the table; requiring that the plan include an implementation program for the towns; and seeking to build receptiveness in the three town governments by mandating their involvement as planning proceeded. It was not insignificant for this approach that the LIRPB, the bicounty agency explicitly named in state law to do the planning, had close, long-established relationships with local governments on Long Island.[40] Finally, oversight was maintained by requiring that the resulting comprehensive plan for the Pine Barrens be accepted by the state Department of Environmental Conservation.

Either by neglect or design, there was no deadline in state law for the LIRPB to complete its comprehensive management plan for the Pine Barrens. With no result in hand or in the offing two years after the law passed, environmentalists grew increasingly concerned that the regional ecosystem and an irreplaceable drinking water source for Long Islanders might suffer irreversible damage if development proceeded unchecked while this study was under way. Moreover, it appeared likely that a site at Calverton in the Pine Barrens, where the Grumman Corporation had built and tested jet aircraft, would be recommended for use as an industrial park as a result of a separate LIRPB study. For this and other reasons, leaders in the Pine Barrens Society distrusted what they regarded as a close relationship between the LIRPB and development interests on Long Island.

Therefore, the Pine Barrens Society decided to proceed with a lawsuit. Its argument to the court was that the 1987 law triggered a higher level of environmental review for special ground water protection areas like the Pine Barrens and that a detailed, comprehensive, regionwide environmental impact study was required for such areas before the development of any single site could be permitted. The effect of proposed projects in the Pine Barrens had to be considered not separately by each town, the society said, but cumulatively and on a regional basis.

Judge Baisley dismissed the suit because he found the proposed development projects insufficiently related for their cumulative impact to be considered and because an approved comprehensive plan was not yet in place.[41] At the appellate division level, the Pine Barrens decision was a close call. The four judges who originally heard the case found themselves split 2–2; they had to call in a fifth colleague to break the deadlock. Writing for the three-judge majority, Justice William C. Thompson noted that a cumulative impact study before development was required because, though "functionally unrelated," the projects proposed for the Pine Barrens were "linked by virtue of their potential to adversely affect an irreplaceable natural resource located within a discrete, geographic area."[42] For the majority, it was the underlying geographical integrity of the region that was crucial. This was a real breakthrough for environmentalists. The court's reference to the defined region in this way not only provided an important victory for them in the immediate battle, but potentially enabled the establishment of a broad rationale for a regional alternative to local land-use control, which the legislature was so reluctant to provide.

Development advocates responded both in the legislature and the courts. An attempt to undo the appellate division decision through state legislation—colorfully characterized by Richard L. Amper, executive director of the Pine Barrens Society, as "the desperate acts of special interests"—received little support, suggesting that many assembly and senate members from Long Island in both parties were not at all unhappy that the court's decision pressured localities for coordinated regional action on Pine Barrens development.[43] Because of their common interests, developers were allied with the local governments (and not, as was the case in New Jersey and Connecticut, with advocates of regionalism); they backed the towns in their final appeal to New York's highest court, the Court of Appeals. Southampton, however, withdrew; its new supervisor, Fred Thiele (later an assembly member), had just been elected on a strong pro-environment platform.

Even before the Court of Appeals heard oral arguments, the uncertainty of the outcome caused environmentalists, developers, and town officials to begin exploring the possibility of a settlement. Auspices were provided by the Long Island Association, a regional business group headed by James Larocca. Larocca was widely respected among elected officials, policy advocates, and business leaders on Long Island; as a former state commissioner of both the departments of energy and transportation, he was also very well connected in Albany. (He later unsuccessfully sought the Democratic nomination for governor.) In a series of luncheon meetings in the association's offices in Commack ("I just served the sandwiches," Larocca later said), agreement was tentatively reached on the scope of a comprehensive impact study, but the issue of dividing land-use power between local governments and a regional entity proved intractable.

Environmentalists publicly floated the idea that an approval role for Pine Barrens projects be given to the Advisory Council of the Pine Barrens Maritime Reserve, a group dominated by state appointees and created in accordance with a state law passed in 1990.[44] However, according to Lee Koppelman, executive director of the Long Island Regional Planning Board, the idea of "taking town powers and zoning board powers away from the towns and villages and giving it to a regional entity had minus zero chance of working."[45]

On November 22, 1992, localism had its victory: the state Court of Appeals unanimously decided that "cumulative impact review" for the Pine Barrens was not required in the absence of the adoption of the formal comprehensive management plan explicitly authorized by the legislature in 1987. Writing for the court, Judge Vito Titone decried the fact that the LIRPB had not yet completed this plan. Although the court was unwilling to do the legislature's job, it was quite willing to remind it of a responsibility that had been identified in previous decisions. "The existing system of land-use planning in the region is plainly not equal to the massive undertaking that effective long-range planning would require," Judge Titone wrote, "and some other system devised by a larger planning entity must be substituted." The court urged the legislature to "create sensible deadlines and mandate prompt action by the designated planning bodies to address this matter of urgent public concern."[46]

Each side had experienced victory and defeat in the courts. From the environmentalists' perspective, there was still no effective mechanism in place for ensuring that local land-use powers would be used in a way that considered regional needs. For their part, developers now faced the prospect of projects being tied up in the courts one at a time. *Newsday*, the powerful Long Island daily, called for an islandwide summit to find a compromise approach to land use in the Pine Barrens that protected vital water supplies while allowing development to proceed.[47] A conference entitled "Why Can't Long Island?" was held, also focused on compromise. Meanwhile political activists were mobilizing in favor of a possible referendum to require comprehensive planning before any development could proceed.[48]

Larocca went back to work, with help from Michael LoGrande, head of the Suffolk County Water Authority, and advice from the heads of the New Jersey Pinelands Commission and Massachusetts's Cape Cod Commission. A very important push for accommodation came from influential majority state legislators from the region. Senator Kenneth LaValle, a Republican, and Assemblyman Thomas DiNapoli, a Democrat, insisted on having a widely supported local compromise bill that they could sponsor before introducing anything in their respective houses. LaValle and DiNapoli knew that their colleagues from elsewhere in New York would defer to them on a local matter if local interests were aligned. By taking this stand, they ensured that the state legislature would not be a potential alternative arena for local combat but a force for local accommodation instead.

This approach worked; the Long Island Pine Barrens Protection Act, passed unanimously in Albany in 1993, made the central Pine Barrens the state's third forest preserve. Like the Pinelands in New Jersey, the

Pine Barrens preserve was divided into two parts, with 55,000 acres designated for preservation and the rest for compatible development. (These two large areas were demarcated during the compromise negotiations on Long Island on what came to be called the "Larocca map.") Development of the Core Preservation Area—about half of it already publicly owned parkland—would be strictly limited, with landowners of the private portions compensated for their losses through public purchase of their property or sale of development rights. Local governments were also to be reimbursed for their loss of revenues as a result of land being left undeveloped. Development in the Compatible Growth Area would continue but in ways sensitive to environmental concerns.[49]

To balance the need for local and regional control, the act also created the Central Pine Barrens Joint Planning and Policy Commission to write a land-use plan for the area. Significantly, four of this commission's five members were local elected officials: the Suffolk County executive and the supervisors of the three towns. (The fifth was a gubernatorial appointee.) Other parties were to be heard through their membership on an advisory board, also provided for in the legislation. The commission was given twelve months to develop a draft comprehensive land-use plan and generic environmental impact statement for the plan. Portions of the plan that impacted land within each of the towns had to be adopted by the town's board before they went into effect. If these were not approved by the towns and the commission by February of 1995, the law establishing this process would expire. (Importantly, town approval, once given, could not be withdrawn.) Then the towns had three months to bring local land-use law into conformance with the plan, subject to commission approval. Authority over land use remained with the town, except that the commission retained a role in matters of regional importance or when a single commissioner petitioned to take up a project. Rather than forcing a regional land-use policy on the towns, the state used these structural arrangements to bring them into the process of developing and adopting such a policy.[50]

A final barrier concerned the financing of the plan. Suffolk County had $10 million set aside for the acquisition of land and development rights in the Pine Barrens, but an estimated $50 to $75 million was needed. Repeated attempts to establish an environmental trust fund were blocked in Albany. Majority Leader Ralph Marino, himself from Oyster Bay on Long Island, had earlier given Senator Ron Stafford a veto in this broad policy area in order to gain Stafford's backing for Marino's successful senate leadership bid. Stafford was from the North Country, site of the Adirondack Preserve—the only region where the state had ever approved regional land use. Therefore, Stafford was dead set against voting funds for further public land acquisition. But a bipartisan local consensus had been reached in suburban Long Island, which was a part of the Republican heartland. Since all of Long Island's eight state senators were in the Republican majority, action was expected of them. Stafford finally gave way, and the trust fund bill was passed and signed in July 1993.

In this instance state policy persistently supported regional planning but did not impose it on localities. Environmentalists presented local citizens and leaders with a compelling, self-interested reason for regional action—the protection of vital drinking water supplies. Litigation gave the contending interests in the policy contest selective victories, but it also promised each continuing costs and the likelihood of persistent conflict without real issue resolution. A broker trusted by all local parties and state decisionmakers, Jim Larocca, was available to bring the contending parties to the table.

At the state level, the courts and the legislature did not square off. The highest state court was respectful of legislative prerogatives but also functioned as a powerful advocate for the need to find a regional solution. In fact, pressure from the courts allowed legislators more leverage to insist on a compromise accommodating both local and regional approaches in the Pine Barrens. Thus key state legislators with strong local bases insisted upon local agreement as a condition for passing legislation needed to put the local agreement into effect and to fund it.

Herbert Balin's review of this case argues that because the three towns involved in the creation of the Pine Barrens plan were all given veto power over the plan, their authority was not challenged, and thus they voluntarily complied with the resulting plan's requirement that they alter their land-use and zoning policies.[51] It was a win-win-win situation: environmentalists, property owners, and local municipalities all made gains. Environmentalists succeeded in protecting the Pine Barrens; property owners gained clear rules by which they might proceed with development or, if development was barred, receive fair compensation; and local jurisdictions protected their revenue base and maintained control over the land-use plan. In addition, by helping shelter the towns from the legal claims of landowners or potential developers that might have arisen from the Pine Barrens land-use plan, the state provided an incentive for local governments to support restricted use of lands in the region. Thus was regionalism for the Central Pine Barrens facilitated, rather than commanded.

Encouraging Multigovernment Collaboration: The Emergency 911 Phone System

A small child dials 911 and says, "Our house is burning!" Firemen are dispatched immediately to the exact location, although the panicked child does not know—or cannot remember—her address. Another call to 911 is initiated in the heat of a domestic dispute—and then disconnected. With the origin of the call evident through the enhanced system, the dispatcher at the communications center calls back; it takes seconds. If unsatisfied by the response he or she receives (or if there is no answer at all), the dispatcher immediately sends a police officer to the exact address linked to the phone number.[52]

In the wake of the urban unrest of the 1960s, the first universal emergency telephone number (911) was established in 1968 on the recommendation of the President's Commission on Law Enforcement and the Administration of Justice, to improve response time across the nation in health and public safety emergencies.[53] By the late 1990s, four of five Americans were served by enhanced 911 emergency response telephone systems. Enhanced systems, made possible with advances in telecommunications technology, automatically display for an emergency service dispatcher a phone number and associated address from which a call is initiated. This allows rapid response to an emergency situation based on the connection alone, without any further information being communicated (although it is, of course, more efficient if the nature of the emergency is made known).

Rapid response means fewer lives lost in medical emergencies, more criminals apprehended, a greater likelihood of intervention in civil disputes before they turn violent, and less property loss from fires. Additionally, the National Emergency Number Association states that "an important but somewhat less visible benefit of enhanced 911 is the more efficient, more cost-effective, use of scarce emergency service resources for the public benefit."[54]

The Bell System—then a national telephone monopoly—paid the central office costs for bringing 911 on line from its general rate base. Other expenses were to be borne directly by subscribers or by state and local governments. Thus this was not a national emergency response system but a national phone number for a system that was based in and paid for at the state and local levels. It was only available in those places that would support it with local resources.

New York State's approach was to locate local governmental responsibility for 911 in counties, provide them access to a potential resource base, and create the probability of local political demand for change that altered how and by whom a key local service—emergency dispatch—was performed. In 1989 the state legislature authorized *counties* to impose a monthly telephone line surcharge of thirty-five cents to pay for the "system costs" of establishing telephone-based 911 emergency response systems.[55] Note that this was not a state tax to be distributed to localities, nor was its imposition by localities required by the state. At the same time, it was the state's counties—not other local governments already delivering emergency services or with communications systems in place—who were identified in the law as the only jurisdictions authorized to implement 911.

Enhanced 911 made a good deal of sense for Ulster County. With a population of 165,165, it could expect 200 or more emergency calls a day, with the number rising as settlement continued to push out from the tri-state region's urban core.[56] The county's land area is the size of Rhode Island, and it is served by fifty fire departments (mostly volunteer), seventeen police agencies, and seventeen ambulance corps. An enhanced system was likely to make the delivery of thinly spread emergency services more efficient. In sum, rapid action to bring enhanced 911 on line was likely to save lives and property.

There were also political incentives to move fast. Once the county started collecting the 911 surcharge in January 1991, everyone with telephone service was reminded monthly (when their bill arrived in the mail with the 911 surcharge clearly identified) that they were paying a "new tax."[57] Citizens began demanding something for their money—right away. In Ulster Mrs. Helen Delaney emerged as a particularly effective advocate for 911 in appearances before the county legislature during regular monthly public comment periods. Her late husband would still be alive, Mrs. Delaney said again and again, if 911 had been in place when he experienced his heart attack at home.[58] This sort of testimony, along with progress reported in the media on 911 in other counties in the state (that is, the presence of the interjurisdictional competition of which public choice theorists are so fond), added to the pressure on county decisionmakers. But planning and preparing for implementation was a vast job. For example, for the system to work, every occupied structure in a jurisdiction had to have a unique address that clearly identified its location; rural route mailbox numbers, traditionally used in less developed areas, were not enough. That meant doing a physical inventory of all structures in the county, using the real property tax system, U.S. Postal Service routes, and local fire department identifiers as a base. It also meant changing some old addresses and inventing new ones, as well as fielding the reactions of angry citizens who liked things the old way or were annoyed at the inconvenience of having all their correspondents adjust their address records.

As noted above, state law gave the county final say over the configuration of the 911 system, but emergency services were usually already organized at the city, town, village, and fire district levels. This meant that lots of cooperation among numerous jurisdictions was required to create the 911 system and make it work. Within each jurisdiction, volunteers and paid staff who actually provided three different services—fire, ambulance, and police—had to be involved.

Ulster County's first move was to include the entire range of interested parties in the 911 decisionmaking process. An elaborate advisory board, including the chairs of key county legislative committees, was created to provide advice. Consultants were hired, and county staff already involved in dispatching and overseeing emergency services were given the lead liaison role. Meeting the needs of fire departments and ambulance corps was relatively easy. There were some technical issues: Ulster County, in the heart of the Catskill Mountains, had some "dead spots" that could not be reached by signals on frequencies commonly used. But with these matters addressed, activists in these services, staffed mostly by volunteers, came to relatively quick agreement about the design of the 911 system. They were accustomed to centralized dispatch, worked within clear geographical areas of responsibility, and already had in place detailed, tested mutual aid protocols.

The police were different. The elected county sheriff and the state police had jurisdiction throughout the county. The City of Kingston and some larger towns and villages had full-time police forces; other communities made do with part-time officers; and some had no local police at all. With geographical responsibilities overlapping, informal arrangements divided the work, but rivalries and competition for the "best calls" were long-standing. Several departments were attracted, too, by the large pot of money piling up in the 911 account; they saw the possibility of lots of new communications and communications-related equipment coming their way.

Ulster County Sheriff Mike LaPaglia's effort to control the system was resisted by the city and town forces and the state police. He, in turn, opposed the location of primary or backup dispatching facilities with the city, town, or state police. The county legislature had final authority; but if local volunteers, local police, state police, and town and city officials were unhappy, they had the political clout to block action.

Finally, after months of wrangling, the political leadership of the county government stepped in. It endorsed a plan that kept primary dispatching responsibility with the county government on Golden Hill in Kingston, but not under the sheriff's control. Backup capacity was located in New Paltz, fifteen miles away (and the hometown of the legislative chairman). A protocol establishing priorities for police dispatch and response was to be approved by the police and then used by the county. Regular meetings by a representative oversight committee would be held to see how the system was working and to deal with complaints and problems.

This was the plan finally passed by the county legislature. An extensive consultative process had included the range of interested parties and incorporated their concerns; most participants were satisfied. As public pressure grew, those who resisted the final plan, which took many months to complete, came to be viewed as self-interested and obstructionist. And most importantly, the county government had clear authority to act under state law and also had control of the money accumulating in the special 911 account.

The second Woodstock Festival, publicized worldwide, was scheduled to begin in the Ulster County town of Saugerties in August 1994. The county's chief elective officer, legislative chairman Daniel Alfonso, directed that 911 become operational in time to deal with the hundreds of thousands of music fans who would be flooding the county on that weekend. Among those who thought this was impossible were the representatives of NYNEX, the builders of the system. But they were wrong: 911 in Ulster County was up and running on July 17, 1994.

Creation and Reform of Networked Regional Institutions: BOCES

"Providing educational instruction and services which the individual districts themselves could not provide efficiently" was New York's stated purpose in establishing a regional approach to schooling in the late 1940s.[59] Enhancing prospects for economic development was another goal. Vocational counseling and training—for both traditional high-school-aged students and adults, many of them military veterans—were among the key services that could not be delivered without interdistrict collaboration, especially in rural areas. Given that today most troubled schools are in older industrial cities, it seems ironic that the New York State Education Department felt the need to encourage regionalism to help *rural* children. But back then rural areas were served by small, poorer school districts, and the department wanted to provide them with the same educational options that were only available to children living in large cities.

The state's approach half a century ago was two pronged. It confronted school districts with increasingly demanding curriculum and programmatic requirements—what we now would call mandates—and then offered a state aid package designed to make meeting these mandates fiscally irresistible if the districts collaborated through a regional education agency. After laying the groundwork with an extensive study by a council on rural education, the State Education Department (SED) sought to create intermediate school districts. These were to be "based on existing economic, social and cultural relationships, rather than on political boundaries . . . [and to] . . . furnish better or at lower cost the services presently offered by local districts—and undertake to provide services that none of the districts can presently offer."[60] These new districts were to replace the department's supervisory districts, which had been operating since 1910. At the same time, as a temporary measure, legislation was sought to encourage school districts to form cooperative boards, administered by existing district superintendents, to "get people working together across district lines." (District superintendents throughout New York State provided professional oversight for the State Education Department in the field but had no authority to deliver services.)

In 1948 the state legislature supported both approaches, allowing creation of up to five intermediate school districts and simultaneously authorizing each existing supervisory district to establish a Board of Cooperative Educational Services (BOCES).[61] Then localism asserted itself, and the best-laid plans of the SED went astray. Few intermediate districts—to be created from scratch, with their own taxing authority and elected boards of education—were established. Instead, the number of cooperative boards, which were controlled by existing districts and run by the existing district superintendents, grew like wildfire. Under the plan, if a BOCES was created, the district superintendent would wear two hats and get two salaries: one from state funds as a State Education

Department official (his or her old job) and one from local funds as the head of the BOCES in the supervisory district (his or her new job).[62] Because each BOCES was created by the local districts (and not, like the intermediate districts, created by referendum), its board members were chosen by the boards of the constituent districts, not by popular vote.[63]

It was an era of great credibility for the State Education Department: smaller school districts accepted the idea that regionalism was needed to enhance services at relatively low cost. But this was also a period when the state was pushing hard for school district consolidation. (See chapter 8.) A time could be envisioned when intermediate districts might not just augment but replace the smaller existing ones. Given a choice, localities opted for a regional structure that could not only provide economies of scale but also maximize their control and prospects for survival.

Within the BOCES structure, the state still tried to create and maintain a network of regional educational institutions. State subsidies for services and administrative costs were paid directly to the BOCES and not to the school districts, and these funds were not available for comparable services purchased by districts from other sources. Moreover, a school district's decision to join a BOCES was irreversible and carried with it a continuing commitment to share in the regional agency's administrative costs, regardless of how much or little the district actually used the BOCES services. This was an incentive to buy services through a BOCES because each purchase lowered unit administrative costs by spreading them over more units of service; it was also a barrier to competition because administrative costs had to be paid, even if a service was obtained elsewhere.

The BOCES system accommodated localism by making entry a local choice. No school district was displaced nor was any required to join (although that was the only way it could benefit from cost sharing for the programs and services that the state was requiring to improve educational quality). There was local choice, too, in the operation of the system. Under the state plan, each district received and paid for only those services it requested and used from the BOCES. At least two school districts had to agree to pay for a BOCES service in order for it to be made available. One of these, however, could be the BOCES itself acting as consumer rather than provider. Some felt this arrangement allowed for the flexibility needed when interest in a new service was being tested; others said it contravened the spirit of the "rule of two" and undermined the initial purpose of the BOCES system.[64]

Under the current system, services are requested annually by component school districts from a list provided by the BOCES. After approval is gained from the state commissioner of education (state aid is provided only for approved services), the BOCES informs districts of a tentative price for each service. The districts then decide which services they want, and this constitutes a reasonably firm commitment. The total demand from all districts is determined by the BOCES, and a final price is set. After each BOCES receives these requests, it files an amended operating plan with the State Education Department. The execution of contracts for services follows.[65]

Equity, too, was a goal, which the state pursued not only by enhancing the quality of available education through regionalization, but also by means of an equalizing element in the BOCES aid formula. For each service approved by the commissioner, the subsidy was higher for school districts with smaller property tax bases, thus lowering the "price" of BOCES services (in *local* taxes) even more.[66] Also, administrative costs are proportionally allocated in accordance with district enrollments: this means that larger districts pay more.[67]

Currently, all but 8 of the 705 New York school districts that are eligible are members of a BOCES. (The dependent school districts in New York City, Yonkers, Syracuse, Buffalo, and Rochester cannot join; it is assumed that they meet economy-of-scale requirements on their own.) A unique provision of the BOCES law requires that each time there is a vacancy in a district superintendency, a study must be done to determine if the job should be eliminated and the district be merged with another. This incremental approach to regionalism puts time on the regionalists' side without provoking opposition from anyone in power when the change process began. When the statute authorizing the BOCES was passed, there were 181 supervisory districts; now there are 38. Although school districts in New York are not organized along county lines, over time and by attrition almost all BOCES came to serve county or multicounty areas.

The flexible design of the BOCES has allowed a fundamental alteration of focus over the last fifty years as the state, its school districts, and its school-age population have changed. The BOCES now serve school districts that are more likely to be in suburbs or small cities than in rural areas and are larger in size, more complex in function, and far more likely to be educating a diverse school population with a much broader array of needs. When federal and state programs and mandates arose throughout the 1960s, 1970s, and 1980s, the BOCES in New York were already well established and able to provide a singular regional locus of response (unlike the situation in New Jersey, where multiple regional organizations existed). Thus regional educational services are funded not only in the manner initially devised but also with grants from the national government, private foundations, and a variety of other state agencies.

After half a century of growth, change, and development, this system of very powerful regional educational agencies annually receives and spends over $1.3 billion, about a quarter of this from state aid provided directly to BOCES districts. (To put matters in perspective, this is more than is spent for *all* elementary and secondary education in more than a fourth of the states.) The ten Boards of Cooperative Educational Services located in the nine New York counties in the tri-state region outside of New York City—three on Long Island and the rest in the Lower and Mid-Hudson Valley—together spent $569 million in 1996, 43.8 percent of the statewide BOCES total. The largest BOCES in the region, Suffolk I, spent more than $144 million; the smallest, in Sullivan County, had a budget less than 10 percent that amount ($13.7 million).[68]

Initially BOCES-provided services were delivered by itinerant teachers and other professionals in such fields as art, music, drivers' education, and school nursing; however, suburbanization changed this. Priorities now differ from region to region, but generally, special education for students with more severe disabilities now accounts for about two-fifths of all BOCES spending. Vocational education absorbs another fifth. Other major focal points are instructional support (classroom resources and training for teachers), administrative and management support for school districts, and general education (alternative schools, distance learning, gifted and talented programs).

Today, a BOCES is a major organization in suburban and rural areas throughout New York, and consideration of one's dissolution is likely to be pro forma. But under the right political conditions, change can occur. Recently, for example, two BOCES were combined in Suffolk County, where the Murphy case unfolded.

BOCES GETS A BAD NAME: THE MURPHY CASE. "Grotesque," said the governor. "Grossly excessive," agreed the commissioner of education. "An astonishing example of greed run amok," echoed the attorney general.[69] These were the reactions when Edward J. Murphy, district superintendent of the Western Suffolk BOCES on Long Island, retired in 1992 with a $960,000 golden parachute.

Until the news broke, Murphy was a respected educational administrator with forty-two years of experience. His annual salary of nearly $225,000 was far more than that of the governor, the education commissioner, or the attorney general, and he had convinced the seven-person Western Suffolk BOCES to alter his employment contract eight times in order to sweeten his retirement. (As mentioned earlier, BOCES members are appointed, not elected as are members of traditional school boards in New York.) Under the final agreement, the outgoing superintendent received $114,000 as a retirement incentive, $1,044 a day in compensation for 800 accrued sick and vacation days, and lifetime health insurance coverage for himself and his wife. Those vacation days were accumulating at a rate of ninety a year at the end, and the contract provided that the sick leave would pile up between 1987 and 1990, even if Murphy died.

According to the New York State Comptroller's Office, which operates the teacher retirement system, Edward J. Murphy achieved the distinction of getting the highest retirement award in the history of the state—and he was in line for at least a $150,000 annual pension. That figure might go up to $300,000 a year, some speculated, if the final lump-sum payment was factored in.

The Murphy case gave New York Governor Mario Cuomo the metaphor he needed to dramatize one of his favorite themes: the excessive administrative costs in school districts on Long Island. Maximizing state aid to education was a persistent priority of suburban Republican Long Island state legislators, who saw it as a way of controlling the property tax burden. The governor was *not* Republican, his political base was *not* in the suburbs, and like most of his predecessors, he resented all the school aid pouring out of Albany without any real state controls to ensure efficiency or effectiveness in spending—especially when other programs had to be cut back.

The barn door was closed after the horse was gone: in 1993 the state capped BOCES superintendents' salaries, placed controls over administrative budgets, and changed the terms and manner of selection of BOCES members. But for people who had never previously heard of the BOCES system—and that was most New Yorkers—a negative image remained. Yet these agencies offer a vital example—both for education and for general-purpose government—of an innovative structure that helps solve the size problem in local government.

BOCES REFORM: REGIONALISM AS A PROCESS, NOT AN OUTCOME. Larger, wealthier suburban school districts in Westchester and on Long

Island have been vociferous critics of the BOCES system; the wealth-equalizing BOCES aid formula helps them least.[70] (In Connecticut, by contrast, regional education agencies are reimbursed by the state for some mandated services at an average rate for all participating districts, a practice that rewards wealthier districts if they use a regional approach.) Moreover, to a greater degree than their smaller, less affluent peers, these suburban districts that are legally committed to pay BOCES overhead every year actually do have cost-effective alternatives: providing specialized services directly, finding them in the market at competitive prices, or entering bilateral or multilateral agreements with other school districts or governments without BOCES participation. In sum, this argument claims that the BOCES system as it currently operates has an unfair competitive advantage over nonprofits, for-profits, and even school districts themselves. According to opponents the only reason school districts pay less for services provided by a BOCES is because of state subsidies, which means that taxpayers still end up paying more overall.

Critics also argue that the growth of Boards of Cooperative Educational Services has been rampant. These regional boards, they say, are providing a broad array of services not anticipated when the system was created, competing with other providers and expanding their budgets and staff size. Relatively high salaries and benefits paid to unionized employees make them high-cost service providers. Moreover, educators and professionals at a BOCES are predisposed to offer service packages that are more extensive than necessary to meet state or federal requirements.

The critics have a point: the BOCES system has grown enormously and is more than half a century old. Remember Peter Drucker's advice, previously cited: organizations that have grown far beyond their original size or have reached the age of fifty ought to be restructured.[71] The Boards of Cooperative Educational Services agencies are no longer new and fragile; they do not need special subsidies to ensure their continued viability. Of course, care should be taken not to "throw out the baby with the bath water": the gains in equity, efficiency, and effectiveness in service delivery should be protected and expanded. But now that the BOCES are well institutionalized, both they and the state educational system as a whole might benefit if these regional agencies were thrust into a more competitive environment.

A 1993 New York State School Boards Association survey of 722 school superintendents on "Cost Saving Strategies and Shared Services" showed that cooperative arrangements through a BOCES often produced real economies through sharing personnel, pooling insurance needs to spread risk, and purchasing larger quantities of supplies and equipment at lower unit costs.[72] But in other cases, "economies" in business operations were achieved not because of lower costs, but because the use of a BOCES made activities "aidable," allowing expenses formerly paid entirely from local sources to be partially shifted to the state. In several instances, too, school districts reported that economies were achieved by leaving the BOCES system and relying on consultants or in-house operations for business functions and other computer applications.

Interestingly, reported interdistrict cooperation outside a BOCES was greatest in providing school busing, an area in which state aid does not flow through the BOCES but goes directly to school districts. On the service side, for special education, occupational education, and certain more specialized instruction in high schools, some districts reported that cooperative arrangements outside a BOCES produced lower costs, even with the BOCES aid forgone. These observations suggest that instead of subsidizing BOCES, the state might do better to place purchasing power in the hands of school districts and thus give them access to alternative service suppliers, which could create a quasi-market situation and reduce costs.

In accord with this thinking, one idea is to emulate the recently enacted, revolutionary federal approach to welfare by giving "block grants" directly to school districts (rather than passing the dollars through a BOCES) and letting the districts buy services in the market. Under such a plan, each BOCES would be one potential supplier but would not be specially advantaged (as it is now) by having its overhead defrayed or its price for a service subsidized by the state. State costs would be capped, and local districts could not reduce their share by shifting the burden to the state.

Research in general-purpose local government shows that when privatization occurs in this manner, and when the government agency that formerly was a sole provider competes to keep its business, that agency does quite well.[73] A BOCES certainly would have an advantage under such a plan in those service areas, such as occupational education, that require very large investments in equipment. But even here there might be actual or potential competitors already in the market. And in general, each BOCES would be required by such an approach to more closely monitor and control its prices while maintaining service quality.

One concern about a market-oriented approach using block grants, however, regards the level at which the state government, interested in reducing its own costs, would fund these grants. Under the guise of reform, the state might support "less for less" instead of "more for less." Another potential problem is the possibility of a "race to the bottom" in service quality, that is, market discipline might reduce costs at the expense of quality.

A recent review of the use of competition among regional education agencies, for-profit companies, and non-profit agencies to provide lower-cost transportation for special education children in the Connecticut portion of the tri-state region, for example, showed significant differences in driver qualifications, vehicle sizes and types, trip lengths, and the student mix on school buses. After reviewing a range of bids, the Norwalk School District considered the regional education agency's higher costs for more qualified drivers, smaller vehicles, and shorter trips to be "like buying a Cadillac when a Chevy will get you there." But another school district returned to the regional agency for transportation services after a special needs child was injured while being transported to school, and the parents sued for $25 million for lack of compliance with state school transportation regulations.[74]

Furthermore, skeptics point out that the change to a market-oriented approach may not work well, or at all, in places where there are no alternative providers and thus no market. Finally, under the BOCES system now operating, smaller jurisdictions with less purchasing power pay the same price for services as do bigger ones. Under a more market-like system, they may be hurt by their limited purchasing power. Thus the equity goal of the regional approach would be compromised.

In light of these criticisms, it becomes the special responsibility of state government to ensure that equity is not sacrificed as this established regional system is reformed to achieve greater efficiency. An intergovernmental system is most likely to be effective when the state government establishes quality and performance standards for local governments and customers and then backs them with rewards for success and consequences for failure. This means, for example, state aid formulas linked as much as possible to measures of outcomes. It also requires an integrated state-local fiscal system that focuses on costs-for-benefits—what is being bought—rather than on who is paying the bill. With the state taking this role, an accountable local government will not just seek the cheapest service from a regional provider but will be attentive to the cost-versus-quality trade-off involved when it buys services.

Moreover, only state government can guard against market failure. Where there are a few service providers and they are nongovernmental, the state may have an interest in sustaining regional governmental entities to ensure quality and to provide a baseline from which to measure performance. In places where the market produces no alternative regional providers for needed educational services, the state must ensure that these governmental agencies remain viable.

Insofar as the reforms proposed here align the fiscal interests of state and local government—by focusing on lowering costs rather than shifting them—they promise to diminish the need for taxes and by so doing, advance economic competitiveness. By concentrating as much decision-making as possible in local school boards or other elected local government officials, these proposed changes are also very respectful of the community value.

The BOCES experience shows that in pursuit of efficiency and equity, the state can induce and sustain effective, flexible governmental systems for collaborative regional service delivery while still accommodating localism. It also shows that any institutional arrangement for regional service delivery must have within it the capacity to adapt as conditions change and as more efficient approaches are discovered or devised. The incentives essential to creating and building a regional service delivery system where none exists are likely to be inappropriate for achieving efficiency in an existing, fully developed system. Regionalists must understand, therefore, that they are involved in a continuing process and are not in pursuit of a single, final governance outcome.

Conclusions

Legislatures and governors can and do advance regionalism. In some circumstances, where the political support is strong, the economic arguments are compelling enough, and the consequences of failing to act are unacceptable (as illustrated in the next chapter), they may even impose it. But this is rare. For state approaches to work in advancing regionalism, they must be more subtle and generally in accord with public opinion and local values. First, there should be a local reason, and better yet desire, to act regionally, one that is easily demonstrated and makes sense to people in their communities. Examples are preserving a vital local resource (drinking water in the Pine Barrens, for example); maintaining or enhancing service levels while keeping property taxes down (the case of 911); or protecting or building the local economy (providing occupational education and counseling through a BOCES). This having been said, it is also important to remember that there is more than a grain of wisdom in the bumper sticker advice: "Think globally, act locally." A larger national or statewide movement (the environmental movement is a good example, as the Pine Barrens case illustrates) may provide a strong rationale for regional action supported from the top, but it is much better if there is also a benefit that is palpably local.

Most sensitive of all, making social equity the primary goal of regional reforms can be confrontational, involving the competing interests of the haves and the have nots and, as in the New Jersey case, racial differences as well. Such an equity purpose for regionalization often challenges rather than mobilizes local feelings. State politicians often avoid such an approach because it is unlikely to work and has major political costs. That is why we stress that regional reformers who pursue equity should seek it as a result, not as a cause or main motivator, of regional action. One might call this a "stealth approach" to regional reform.

In reality, bottom-up and top-down regional reforms often go together in ways that can help political leaders achieve their aims. In policy areas where the community value is strongest, if a local rationale for regional action is present or can be developed, possibilities for state-induced, top-down regionalism are likely to be enhanced. Diverse strategies and combinations of strategies are available to state governments; some of these have been discussed in this chapter; others have been touched upon elsewhere in this volume. The state can provide access to new resources and can create political conditions that encourage local governments to act together (the 911 case). It can break down barriers, for example, by providing or paying for studies that demonstrate the feasibility and desirability of regional action (the Pine Barrens case). It can establish regulatory conditions that encourage collective action by local governments or discourage go-it-alone alternatives (the BOCES case). It can provide revenue streams (emergency-911 accounts) or subsidies from state sources (BOCES) to induce the shift of an established governmental function to a different level (and scale) or the creation of regional institutions that reduce local costs for required or needed services and thus decrease demands on the local property tax base.

Throughout this chapter the theme common to both bottom-up and top-down approaches to regional reform is that for a program or structural change to succeed, it must be politically astute and doable. Citizens who want to reform local governments should not only carefully evaluate and blend the goals and values involved; they also must find a popular proposal as a focus that will enable them to form coalitions for regional reform.

PART FIVE

The Nation in the Regional Arena

CHAPTER TEN

The Case of Solid Waste

In March 1991 a large semitrailer hit an overpass on the Palisades Parkway in New York, about an hour's drive from New York City. The truck belonged to C. A. Carbone, Inc. It was carrying twenty-three bales of waste from Clarkstown, in Rockland County, New York (part of the outer suburban ring of the tri-state region of New York, New Jersey, and Connecticut), to a landfill in Indiana. As it turned out, this was no ordinary traffic accident.

First, no truck of this size should have been on the Palisades Parkway at all. Built just after World War II as one of the region's last "scenic highways," on parkland donated by John D. Rockefeller Jr., the parkway was conceived as a sort of "garden for machines." Although by the 1990s "the Palisades" had become a major commuter path into and out of New York City, this road was actually originally designed for sightseeing and recreational driving, and access to it was limited. It simply could not accommodate big trucks. Its overpasses were too low and its lanes were too narrow. That is why it was restricted by law to automobiles.[1]

But the Carbone Company was not particularly strict about playing by the rules. Carmine and Salvatore Franco, who ran it, were later convicted of running a racketeering enterprise and of defrauding the Bergen County Utilities Authority of $22.5 million and the State of New Jersey out of $443,966 in taxes. Alleged by the New Jersey Attorney General's office to have ties to organized crime, the Francos were barred from the carting industry in the state in the mid-1980s, but they continued to operate their business in defiance of the law.[2]

The Palisades Parkway accident made Clarkstown officials suspicious. What exactly was in this truck, and why was it heading for Indiana?

In 1989 Clarkstown had entered a consent decree with the New York State Department of Environmental Conservation to close their landfill on Route 303 in the Village of West Nyack and build a new solid-waste transfer station on the same site. Recyclables were to be separated out there. A private contractor agreed to build the facility, operate it for five years (at a cost of $1.4 million), and then transfer ownership to the town for $1. But he would do this only if Clarkstown guaranteed delivery of at least 120,000 tons of solid waste a year and permitted a "tipping fee"—a charge to those depositing waste—of $81 a ton. Town leaders agreed, and to meet these conditions they adopted Local Law No. 9 of 1990, a "flow control" ordinance.[3] This statute required all nonhazardous solid waste within the town to "flow" to the newly constructed transfer station. The penalty for noncompliance—that is, for Clarkstown residents or businesses who bypassed the transfer station in disposing of solid waste—was a fine of up to $1,000 and up to fifteen days in jail.

This penalty was not enough to deter the Carbone Company—which, as it happened, was already operating a recycling center in Clarkstown, where it sorted and baled solid waste (mostly cardboard) from out of town and shipped out recyclables. That was fine with Clarkstown, as long as Carbone brought nonrecyclable waste to the transfer station and paid the tipping fee. But the cargo of the truck that hit the Palisades Parkway bridge was not recyclable cardboard; it was garbage that should have gone to the Clarkstown transfer station but that Carbone could dispose of more cheaply in the Midwest.

Clarkstown sued to enforce its local law and was successful in the New York courts. But Carbone appealed. And in 1994 the U.S. Supreme Court decided that the local flow-control ordinance had a clearly limiting effect on interstate commerce, and overturned it.

In earlier decisions the Supreme Court had found that local attempts to keep *out* garbage from other jurisdictions were unconstitutional. In this decision the Court used similar reasoning to prevent localities from keeping their own garbage *in* or exerting control over where it went. Justice Anthony Kennedy wrote for a majority of the Court, "State and local governments may not use their regulatory power to favor local enterprise by prohibiting patronage of out-of-state competitors or their facilities."[4]

Flow Control, Federalism, and Privatization

A key goal of the founders when they wrote the U.S. Constitution was to create a common market. The national government was given sole control over regulation of private-market economic activity in interstate commerce in order to nurture a truly national economy. The commerce clause was written so as to allow private business activities to proceed unimpeded by levies or other burdens that experience showed might be imposed by the states and their localities. In the earliest days, the collection and disposal of waste was local and—although part of the private economy—hardly a matter of interstate commerce. Over time, concerns about public health and safety, especially in more densely settled places, made solid waste an interest of state and local governments—as regulators, customers, or direct service providers. Within the broad framework of state law, the function still remained very local. Garbage was for centuries largely a matter of every city, town, or village for itself.

The *Carbone* decision thus applied constitutional standards designed to create and maintain a truly national, private-market economy with respect to a function that had long been public and local. The timing was critical. At the time *Carbone* was decided, the states, driven by the burgeoning environmental movement, had been seeking efficient, cost-effective alternatives to traditional local methods for dealing with solid waste for at least a quarter of a century. Their approach was to use incentives and regulation to shift responsibility for this function from the local to the regional (or at least the subregional) level, while keeping it largely governmental.

We demonstrated in chapters 6 and 7 that it was market failure that "governmentalized" responsibility for mass transit in the tri-state region: local government was asked to provide an essential service after private companies—some of them national in scope—could not make it profitable. The effect of the Supreme Court decision in *Carbone* was just the opposite. In the name of efficiency, it encouraged the shift of an essential function from the local and governmental spheres to the national and nongovernmental. With state and local regulations removed, private companies, in a direct business relationship with citizens or under contract with governments, might now handle solid waste at lower cost, hauling it long distances for disposal at large privately owned and operated facilities.

Thirty-nine of the fifty states, including all three in the tri-state region, had flow-control provisions in force in 1994.[5] The Supreme Court's decision in *Carbone* upset the legal infrastructure developed in the region and elsewhere by states and localities just as success in regionalizing a key local service appeared to be at hand, or in the immediate offing. As we shall see, one effect of the Court's decision was to dramatically reduce the cost of disposing of solid waste. But was this the best way to balance efficiency with other core values that regionalists seek from local government—especially the value of community?

New Jersey: Relying on the Counties

A 1987 report of the New Jersey County and Municipal Government Study Commission found a solid-waste crisis in the state. Almost all of New Jersey's waste was still being placed in landfills, yet many landfills were closed and others were reaching their capacity. Planned burn facilities were not yet on line and would not be for four years. Other states were threatening to stop receiving New Jersey waste. The study commission reported that counties "have failed to meet state requirements in planning and implementing solid-waste programs," leading to a situation in which "capacity in much of New Jersey will be virtually nonexistent."[6]

State legislation passed in 1970 had created an unusual administrative situation with respect to the development of solid-waste policy in New Jersey. Counties were empowered to build and operate solid-waste facilities; the state Department of Environmental Protection was to regulate the design and operation of these facilities and to help in the development of regional plans. But in a unique arrangement for state governments in the United States, private-sector elements of the waste disposal system were regulated by the New Jersey Public Utility Commission. It oversaw charges for collecting and hauling waste and for depositing it in landfills.

A statute passed in 1975 reinforced the shift of the solid-waste function to New Jersey counties, making them the state's solid-waste planning districts.[7] (The state had considered an approach based on regional "wastesheds"—regions conceived to deal specifically with the solid-waste problem—but "the political and administrative strengths and traditions of counties as regional governments prevailed.")[8] Most counties created public authorities to do the job, although five retained direct control (including Monmouth, Somerset, and Ocean Counties in the tri-state region). In this 1975 act, the state legislature required the executive to adopt a solid-waste plan, approve county plans, and inspect and approve any facilities developed in accordance with those plans. If counties failed to meet their solid-waste planning obligation, the state could do the planning for them—and send them the bill.

Acting in accordance with both state and federal law, the New Jersey Department of Environmental Protection published the state solid-waste plan in 1982. The plan included flow control. As the department's tightening environmental regulations continued to force landfill closure throughout the state, public and private landfill operators sought help in Trenton to meet the costs of new statutory and regulatory requirements.

In response, in the 1980s the New Jersey Legislature passed and the governor signed laws establishing a series of fees and special taxes to help meet closure costs, including those that might arise from damage suits against landfill operators. One approach allowed the creation of landfill operator–controlled contingency funds from a surcharge on the volume of waste deposited. Another required the revenues from fees or earmarked taxes to come to the state, which was to use them to assist with closure. Money might also be used for development of solid-waste facilities or to create "benefit packages" for communities in which waste facilities were sited, but the state government could withhold assistance if no real effort at siting was being made.[9]

By the mid-1980s, landfill closure and increased costs for out-of-state shipment of waste had led to renewed interest in recycling. A 1981 law placed a small surcharge on solid waste deposited in the state to create a fund to finance the development of recycling programs by communities and companies, encourage recycling education, and reward communities that reached targeted recycling goals.

But the use of economic incentives rather than "command and control" strategies did not achieve the target, which was to have 25 percent of the waste stream recycled by 1986. In the crisis environment that prevailed, a mandatory program was therefore enacted. It required New Jersey counties to have a program for yard waste composting in place within six months, and a plan for recycling three of four named materials (aluminum, glass, paper, and plastic) in place within two years. In addition, counties were required to develop markets for recycled waste in order to reach the 25 percent recycling goal within that two-year period—at the risk of otherwise losing state recycling aid. The state surcharge on solid-waste deposits was increased to finance this effort. As a further incentive, a 50 percent credit against the corporate business tax was also enacted for firms that purchased recycling material and equipment.[10]

All did not go smoothly, however. In the 1980s, local governments seeking to avoid siting solid-waste facilities within their limits challenged state authority to redefine the solid-waste disposal system. But the New Jersey courts confirmed the power of the state to prepare plans for counties that identified solid-waste facility sites and to force counties to carry out those plans if they failed to do so.[11] More importantly, they confirmed the authority of counties to site facilities in towns over the objections of the town, removing any doubt about the state's power to regionalize the solid-waste function.

With regard to recycling, great progress was made, notwithstanding opposition of the private waste-disposal industry and crashing markets for recyclables. But when it came to new facilities, the planning took place but the siting did not. The political pressures were enormous. Counties dragged their feet; they sought to distance themselves, to be publicly forced, thus passing responsibility on to the courts and state government.

This was the root of the crisis identified in 1987. According to political scientist Carl Van Horn, "perhaps the greatest single failure of New Jersey political and agency officials in the 1980s was their inability to find ways to gain public acceptance for siting facilities."[12] Even when county power was confirmed and sites were selected, monkey wrenches appeared in the works. For example, under pressure from the state and after only a preliminary environmental investigation, Morris County, in the tri-state region's intermediate ring, bought a waste facility site in Rockaway Township. In 1986, its resistance to the development of this site having been stymied within the state, the township persuaded the local congressional representative, Robert Roe (one of New Jersey's most senior Democrats), to offer an amendment to federal Superfund legislation specifically blocking development of the site.

In another example, the Passaic County Utility Authority, also in the intermediate ring, gained a permit from the state to build an incinerator in 1990. But then, Governor James Florio, acting on a campaign promise, negated the permit because of the proposed facility's proximity to a school and a hospital. Thus the county, which had already spent $40 million to conform with state law, was forced back into the courts to try to implement its solid-waste plan.

The result of twenty-five years of state and local governmental effort to deal with solid waste in New Jersey, remarked federal judge Joseph E. Irenas in 1996 (somewhat ironically, since he was finding it constitutionally flawed on the basis of the *Carbone* precedent), was a "complex system" that was both "environmentally sound, and effective in providing a long-term solution to intractable problems."[13] Elsewhere, the judge described this result of the state's long-term, incremental public policy process

> as a delicate balance—a political compromise—which resolves interests that may at times be compatible and at other times conflicting, such as (i) the cost to the public for waste disposal, (ii) protection of the environment from damage by waste disposal activities, (iii) funding for ancillary activities, (iv) the need for recycling, (v) long-term availability of disposal activities, (vi) protection of neighborhoods in which disposal activities are located, and (vii) protection of the rights of investors who fund the construction of disposal facilities.[14]

Although it did not meet the ambitious recycling goals it set for itself (50 percent of its municipal waste stream recycled by the end of 1995), New Jersey's 41 percent recycling rate far exceeded the national average. Polluting landfills were closed, and twelve sanitary landfills were operating. Five waste-to-energy plants were brought on line between 1988 and 1994, three of these in the tri-state region (in Essex, Union, and Warren Counties).

But tipping fees in New Jersey were among the highest in the nation; in several of the region's counties they exceeded $100 a ton. Nor did New Jersey achieve self-sufficiency in solid-waste disposal; statewide, more than a third of the waste stream was still exported. Although five counties in the tri-state region (Middlesex, Monmouth, Ocean, Sussex, and Warren) disposed of all their waste within the state, three counties in the region (Mercer, Morris, and Passaic) exported all their garbage. There was some facility sharing across county lines, but not much. In the region, Hunterton and Somerset Counties sent some waste to the Warren County burn plant and used the Atlantic County landfill. Additionally, some of Bergen County's waste was burned in the Union County facility. And the very large Essex County facility, built by the Port Authority, took some New York City trash.[15]

Connecticut: Creating a State Authority and Making Burning Work

Charles Atkins, a long-time official of the Connecticut Department of Environmental Protection, noted,

> It is remarkable how close the state's solid-waste system in 1995 is to the plan devised in 1972. It took a long time to implement. Privately, town leaders wanted the state to take over solid waste; but publicly they felt that they had to assert home rule, independence. The department was new, and not well equipped to move the plan along at first. We had to create a public authority as the implementing tool. The [Connecticut Resources Recovery Authority] now runs several plants, ashfills, and transfer stations.[16]

The Connecticut Department of Environmental Protection (CDEP) was established in 1971.[17] The law creating it moved responsibility for solid waste from the state health department, transferred responsibility for advancing long-term solid-waste solutions from towns and cities to the state government, and mandated a statewide plan for managing solid waste in every region by July 1, 1973.

A solid-waste plan drafted earlier by the health department was adopted by the CDEP in 1971. It focused on the need for towns to cooperate regionally. To meet the statutory mandate for a statewide plan by 1973, the department retained the General Electric Company as a consultant. The resulting "Proposed Plan of Solid Waste Management for Connecticut" emphasized a regional approach to resource recovery and recycling, with the use of landfills to dispose of the residual waste ash from planned burn facilities. The state was to be divided into "wastesheds," with garbage from each town being delivered to a transfer station, from which it would be taken to the appropriate resource recovery facility and materials recovery facility for sorting and burning. The 1973 plan projected a need for between five and eight resource recovery facilities; for five materials recovery (recycling) facilities; for forty-five transfer stations; and for eighteen new residual disposal sites.

The plan also called for the creation of a statewide agency for implementation. This was the origin of the Connecticut Resources Recovery Authority (CRRA), established in 1973. Its mandate reinforced the need for a regional approach and anticipated a public/private partnership in the state for finding a solution to the solid-waste problem. The CRRA has the power to borrow, but it is financed entirely from fees and charges for services; it may levy no taxes. It contracts with private industry to build and operate facilities; enters into agreements with municipalities to channel waste to these facilities for disposal; and charges these local governments (and private haulers) a fee for doing so.

The CRRA is not the only player in solid-waste disposal in Connecticut. The Ogden Martin Company built and operates a major burn plant in Bristol in the east-central part of the state, and Oxford Energy has a tire burning facility in Oxford. But the CRRA is the major player, with responsibility in law to "develop and implement a plan for the design, construction and operation of a statewide network of regional systems, in conjunction with private industries, utilizing the best available means of resource recovery, to resolve the solid-waste disposal problems of the cities and towns in the state."[18]

Connecticut's brand of regionalism in solid-waste disposal—state-centered action in newly defined regional areas—developed unevenly. A town and city backlash to early-1970s legislation led to the passage of a bill in 1978 that confirmed localities' authority in the area of solid waste and required that the CDEP identify an alternative site for waste before local landfills could be closed.[19]

In 1981 CDEP officials expressed worry that the CRRA would engage in "spot implementation" of the overall solid-waste plan. "Inability to obtain town cooperation in time," they wrote, "was leading the CRRA to try to put together less than complete systems where the need was immediate." This approach, they said, was "guaranteed to lead to problems, high cost, and perhaps, inability to serve some waste flows some years from now." The legislature could not be induced, however, to require by law that towns become members of one of seven regional wastesheds.[20] (And as noted, many towns did not participate in the regional system until they could absolutely no longer operate their landfills or incinerators.) Later, however, the state did subordinate local interests to regional needs in a law that allowed the CRRA to site ash fills on approved sites without the consent of the host municipality, as long as a host benefit package was negotiated.[21]

While New Jersey raised fees and levied earmarked taxes to generate the money to enable limited state assistance to localities for new capital costs, Connecticut—perhaps because of its state-centered approach—borrowed against its own credit to partially finance equipment for sanitary landfills or transfer stations. As an incentive to intermunicipal cooperation, the state paid an additional 10 percent of the costs incurred by each municipality (up to a total of seven) that participated in a group or regional approach. By 1991 Connecticut had expended $98 million on solid-waste management activities, including landfill operating equipment, resource recovery feasibility studies, and recycling program grants.[22]

Recycling in Connecticut remained voluntary until the mid-1980s. A $10 million recycling trust fund to support planning was established by the state legislature in 1986. Mandatory recycling came the year after, at about the same time as in New Jersey. In 1987 the legislature directed the CDEP to add a recycling component to the solid-waste management plan. It was to include "options for local compliance of municipalities with recycling requirements," but it permitted the commissioner to assign localities to regional programs and direct their participation in specified intermediate processing centers if they refused to cooperate.[23]

Eight regions were proposed in the department's plan, each with an intermediate processing center (except the capital region, which was to have two). Most of these were to be privately run. Ancillary facilities included transfer stations and sites for leaf composting facilities, scrap metal storage, and waste oil collection. The target was the recycling of 25 percent of the municipal waste stream by 1991. By 1995 Connecticut had in operation 104 regional and municipal transfer stations and 6 intermediate processing facilities; its municipal solid-waste recycling rate was 23 percent.

The last year a municipal landfill was permitted in Connecticut was 1978. Although towns resisted on financial and home-rule grounds, a wave of closures followed every tightening of regulatory requirements (and therefore simultaneously increased local costs). More than one hundred municipal landfills were shut down in Connecticut during the 1970s and 1980s; another forty succumbed after tightened federal regulations were adopted in 1991. By 1999 the town of Windsor, north of Hartford, was operating the only remaining municipal facility in Connecticut that was accepting municipal solid waste.

The CRRA's initial effort to build a regional solid-waste facility was abortive. In 1977 the agency contracted with Combustion Equipment Associates for a combined recycling and "refuse-derived-fuel" plant, to be located in Bridgeport. Based on a relatively untested technology, this plant was plagued from the start. Cost overruns were in the tens of millions. The plant never ran at anywhere near full capacity, and in early operation it produced fuel with too much sulfur content to meet air quality standards when burned.[24]

Combustion Equipment Associates declared bankruptcy in November 1980. Chastened by this experience, the CRRA turned to more conventional refuse-to-energy plants. By the mid-1990s, the agency had built, and was contracting with private vendors to operate, four major facilities: Mid-Connecticut (Hartford), Bridgeport, Wallingford, and Southeast (Preston). A non-CRRA facility built at Windham and first permitted in 1981 was shut down in 1994. Another, at Lisbon, came on line in 1997.

Each CRRA project is now a network composed of a major resource recovery facility, landfills, transfer stations, and recycling centers (figure 10-1). For example, the Bridgeport project, which serves eighteen municipalities in the tri-state region, includes a mass burn facility, eight transfer stations, a regional recycling center, and two landfills. The burn facility was completed in 1988. It has a capacity of 2,250 tons per day, annually disposes of more than three-fourths of a million tons of garbage, and produces fifty-five megawatts of electricity.[25]

CRRA member towns were assured a solution of their solid-waste disposal problems over a long term at a predictable price. In return, they allowed their full faith and credit to be used to back CRRA bonds before the agency had a track record in the market, and entered into "put-or-pay" municipal service agreements, under which localities either delivered a guaranteed weight of waste for burning at the contracted rate per ton or paid a minimum total fee for disposal. (That is, they either "put" the burnables in the furnaces or "paid" the waste facility anyway.) Combined with flow control (until the *Carbone* decision), these agreements allowed the CRRA to borrow the money it needed to go into business.[26]

The terms of the CRRA's contracts with the towns took on added significance in 1989, when reduction in the size of the waste stream became a Connecticut priority by law.[27] Towns that worked to comply with state policy, and succeeded, found themselves obligated to pay the CRRA for services they no longer needed. Bad economic times also had their effects, cutting down on the amount of waste produced. Delivery of waste by member localities to CRRA facilities dropped by about a third between 1990 and 1994. In 1990, for example, the eighteen member local governments delivered 532,767 of the 715,309 tons (just under three-fourths) of the municipal solid waste burned at the agency's Bridgeport facility; in 1994 they were the source of 396,349 of 772,854 tons (a little over half) burned there (see figure 10-1).

Thus even before the *Carbone* decision, the decline in the amount of waste to be processed in the state required that the CRRA aggressively

Figure 10-1. *Connecticut Resource Recovery Agency Project Zones*

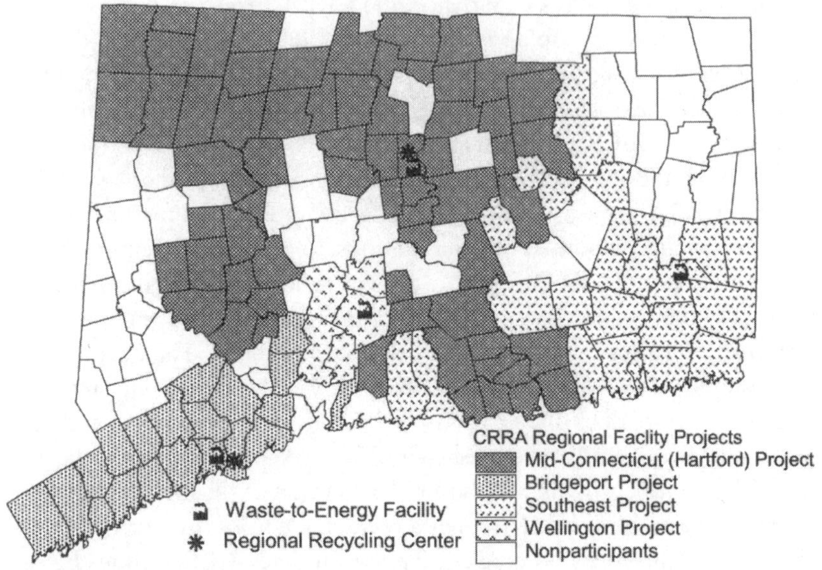

Source: Connecticut Resources Recovery Authority, *1997 Annual Report* (Hartford, Conn., 1997).

compete in the short-term market, even out of state, to keep its facilities operating and meet its financial obligations. But in doing so it had to take care to ensure that member towns did not become disaffected. With municipal facilities now almost all closed as a result of state requirements, nonmember towns (a number are in the tri-state region's outer ring, in Litchfield County) may contract with the CRRA over a five- to ten-year term—making cost and disposal more predictable, but at a higher-than-market price—or they may simply rely on the spot market, paying the prevailing price when the waste is delivered.

These operational issues notwithstanding, from the perspective of the mid-1990s, the regionalization of the solid-waste system in Connecticut seemed a major success story. The Connecticut Office of Policy and Management wrote with pride in 1995 of "a statewide, integrated recycling, composting, resource recovery and landfill system."[28] The planning focus had clearly shifted to fine-tuning a solid-waste system already in place and operating: increasing the range of recyclable materials, expanding markets for recyclables, adjusting the waste flow between towns and regional burn facilities "to promote the lowest cost long-term management of the waste stream," and "assisting the remaining towns that may suddenly find they can no longer meet their disposal needs on their own."

Connecticut and New Jersey Compared: Structure Makes a Difference

Like New Jersey, Connecticut—both on its own and as a consequence of federal law and regulation—proceeded along parallel courses to

—induce the closure of local landfills by ratcheting up environmental requirements and providing financial support and incentives;

—make it more difficult to permit new municipal landfills; and

—provide for waste disposal through fewer, larger-scale regional facilities.

Unlike New Jersey, however, Connecticut's approach was based on wastesheds, not counties. Here we see an advantage to the greater simplicity (and lower level of layering) of Connecticut's general-purpose local government system. With its county governments abolished in 1960 (as explained in chapter 8), the regions Connecticut used to deal with the solid-waste problem did not have to accommodate an existing system of county governments. This, and the large number of relatively small towns in the state, allowed the easier creation by planners of regions specifically to deal with solid waste. Moreover, the relatively small size of the state permitted the key implementing institution for Connecticut's plan to be a statewide public authority established specifically for this purpose (the CRRA).

In contrast, New Jersey—also small in size, but with a layered, general-purpose local government system already in place—employed a far more decentralized approach. There was a state plan, but no statewide entity created to effect it. Although experts thought that eight or nine regions would be optimal for the state, solid-waste planning and the creation of larger-scale disposal facilities was left to the twenty-one counties.[29]

Connecticut's statewide approach to implementation and simpler local government structure also allowed it to adhere more closely to its original strategies and policies and to move with greater alacrity toward self-sufficiency in solid-waste management. Connecticut towns resisted change, but unlike counties in New Jersey were actually required to do relatively little to make change happen. Therefore, implementation of the state's initial commitment to large-scale solid-waste burn facilities was more efficient and, in the end, more complete.

It is more than a little ironic that because Connecticut was relatively efficient in moving toward the goals it set for itself in the early 1970s, adjusting its system to mandatory recycling—a priority it adopted only a year after New Jersey—was harder for it than for New Jersey. Once committed to building a burn facility and making it work financially, leaders were slower in starting recycling programs that might require them to pay twice: once for the waste they guaranteed to "put" in the burn plant, and again for the recycling program itself.

In New Jersey burn plants had to be built by counties or agencies responsible to county governments. These were, of course, headed by elected officials, people far more responsive to local opinion than the heads of Connecticut's statewide public authority. Resistance to burn plants delayed the achievement of state self-sufficiency but also allowed recycling to be considered more seriously as an alternative (rather than an add-on) in New Jersey, because burn facilities were not yet in place.

The key intergovernmental relationships in Connecticut were two-way, between municipalities and the state.[30] The Connecticut legislature was reluctant to do all that its experts wanted; it would not, for example, mandate town participation in specific solid-waste regions, leading to considerable disorder in deciding which town participated where. But the state's home-rule tradition notwithstanding, Connecticut state government did give statewide actors considerable power to impose their will on localities. The CDEP commissioner could compel towns into recycling regions. The CRRA, although it is reluctant to do so, is authorized by law to site ash fills without local consent.

In New Jersey the very authority of the state to shift responsibility for solid waste to its counties was challenged by towns, townships, and counties and ultimately had to be established in the courts. New Jersey's three-way intergovernmental political dynamic was much more complex, with towns, townships, and boroughs becoming governmental focal points for resistance to siting decisions and other actions by often reluctant counties or newly created county-based public authorities. The result was that the capacity to perform the solid-waste function regionally in New Jersey seriously lagged behind the shift of responsibility for this function to the regional level.

As in Connecticut, the New Jersey Legislature developed a range of incentives to align localities with state priorities. But New Jersey raised the resources it used more from fees and taxes than, as Connecticut did, from borrowing. Both states spent state funds on planning grants, assistance to localities with capital costs, and recycling programs. But New Jersey did not compel local action or bypass local powers by law or regulation to the same degree as did Connecticut.

National and Private Sector Responsibility for Solid Waste

"As governor," Christine Todd Whitman of New Jersey told a U.S. Senate subcommittee considering how to deal with the results of the U.S. Supreme Court's decision in the *Carbone* case in March 1995, "I am faced with the prospect of the destruction of a waste management system that has taken twenty years to create."[31] When flow control was struck down, outstanding debt for solid-waste facilities in New Jersey totaled $1.955 billion (including Port Authority obligations for the Essex County plant in Newark). In June 1995 Moody's Investment Service downgraded the debt of six solid-waste facilities to junk bond status because of the loss of flow control. Five were in New Jersey.[32]

New Jersey was not alone. In Connecticut, as noted, the debt incurred to build regional solid-waste facilities totaled almost a billion dollars. On Long Island, where drinking water concerns (like those raised in the Pine Barrens case, chapter 9) and other local conditions led to the construction of half the waste-to-energy plants in New York State, several hundred million dollars were borrowed and invested in these and other facilities, "all secured by local laws enacted to assure the steady flow of waste from the public, through the collection industry, to municipal disposal facilities."[33]

Faced with declining revenues from tipping fees and diminished fuel supplies for its burn facility, Dutchess County, New York, in the tri-state region's outer ring, was required to subsidize its resources recovery authority to the tune of $3 million in 1995. (This was the equivalent of 6 percent of the county's annual property tax levy.) By the late 1990s, public authorities throughout the New York and New Jersey portions of the region were receiving financial assistance from counties—and the counties from state government—to help meet their obligations. In November 1998, for example, New Jersey voters approved a statewide ballot question, advanced by the governor and state legislature, that forgave $175 million in state loans to counties for incinerator and landfill construction costs.[34]

The *Carbone* decision made solid-waste debt more risky by making revenue flows to agencies far less certain. Without the local monopoly control that flow control produced, regional solid-waste facilities had to compete in the national market, and they were hard pressed to do so. In 1995, for example, Bergen County, which exported about half its garbage and contracted with Union County to burn the rest, obtained a three-year level contract with Chambers Development Corporation for trash disposal that *dropped* its rate by 32 percent, to $42.75 a ton from $63.00 a ton. Chambers transports the waste by rail for burial in its landfill in Charles City, West Virginia.[35] The company's rate to Bergen County was less than half the average cost per ton to dispose of solid waste in New Jersey in 1995; about half the average cost in New York; and just under two-thirds of the cost in Connecticut. In fact, Chambers's rate was 22 percent lower than the lowest rate charged at any CRRA facility in Connecticut in 1995.

Following the maxim that "no good deed goes unpunished," the places that had worked the hardest and succeeded best at complying with national and state priorities—moving their solid-waste functions most quickly and fully to the county level, planning and building facilities, taking on and overcoming local resistance to siting—were locked into bond service obligations, and therefore were the least well situated to take advantage of the lower tipping fees available at privately owned mega-landfills outside the state. Connecticut towns unilaterally lowered their tipping fee payments—put-or-pay contracts notwithstanding—only to be sued by the CRRA or the contractors operating its facilities.[36] Connecticut's U.S. senator Chris Dodd had it right when he remarked that his state and others were "now being asked to pay a price for being responsible and proactive."[37]

The initial response of the region's states was two-pronged: to seek congressional action reversing the Supreme Court's decision and restoring flow control; and to seek a constitutional means, even without this action, to ensure a flow of solid waste to already built regional facilities, so that they could remain economically viable in this new, national-market environment. Each of these goals demonstrated the degree to which solid waste had been transformed from a local governmental function to a national business.

Congress Fails to Act

Virtually from the day flow control was struck down by the Supreme Court, efforts began in Congress to restore it. Proponents included state and local governments with investments in solid-waste facilities now in peril, along with investment bankers who feared the impact on the municipal bond market of a series of defaults by solid-waste agencies. Opposition was led by private waste haulers and disposal-facility operators. They were joined by potential customers (for example, local governments without their own facilities) that stood to benefit from the lower prices for disposal likely to result from greater competition in the marketplace.

The CRRA was in favor of flow control, it said, because without it towns and cities in Connecticut were much less likely to be able to deliver the amount of solid waste they had guaranteed under put-or-pay contracts, and therefore they were much *more* likely to have to pay for something they were not getting.[38]

Why would the waste not simply flow to these facilities anyway? For the same reason that the Carbone Company was sending garbage to Indiana in the first place. Someplace else was cheaper. And this was true even with transportation costs factored in. One expert witness in the follow-up federal lawsuit challenging flow control in New Jersey in 1995 estimated that waste generators there "spent an average of $110 million per year in excess tipping fees, compared to competitive market prices, due to flow control."[39]

According to Brett Schundler, Republican mayor of Jersey City, waste disposal costs in the parts of New Jersey where flow control prevailed were more than 2.5 times the national average.[40] He for one, Schundler said, did not want to be forced by state or national law to subsidize what he regarded as others' mistakes and inefficiencies. Several hundred New Jersey mayors, organized in 1995 in a task force against flow control, agreed with him.

For counties, county-based public authorities, or regional agencies with responsibility for waste disposal, flow control was necessary to get the job done; it ensured effective home rule. But as Schundler's comments indicated, leaders in those localities without this responsibility argued just the opposite. Ed Farrell, head of the New York State Conference of Mayors, told a congressional committee that "flow control deprives local governments of a basic tenet of home rule, the ability to make decisions on the local level in the best interests of the local citizenry."[41] Before *Carbone,* Farrell said, villages on Long Island (some with, some without, municipal sanitation departments) had to pay tipping fees set in accordance with the Town of North Hempstead's flow-control law. These fees had gone up by more than two-thirds in the five years from 1990 to 1994, even though no solid-waste facility had been built by the town.

As we noted earlier, the argument about costs and fees is not as simple as it seems. Flow control advocates point out that the tipping fees set under these laws pay not only for disposal but for socially desirable outcomes that may not always pay for themselves, such as "recycling programs and other environmentally friendly recovery projects, and developing long-term disposal plans."[42] Supporters of flow control emphasize the need for communities to control their own fate in this critical service area. They also note that commodity markets (and solid waste is a commodity) can be very unpredictable, offering attractive prices now but at the risk of budget-busting costs later. National laws or regulations might change, they argue, allowing states to bar out-of-state garbage, thus making capacity scarce and driving prices up.

In theory, state and local officials are attracted by the idea of local control. But lower prices today help balance budgets now, and relatively short terms in office do not encourage long-term thinking. The differences in rates—between those extant in the regional governmental system (created by regulation and supported by flow control) and those obtainable in the private market—were just too great for defense by politicians whose constituents were among the most highly taxed in the nation (table 10-1.)

Moreover, there was an emerging view that questioned whether recycling and waste reduction—the money-losing but socially desirable programs served by flow control and higher, mandated tipping fees—were in fact desirable. During the same week in the summer of 1996, John Tierney published an essay in the *New York Times Magazine* that argued that recycling was more trouble than it was worth, and Mayor Rudolph Giuliani announced cutbacks in New York City recycling efforts to save $29 million in the city's budget.[43]

The debate over flow control was introduced into a congress that had for years been roiled by another solid-waste transportation issue—"non-importation." As interstate transportation of waste grew in response to the environmental reforms of the 1980s that closed more and more landfills, so did public resentment in waste-receiving states such as Indiana and Pennsylvania against becoming "dumping grounds" for the large waste-producing states. One 1997 estimate was that about 25 million tons of solid waste crossed state lines each year.[44] Efforts led by Senator Daniel Coats of Indiana to give state governments authority to block the entry of waste at their borders had since 1988 been one of the major road-

Table 10-1. *Effect of the End of Flow Control on Tipping Fees in New Jersey Tri-State Region Counties, 1997–98*[a]

Dollars per ton

	Tipping fee	
County	*November 12, 1997*	*October 10, 1998*
Bergen	101.88	54.00
Essex	72.75	50.00
Hudson	63.27	58.50
Hunterdon	93.50	65.00
Mercer	117.81	98.25
Middlesex	55.42	51.00
Monmouth	75.10	55.15
Morris	88.40	83.40
Passaic	104.74	49.25
Somerset	132.93	72.85
Sussex	108.55	58.00
Union	83.05	50.00
Warren	100.26	48.00

Source: New Jersey Solid Waste Bureau (www.state.nj.us/dep/dshw/recycle/8696trnd.html [Summer 1999]).

a. The effect of the *Carbone* decision in New Jersey was delayed for two years while litigation proceeded in federal court on its applicability in the state.

blocks to reauthorization of the federal Resource Conservation and Recovery Act.

When flow control was overturned by the Supreme Court, a new basis for a natural alliance was formed—between receiving states, who wanted federal authority to keep waste *out,* and states and localities heavily invested in solid-waste facilities, who wanted federal authority to keep their waste *in.* (Interestingly, members of Congress from jurisdictions in the latter category, places that were still net exporters of waste, had until the *Carbone* decision opposed Coats's efforts to pass nonimportation legislation as being against their areas' interests.) After extensive hearings and complex negotiations among competing interests, a tightly crafted compromise bill was drafted that included two grandfather provisions. It established nonimportation, but only for new solid-waste sites; facilities that had received interstate waste before 1993 could continue to do so unimpeded. And it reinstated flow control, but only for places that had it before the Supreme Court decided *Carbone.*

This bill came within a whisker of passage in the last days of the 103d Congress in 1994. It was blocked by a parliamentary maneuver: Senator

John Chafee of Rhode Island, an exporting state, denied unanimous consent for its rapid consideration. Chafee had no problem with flow control, but he did object to the power given in the bill to local officials to block the use of new sites in their jurisdictions for the disposal of interstate waste.[45]

With the election of a Republican-controlled Congress in 1994, flow control faced new problems. Many conservative Republicans, already predisposed in favor of business and against governmental solutions to problems, objected on ideological grounds to what they regarded as monopolistic restrictions that flow control placed on the free market. Ideology notwithstanding, the Senate again passed a compromise bill that included both some restrictions on interstate waste disposal and flow control for localities that were "out there holding the bag" when the Supreme Court acted.[46] But then the compromise came apart. An attempt, in response to pressures from the New Jersey delegation, to separate the flow control and interstate transportation parts of the bill and pass only the former in the House was roundly defeated in February 1996 by a vote of 150 to 271. Some House members again objected on ideological grounds. Others would not support a bill that did not simultaneously address the interstate transportation issue. Still others objected to the failure of the bill to include the "special fix" for problems in their districts that it provided for others.[47]

With a congressional election in the offing, an attempt to bring flow control back during the fall 1996 federal budget negotiations again failed. At hearings in the spring of 1997, New Jersey's senior senator, Frank Lautenberg, while accepting that the "new post-*Carbone* reality" had brought a "free marketplace that was bringing benefits to local communities," argued that relief was still needed for regional facilities formerly dependent on flow control.[48] But the energy was out of the issue. The fragile coalition between advocates of nonimportation and champions of flow control was coming apart. The passage of time produced a new status quo, and made unlikely Congress's restoration of the premises of the old regional service delivery system.

Local Actions to Bolster the Regional Role

The availability to localities of alternative financing mechanisms to pay for solid-waste systems—including straightforward taxation—was critical to federal judge Joseph Irenas's decision applying the Supreme Court's flow control precedent in New Jersey. Experimentation with a number of alternatives produced at least one approach that is working and has proved acceptable to the courts.

On Long Island, the Town of Babylon's response to the *Carbone* decision was the creation of a special "garbage district" to handle commercial waste. Businesses are taxed by the district for the service; the district in turn contracts with a hauler to remove waste. Such an approach takes advantage of the fact that "the Supreme Court has developed an exception to the broad reach of the commerce clause to address situations where a state or local government is acting as a participant in the market, rather than as a regulator."[49] The hauler may bring the town's waste anywhere —meeting the requirements of the Supreme Court's decision—but uses the town facility because there is no charge if it is taken there. (The tax levied to support the garbage district allows the town to pay directly for both hauling and disposal.)

Also on Long Island, the Town of Smithtown has created ten garbage districts that take ownership of municipal waste at curbside. From there, as owner, government can direct its flow. Both the Babylon and Smithtown practices were challenged and upheld by the U.S. Appeals Court for the Second Circuit, with the Supreme Court declining to review. An approach by Stonington, Connecticut, modeled on that used by Babylon and Smithtown was similarly upheld in federal court.[50]

For their part, regional solid-waste agencies, after having achieved success in a highly regulated, rule- and law-driven environment, now find themselves not local service deliverers, but participants in a national market. They are adapting. For example, only about half of the 985 tons of trash a year burned in the Essex County incinerator in Newark—the only one in the state operating at capacity in 1998—was from localities in the county; the rest was from New York City.[51] Industry advocates are right when they observe that the discipline of the market has led to greater efficiency, "lower tipping fees, elimination of unneeded expenses, slimmed-down agencies that are becoming cost competitive."[52]

But there are other results. State and local governments are left to subsidize those aspects of the system wherein the market does not perform well but public expectations must be met—recycling programs, for example. And as the debate in New Jersey over possible subsidies for county solid-waste agencies in 1998 demonstrated, they are also left with the payments for investments they made to meet a compelling need when the old rules were in force. And the costs of unplanned transition from a local government service to a national, market-based system are highest for those who acted in good faith to comply in a timely fashion with federal and state requirements.[53]

Regionalism: To What End? For What Price?

When the first Earth Day was celebrated in 1970, 60 percent of all solid waste in the tri-state region was being buried.[54] There were 1,600 open dumps in New York, 147 in Connecticut, and 400 or more in New Jersey. When it came to disposing of garbage, each city, town, village, or borough was largely on its own. Indeed, few jurisdictions would accept garbage from elsewhere; many even passed laws barring burial of others' trash.

By 1994, the year of the *Carbone* decision, the three states—sometimes anticipating federal requirements in law and regulation, but more often reacting to them—had all shut down the long-established, highly localized, every-place-for-itself system of solid-waste disposal.[55] Many localities resisted, but they ultimately gave way before the force of the environmental movement. The number of active landfills in the tri-state region's three states was reduced by an astonishing 96 percent: New York had sixty-four; New Jersey, twenty-four; and Connecticut, six. Throughout the tri-state region, cities, towns, villages, and boroughs were out of the solid-waste business, or on the way out.

In Connecticut over three-fifths of the waste stream—almost four times the national average—was being burned in energy-producing plants serving regional "wastesheds," run by the CRRA. In New Jersey, solid waste had become regionalized to the county level. Counties were the responsible governments for solid waste in New York as well, except in New York City (which, of course, encompassed five counties) and on heavily populated suburban Long Island, where the function remained with the towns.

This shift in the scale and locus of delivery for solid-waste disposal—a most traditional local function—was difficult and represented a real achievement for regionalization. State-induced change involved the alteration of complex intergovernmental and public-private relationships. The routines and practices of literally thousands of municipalities and hundreds of private businesses—waste haulers, landfill and incinerator operators, engineering and construction firms—had to be altered. Existing local governments took on entirely new responsibilities. Additionally, dozens of new local governments—public authorities—were created.

Ironically, however, in achieving regionalization to meet environmental goals, the more general underlying values of the regionalism movement were seemingly forgotten. Concerns for social equity and economic development did not figure prominently in the debate. Solid waste proved to be a function that was easily given away. With one very serious exception, the massive resistance of places targeted as sites for regional facilities, regionalization produced no great outcries for the return of local control.

But when community sentiment was aroused, it was powerful. Years of delay, and increased costs, resulted from localities' battles against the location of regional facilities in their back (or front) yards. Regional entities—confirmed in their responsibility for managing solid waste and having developed expensive, elaborate plans to do so—found themselves unable to implement their plans.

Local resistance to the siting of regional facilities was one reason that, as the community value was slowly overcome in the area of solid-waste policy, there was no gain in efficiency. But more important for the failure to achieve efficiency was the reliance on governmental power to establish monopoly conditions to permit the building and sustain the operation of larger, regional solid-waste facilities. Regional monopolies created by state and local law and regulation allowed the establishment of a price for waste disposal that paid for many of the ancillary costs of the conversion from a local to a regional system without increasing state or local taxes. These costs were driven, in turn, by ever more rigorous state environmental standards. Capping and sealing old town dumps in accordance with state regulatory requirements, for example, was a very expensive proposition.

In addition, an administratively established tipping fee allowed responsiveness to evolving public demands for environmentally sensitive, socially responsible solid-waste policy while also meeting the financial commitments that regionalization required. Although they were popular and virtuous (and therefore a political necessity), recycling, composting, and other reuse programs rarely paid for themselves. Where they were successful, moreover, these programs took material out of the waste stream, reducing the flow to regional facilities below levels that were assumed when these facilities were financed and built. Throughout the tristate area, the regional monopolies sustained by flow-control laws allowed the cost of recycling and reuse programs to be covered not from property taxes but from administratively established tipping fees, while also ensuring the financial viability of costly regional facilities built to meet national and state requirements.

The Trade-Off: Community versus Efficiency

In opening his subcommittee's hearings in 1996 on restoring flow-control authority to states and localities in the wake of *Carbone,* U.S. Senator Robert Smith, a conservative Republican, remarked, "I find myself in the very difficult position of having to choose between two very attractive philosophies: strong state and local control, and at the same time, the free market mechanism."[56]

New Jersey's governor, Christine Whitman, like Senator Smith a Republican, was a leading proponent of privatization of governmental functions to achieve economy and efficiency. Yet she appeared before Senator Smith's committee defending a public-sector approach that had produced the highest tipping fees for solid-waste disposal in the nation. The governor's reasons were simple: she believed that New Jersey's fate should be kept in New Jersey's hands, and she thought that ultimate responsibility for solving this problem should lie with state and county (that is, regional) elected officials. Although "a waste management company headquartered in a distant state can provide a prescribed service for a specific county in my state," Whitman said, "it cannot be expected to look after that county's long-term needs in waste management. That long-term planning," she continued, "is the duty of our elected freeholders and county executives."[57]

Nationally in 1997, about 10 percent of all solid waste was in interstate commerce. From both Connecticut (where sufficient within-state capacity was developed to meet state needs) and New Jersey (where self-sufficiency was never achieved), more waste has been exported in the years since *Carbone* was decided.

The year 1998 saw major corporate consolidations in the solid-waste industry.[58] The percentage of the waste stream traveling between states will surely rise as the solid-waste industry consolidates further and additional, large waste-producing jurisdictions—New York City, for example—enter the market more fully, as they plan to and must, in the years immediately ahead.

Faced with the necessity of closing Freshkills on Staten Island—the nation's largest landfill—by December 31, 2001, New York City has become one the nation's largest solid-waste exporters. Interested in avoiding local resentment in waste-receiving communities, the city wisely insists, in contracts with private solid-waste companies, that they have in place host community packages that provide concrete benefits to these jurisdictions. Surely this practice will be followed by other large waste exporters as well. Nevertheless, experience shows that tensions are inevitable—if not with the locality in which a landfill is located, then with surrounding localities, or the receiving state. And this may be especially true when waste from the New York region is involved.

Two examples are indicative. In December 1998, after Mayor Rudolph Giuliani announced a plan to ship most of New York City's residential waste out of state through two transfer stations in Newark and Carteret, New Jersey, Governor Christine Todd Whitman responded with a press release in an evocation of one of the *New York Daily News*'s most famous headlines, titled, "Whitman to New York's Garbage Plan: Drop Dead."[59]

Just a month earlier, in reaction to new contracts signed in 1998 by private companies with facilities in Virginia to take more New York City garbage, Virginia governor James Gilmore III said that he did not want his state to become a "dumping ground," and imposed a moratorium on landfill construction or expansion.[60] Gilmore later endorsed proposals for a ban on the transportation of trash by barge and limits on the amounts of out-of-state garbage coming into his state.[61] These positions reflected overwhelming public sentiment. A Virginia Commonwealth University poll released in early 1999 reported that 87 percent of Virginians asked favored limiting the amount of out-of-state garbage coming into their state.[62]

Anyone who has seen garbage piled high in the streets when it has not been picked up for a while—for example, during a strike, or a series of massive snowstorms like those experienced in the tri-state region in 1996—needs no convincing that the proper performance of this function is essential to local public health and safety. A national market has brought lower waste-disposal prices, partly because it has encouraged efficiencies and partly because it has forced the return of some capital and program costs—formerly paid through elevated tipping fees—to local and regional governments, to be met from general revenues. Clearly, in this area of policy, the question of the proper balance between the efficiency of the national market and the desirability of community solutions at a regional scale still remains an open one.

PART SIX

Conclusion

CHAPTER ELEVEN

Lessons for the Future

The tri-state region is singular in the size and scope of its local governments. At its core, New York City spends more every year than all but three governments in the country: the federal government and the state governments of California and New York. The range of the city's functions, although now diminished, remains unrivaled among American localities. In addition, three of the region's suburban counties rank among the nation's largest, with billion-dollar-plus budgets. Even the tri-state area's special-purpose governments are among the nation's largest.

The focus of this concluding chapter is not the region's special character, however, but the general lessons it provides concerning the nature of and prospects for regionalism in America's metropolitan areas. Although New Yorkers may be reluctant to admit this, it is not the region's singularity but its commonalities with other regions that are most important for understanding and reforming local government in urban America. Many of America's largest metropolitan regions, like the tri-state region, stretch across state lines. Most have complex and rapidly changing economies, diverse populations, multifaceted arrangements for local governance, core cities in need of renewal, and often socially troubled outlying areas. Also common to metropolitan regions in the United States is the importance their citizens give to the value of community, that is, political localism.

All of these forces and factors operate in the diverse and fluid environment of American federalism. Federalism by its very nature places intergovernmental relations at the center of domestic government and causes home rule to be a perennial issue for localities and regions. Because of the authority vested in state governments, their decisions regarding the range of responsibilities, powers, and resources given local jurisdictions are crucial for urban regions in America.

Based on these commonalities, we use the experience of the tri-state region to derive thirteen lessons for balancing the three core values of regionalism and reconciling them with the insistent demands of localism. These lessons are organized in four categories: understanding the values of regionalism, regionalism and state government, regionalism and local government, and the politics of regionalism.

Understanding the Values of Regionalism

Lesson One: Regionalism's three core values—equity, efficiency, and competitiveness—often conflict with each other and with the value of community.

The regionalism movement in contemporary America is driven by the three values—social *equity*, governmental *efficiency*, and economic *competitiveness*. The various ways these core values are prioritized produce different and distinct approaches to the delicate political act of balancing regionalism with realism. Those who give primacy to equity tend to emphasize structural measures for linking cities with suburbs. Those most interested in efficiency are likely to favor more cautious, function-by-function approaches to regionalism. Those who emphasize competitiveness are likely to focus less on governmental structure and more on cooperative efforts across sectors (public and private) in the pursuit of regional economic objectives.

In seeking to fulfill goals based on these values, advocates of regional cooperation must come to terms with the persistence of localism as a value in governance across America. Commitment to community, as we have seen from the experience of the tri-state region, is often the reason that structural reforms, especially local governmental consolidation, are resisted. Although many public and private sector leaders believe that social, economic, and technological changes require government to act across ever-larger expanses of urban territory, old boundaries persist.

Localism can be an elitist, even exclusionary, force in politics, but it does not have to be. There is growing support among urban experts and advocates for efforts to build "social capital" through collaboration among public and private organizations at the neighborhood level. They believe this can give meaning to citizenship and promote sharing and mutual respect. Indeed, the objective of building social capital is considered especially important for lower-income and marginal neighborhoods, where achieving social cohesion is crucial for advancing civility and achieving economic progress.

Lesson Two: The goals of regional reform are often best achieved by emphasizing efficiency (not equity or competitiveness) and accommodating (not confronting) the community value.

Although local government boundaries may seem irrational to people interested in changing political structures to advance regional purposes, many citizens carefully pick the places in which they live and work and come to identify strongly with them. The complex, layered web of local governments in urban regions, defended in the name of community, can reinforce or increase racial segregation. However, defense of the community value also arises from positive motivations: the need for cooperation and connectedness through churches and other civic and voluntary organizations, the desire for economic security, and a commitment to family, friends, and ethnic traditions.

Yet even in areas and situations where the community value is strong, regionalism has demonstrated its appeal in the tri-state region. This is largely because local governments are financed substantially through property taxation. As we have shown, citizens in the tri-state region pay some of the highest taxes in the United States. Responding to their concerns about high property taxes, leaders of local governments seek opportunities for tax reduction. For these officials the efficiency argument for regional solutions is attractive insofar as it promises to control costs and reduce taxes.

Lesson Three: Although efficiency is generally the best-received argument for regional action, the goals of regionalism often are at odds with the logic of the private marketplace.

The argument is often made that local governments should abandon old boundaries and organize across a larger territory in ways that maximize their efficiency and at the same time enhance competitiveness in the global economy. Yet there is an unacknowledged tension in this view, between regionalism as a governance strategy and the market paradigm. Regionalism as the basis of governmental action is purposeful, the result of planning. Markets, conversely, tend to change in dynamic ways that are unplanned and less subject—or not subject at all—to government control.

In this respect political and economic trends may seem to be going in opposite directions. The geographical expansion of commerce has proceeded simultaneously with the devolution of many public services from the national level to the states. However, while state government responsibility for many public services has been increasing, the U.S. Supreme Court has protected the flow of interstate commerce in ways that supersede state power. In some areas of increased devolution, governmental decentralization of public services provides opportunities at the local level for greater intergovernmental collaboration. As an example, federal government efforts to give states and localities more flexibility and scope for action under the 1996 national Welfare Reform Act has led at times to increased collaboration among local governments.[1]

Lesson Four: Functional collaboration rather than jurisdictional consolidation is often the driving force of regionalism.

A practical and often successful focus of regional reform is finding the right scale for delivery of services—functional rightsizing. This does not imply that one size fits all; instead it is a matter of the degree of regionalism that exists or should exist in different situations for different governmental functions. Experience in the tri-state region shows that intergovernmental collaboration is most easily achieved for government functions that challenge the community value the least. These include, for example, back-office operations, such as accounting and information processing, or activities in which citizens are less personally or directly served, such as vehicle maintenance, snow plowing, and highway maintenance. Other applicable functions include parks and recreation, transportation (a major area of functional rightsizing), the arts, culture, and sports, all of which involve voluntary participation by some, but not all, citizens. Collaboration is more difficult for hot-button functions such as education and police—services that define the community and are directly, personally, and often involuntarily experienced by many citizens on a daily basis. Significantly, these functions also often involve public employees who are organized in unions and are highly visible and respected in the community, which can add to the political clout of opponents of regional reform.

Regionalism and State Government

Lesson Five: Acting regionally is almost always up to state (not local) governments.

The demand for regional reform almost always arises locally. Local mobilization within the region, it is argued, can overcome parochialism and achieve benefits for everyone. However, experience in the tri-state region suggests that measures to advance regionalism by reforming local governmental structures and functions are almost always accompanied or even dominated by state involvement. This is because despite home rule, localities remain very much creatures of the state. It is in state constitutions and statutes that the authority resides for creating and extending general-purpose governments and for establishing and modifying the role of special-purpose governments in major functional areas of activity. Moreover, state geographical boundaries place an absolute limit on the reach of locally initiated reform.

The role of state government is crucial. Within the tri-state region, functionally organized regional entities have their priorities set by governors and other political leaders in state capitals. They, in turn, are likely to be responsive to perceived statewide needs, not regional or local ones. Agencies that operate across state lines are more likely to be influenced by intense interstate competition for resources than by regional perspectives arising from the regional aspirations of policy planners, program managers, and policy analysts. At the subregional level, within large metropolitan regions, state governments control both the political and financial incentives and disincentives that can influence whether local jurisdictions collaborate or go it alone. They do this by allocating or withholding the power to act collaboratively, issuing directives, awarding financial aid (often with conditions), and providing taxing powers (again, with conditions).

States can encourage regional cooperation within their borders in many ways. These include adopting mandates to reorganize particular governmental functions, removing legal and regulatory barriers to collaboration, financing studies that advance regional collaboration, providing capital guarantees or direct assistance, and establishing subsidies that reduce local costs for services only if they are delivered on a broad geographical basis. More subtly and less visibly, states can act in ways that change the political environment, altering citizens' expectations of localities and thus providing incentives for intergovernmental collaboration at the local level.

Lesson Six: Regional approaches by states typically are ad hoc, not planned, efforts.

Because of the complexity and layering of local government in the tri-state region, the sharing of governmental responsibilities most often arises from *incremental* change, the result of accommodating localism while responding to evolving social and economic conditions. The creation of Greater New York and the elimination of Connecticut's counties as political entities are exceptions to this generalization. The usual practice in the tri-state region is to adapt local government to growth and change by creating additional structures or grafting new powers onto established ones, rather than by undertaking the politically formidable task of replacing the old with new. This has been the case not only at the local level but on the broadest scale, for example, with respect to transportation, which on a national basis is the function most susceptible to regionwide approaches.

The three large-scale, functionally organized transportation authorities in the tri-state area that we considered—the Port Authority of New York and New Jersey (PANYNJ), the Metropolitan Transit Authority (MTA), and New Jersey Transit (NJT)—were not created as part of a long-term plan for regional development. Rather they were added to the region's mix of jurisdictions and governmental arrangements in the midst of crises to address specific problems that were beyond the capacity of existing governments to solve. Through creation of the Port Authority, New York and New Jersey together sought to bring order out of the chaos for commercial rail-freight activities in the New York harbor. New York and New Jersey separately created the MTA and NJT to preserve and hopefully improve commuter transit services when the capacity of private carriers to do this in their respective markets was near collapse.

Lesson Seven: In multistate regions, state governments rarely work together regionally. Large-scale regional functions tend to be organized and run to accommodate the priorities of state leaders, not regional values.

In recent years the need to be competitive in the national and world economies has been a very powerful driving force for the regionalism movement. This was the case with the major changes made in the Chattanooga and Cleveland regions, two examples cited in chapter 2. But in the tri-state region (and probably in other multistate regions as well), interstate rivalries often prevent convergence around regional goals, even when they are compelling. Divided by state lines, the economically integrated New York–New Jersey–Connecticut region is more an arena for interstate economic rivalry than for mutually beneficial collaborative action.

Early in 1999 Sea-Land Service and the Maersk Line, two shipping companies that controlled one fourth of the containerized cargo that passed through the Port of New York, were threatening to decamp to Baltimore, taking a thousand jobs and $100 million annual payroll with them. With long-term leases for their existing facilities at the Elizabeth Marine Terminal in New Jersey coming to an end, and officials from competing ports up and down the Atlantic coast romancing them, Sea-Land and Maersk demanded financial concessions from the Port Authority to keep them in the region. New Jersey wanted to put together a package; New York insisted that the companies were bluffing. An unnamed senior New York official told the *New York Times*, "If we are going to satisfy New Jersey, then we need something, too."[2]

As discussed in chapter 6, the Port Authority of New York and New Jersey did not turn out to be an instrument for a politically independent regional voice. Despite the intention of many of its original supporters that it be an autonomous public authority with billions of dollars in dedicated revenue and the power to borrow, the agency is in fact almost entirely subject in its governance and activities to the often competing policy aims of the governors of New York and New Jersey. Its priorities are set by these and other statewide officials, who as a general rule are expected to place state (not regional) interests first and foremost. Historically, the capacity of the Port Authority's leaders to serve regional transportation and economic development goals has been hampered by the need to be equally distributive between the states.

Governors control appointments to the boards of the MTA, NJT, and the Port Authority and oversee their operations. The need for subsidies makes regional mass transit a major consideration in state budgeting; thus state chief executives and state legislators become key decisionmakers for regional mass transit. Despite the fact that local officials and legislators are players in this game, agency operations are constrained by resource priorities set in state capitals and often determined by people for whom regional considerations are secondary.

Another important point about the values of regionalism needs to be added here. At the state level, equity for low-income citizens, as sought by some regional and local political leaders, is not the principal consideration in allocating transportation dollars. Rather the goals most commonly emphasized concern the distribution of resources across modes of transportation or across states. In New Jersey, with Republicans and Democrats alike representing districts that have a large number of commuters, disputes arise over investing in roads or rail. In New York, with its Republican suburbs and Democratic core, the political bargaining is over subsidies for city subway and bus riders versus those for suburban users of commuter rail.

Despite their many difficulties, the tri-state region's transportation agencies have had important recent successes that link people and places within the region. The "E-ZPass" has integrated the region's toll collection system at the customer level, making commuting quicker and more convenient. Likewise, the "MetroCard" allows variable pricing on New York City buses and subways, helping to boost ridership and revenues.

Regionalism and Local Government

> *Lesson Eight: Achieving regionalism through the creation of a single, integrated general-purpose metropolitan government is almost always a false hope.*

Regions grow and change with disregard for state and local boundaries. Greater New York, one of the first and most ambitious experiments in creating a single, integrated, general-purpose metropolitan government in the United States, was established with lots of growing room. Cows grazed and corn grew within the Greater City's limits. Yet after just a few decades, New York City's boundaries contained a diminishing portion of the region's population and territory.

The *New York Times* said editorially in 1925 that the extension of the Greater City's boundaries was its "manifest destiny." "When Westchester really is a part of New York City, then the consolidation will occur."[3] Three quarters of a century has passed since this prediction was made, and though that quintessential suburban county has been integrated economically into the region, it remains an autonomous government. Moreover, as a jurisdiction Westchester has one of the biggest budgets in the country (spending in 1997 was $1.727 billion), and its 85 cities, towns, villages, and school districts remain autonomous localities despite efforts to combine some of them.[4] Further consolidation of Greater New York has not happened in a hundred years. And it likely never will.

In short, experience in the tri-state region and elsewhere shows that metropolitan consolidation occurs in rare moments, at times and in places in which there is an unusual convergence of political opportunity, will, and power. The creation of Greater New York was such an event. Even if the rules of the game had remained unchanged after 1898, there is reason to think that further boundary and jurisdictional changes would have been unlikely. As we have shown, however, the rules *were* changed: an amendment to the New York State Constitution (to which the *New York Times* expressed indifference in a 1925 editorial) was adopted in 1927. It requires the consent of a majority in *each* affected locality before that area can be annexed to a city (see chapter 5). The successful creation of Greater New York spawned a political reaction and state constitutional changes that render the replication of this act impossible now, or at least extraordinarily difficult. Thus the experience of Greater New York demonstrates that what many regional reformers regard as an optimal outcome is very hard, if not impossible, to bring about.

Unfortunately, the history of the Greater City also shows that advocates can be too optimistic in their expectations for a metropolis once it is created. As best we can tell, the establishment of Greater New York did not lead to long-term fiscal efficiencies. Research by the respected Citizen's Budget Commission (presented in chapter 5) shows that in the Greater City one hundred years later, the costs of delivering local services in the metropolis were greater, not less, than costs elsewhere.[5] We have also noted that the city's share of local spending in the tri-state region persists at roughly the same level even though its share of the regional population has diminished.

The regional value of equity is not necessarily advanced when a consolidation occurs. Disputes over who gets what and how much are not necessarily resolved but instead tend to shift in their locus. Conflicts between and among groups and neighborhoods for services and resources continue, and the same people (middle- and upper-middle-class people with high levels of education and access to decisionmakers) are likely to remain influential. Moreover, the enlarged government remains a *local* government, with limits on its powers to govern, tax, and borrow. Redistributive policies in the pursuit of equity, as New York City's experience shows, entail the risk of becoming less competitive economically.

Lesson Nine: Metropolitanism tends to drive out community.

A general-purpose metropolitan government tends to centralize control; therefore, it is less likely to build on and nurture existing smaller component communities and more likely to reduce their power, threatening their local character. New York's boroughs were accepted in a reluctant compromise by advocates of the "one big city." They were seen as the minimum necessary bow to decentralizers as dozens of cities, towns, and villages were eliminated. That was round one. The artificially created boroughs had their victories, but the net result of political battles over the greater part of the century since then has been their devitalization and marginalization.

Decentralizers in the 1960s and 1970s did achieve the creation of community boards and community school boards. Some community boards (especially in the city's whiter, more affluent neighborhoods) have been effective in influencing land-use decisions, but in general, research shows that their impact on city decisionmaking has been limited. In the wake of patronage scandals (a source of continued vulnerability for localism's advocates in New York City), school decisionmaking is being recentralized, and community school boards are being weakened.

Another case of creeping recentralization is the unsuccessful defense of the Board of Estimate, during the New York City charter reform debates of 1988. Defenders of the board argued that it was empowered and supposed to protect local interests in the Greater City. The board's role in city government and that of the borough presidents was the purposeful aim, they said, of a "metropolitan bargain" struck between metropolitanists and localists when the Greater City was created. But the historical record shows that there was no such bargain when the city was created. The boroughs were empowered later, and then devitalized through charter changes over the course of the twentieth century. We believe that the boroughs have outlived their usefulness, and we urge that ways be considered to rebalance community and regional values in New York City.

Although the city's residents do not have viable local governmental arrangements, there are indications that they want them. The Staten Island secession movement is one such indication. Another is the rise of business improvement districts (BIDs).[6] Although Mayor Rudolph Giuliani initially supported the BID movement, his efforts to bring them to heel in 1998 and thereafter are consistent with the centralizing efforts of his predecessors on similar issues and need to be seen as challenges to localism, that is, the value of community.

Lesson Ten: New York needs real local government, as do all regions.

In chapter 4 we suggest the elimination of existing decentralized elements in the structure of New York City government—the boroughs, community school boards, and community board; they have atrophied. In addition, we suggest the creation of a charter commission to consider new models for local government—for example, urban towns within the city. As part of such an agenda for change, school districts could have boundaries coterminous with these towns, and they would be led by prescreened school board members chosen in nonpartisan elections.

Chapter 4 also discusses the invention of mechanisms for collaboration within neighborhoods. Elected leadership in towns within the city could give legitimacy to local claims on the central government and enhance political representation and competitiveness. Finally, rough coterminality could be established between city council district lines and town boundaries; such geopolitical congruency combined with the term limits for citywide offices now in place would produce a situation in which elected leaders could more easily move back and forth between the city government and town governments, linking them politically.

The Politics of Regionalism

Lesson Eleven: Regionwide elected leadership could provide governance in accordance with regional values, but this is politically unlikely.

A regionwide elected executive and representative board, with a guaranteed resource base controlled from within the region, might advance regional values, but there are few precedents for this in the United States. Presumably, under such an arrangement, elected leaders would depend on the region's voters for their selection and advancement, allowing them to advocate the region's needs and priorities—for example, in mass transit, the nation's most regionalized function.[7] It is possible to conceive of an autonomously governed interstate region for this function or others, one flexible enough to adjust its boundaries periodically to adapt to economic and technological advances and able to have a direct, but not dependent, relationship with both states and the national government. However, the creation of such an entity is *extremely unlikely* under anything like the current political and economic conditions in the nation and especially in the tri-state New York metropolitan region.

To advance regionalism in realistic ways at the local level, trusted leadership is essential. In the tri-state region's partisan political environment, workaday politics is a barrier, although some counterbalance is provided by institutions that have developed relationships across jurisdictional lines. University-based and community-based organizations interested in regionalism, such as the Regional Plan Association, the New York Partnership, the Michelian Institute in Westchester, Mid-Hudson Pattern For Progress, and the Somerset Alliance in Somerset County (New Jersey), serve in this role.[8] They provide studies that examine and promote regional efficiencies and economic competitiveness, and they bring leaders together to consider proposals for collaboration. They can also help assemble political coalitions for change when targets of opportunity arise for regional reform.

Lesson Twelve: To be successful in the environment of American federalism, regional reforms often must have national acquiescence, if not national support.

The great governance debates of the 1990s in the United States were about two questions: "How much government should there be?" and "Which governments should do what?" For most Americans the answer to the first question has been *"less."* In response, public officials at all levels have pressed for lower taxes and a smaller public sector. On the assumption that markets bring greater efficiency, and therefore lower costs, they have sought to privatize government functions. The answer to the second question has largely been, *"The states should do more."* Congress and the president have sought to devolve powers and responsibilities for many public services to the states. When the answers to these questions are combined, the amalgam is state-based policy driven by market-based thinking.

Woodrow Wilson wrote in 1908, "The question of the relation of the States to the federal government, is the cardinal question of our constitutional system. It cannot, indeed, be settled by the opinion of any one generation, because it is a question of growth, and every successive stage of our political and economic development gives it a new aspect, makes it a new question."[9] In these terms, people who seek to advance regionalism can be seen as, in effect, advocating a refinement of the federal system through further devolution—that is, by states to localities. Some federal policies have purposefully incorporated regionally focused objectives; transportation is a good example. According to a 1998 study by the National Academy of Public Administration, "in the 1960's and 1970's, the federal government invested in building a national network of regional councils that prepared loosely linked plans for a dozen different federal agencies." Unfortunately for the advocates of regionalism, the study went on to say that "the federal government abandoned most of this ambition in the early 1980's and adopted no new vision for how it might relate systematically to regions."[10]

Although the states are the principal arena for decisions about regionalism, the role of the national government can be important in general ways, as well as with respect to specific governmental functions. At a minimum, state and local efforts to achieve equity, efficiency, and competitiveness through regionalization both within and across state lines may benefit from a measure of benign neglect from Washington. At the same time, regional approaches ought not to be discouraged by national policies and regulations. Both the executive and legislative branches of the federal government can offer regions and states inducements to regional cooperation. Congress and the president have the authority to provide assistance to states that act regionally, just as states can influence local action, by providing financial aid designed to encourage interstate regional cooperation and by reducing bureaucratic barriers and disseminating information about regional success stories.

Lesson Thirteen: Regionalism is a process, not a result. For states and localities, the task of balancing equity, efficiency, and competitiveness is ongoing.

Measures to create regional entities and institutional mechanisms do not provide permanent solutions to the structural problems of local governments. When it comes to changes in the role, boundaries, and structure of local governments, one generation's answers can produce the next generation's problems. Governments created to encompass large regions, even that of Greater New York, become ossified. Single- and multifunctional region-wide agencies such as the Port Authority of New York and New Jersey and the Metropolitan Transportation Authority can be overtaken by events. Established localities may be given new functions as conditions change, but these must be exercised within boundaries and legal limits that are or can become barriers to the fair and efficient delivery of public services. As we have shown, when it comes to regional structural reforms, it is generally easier politically to add the new to the old rather than replace the old with the new. Unfortunately, the former, though easier, increases complexity and often diminishes accountability.

The Boards of Cooperative Educational Services (BOCES) system in New York offers an example of the constant need for flexibility in approaches to regionalism. Successful in collaboratively extending a range of educational services to rural areas over the half-century following World War II, these regional educational agencies were criticized in the 1990s for their waste and lack of accountability. The suggestions we offer to help preserve this regional system and make it more market-sensitive may be applicable in other areas as well. They include passing state aid through the customers (the school districts) rather than the provider (the BOCES) and allowing school districts more options with respect to how they spend this aid. They also include allowing the BOCES to serve a greater range of customers, including general- and special-purpose local governments, so that they can be more competitive.

The BOCES example serves well to underscore our final point. Regional solutions are not permanent; adjustments must be made continuously as conditions change. Regionalism is best understood as a work in progress. The skills of the leaders who build coalitions around values of regional reform need to be applied to selecting achievable and well-supported goals and to developing popular proposals that advance these goals. Whether it is a collaborative public-private plan for sustained economic development, a new intergovernmental arrangement to integrate services in a major functional area, a mechanism for helping neighborhoods build social capital, or an innovation to realign boundaries and control land use, the ingredient that matters most is political leadership that blends regional values with political realism.

Notes

Chapter 1. The New York Region

1. Robert C. Wood, *1400 Governments* (Cambridge: Harvard University Press, 1961).

2. Robert D. Yaro and Tony Hiss, *A Region at Risk: The Third Regional Plan* (New York: Regional Plan Association, 1996).

3. John Bollens and Henry Schmandt, *The Metropolis*, 2d ed. (Harper and Row, 1965), p. 6, quoting Bureau of the Census, *Tenth Census of the United States, Social Statistics of Cities*, part 1 (Washington, 1886), pp. 531–32.

4. The Regional Plan Association (RPA) was created in the same year to implement this plan and has since been the tri-state region's strongest center of advocacy for regionalism.

5. William H. Frey and Alden Speare Jr., *Regional and Metropolitan Growth and Decline in the United States* (New York: Russell Sage Foundation, 1988), p. 28.

6. Edward W. Soja,"Los Angeles, 1965–1992," in Allen J. Scott and Edward W. Soja, *The City: Los Angeles and Urban Theory at the End of the Twentieth Century* (University of California Press, 1996), pp. vii and 431–32. See also Joel Gareau, *Edge City* (Doubleday, 1991).

7. Jonathan Barnett, *The Fractured Metropolis* (Harper Collins, 1995), p. 3.

8. Yaro and Hiss, *A Region at Risk*, p. 19. The Census Bureau definition excludes Ulster County, New York, from the tri-state region but includes Pike County, Pennsylvania, extending the region into a fourth state. The Census Bureau assigns the Connecticut counties of Fairfield and New Haven to the New England County Metropolitan Area but notes their inclusion in the tri-state region in a footnote. The bureau does not include Litchfield County, Connecticut, in the region.

9. Bureau of the Census, *Metropolitan Areas as Defined by the Office of Management and Budget*, Supplementary Report, 1990 CPH-S-1-1 (Government Printing Office, June 30,1993), stock number 003-024-08738-3.

10. Nielsen includes Pikes County, Pennsylvania, but excludes the Connecticut counties, which it places in a Hartford-dominated region.

11. Cited in Lawrence K. Grossman, "Why Local TV News Is So Awful," *Columbia Journalism Review*, vol. 36 (November/December 1997), p. 21.

12. American Council on Intergovernmental Relations, *Significant Features of Fiscal Federalism, 1995,* vol. 2: *Revenues and Expenditures* (Washington, 1997), table 60, pp. 118–19.

13. Some counties choose to share this revenue with towns, villages, and even school districts, but these entities cannot independently levy a sales tax.

14. Yaro and Hiss, *A Region at Risk.* For a press account of prospects for the region's economy, see Kirk Johnson and Thomas J. Lueck, "Economy in the New York Region Is Recovering but Pace Is Slow," *New York Times*, February 19, 1996.

15. Connecticut Advisory Commission on Intergovernmental Relations, "Connecticut Municipalities in Crisis: Can Regional Efforts Help?" in Connecticut Institute of Municipal Studies, *Property Revaluation Study* (Hartford, Conn.: 1994), p. 6.

16. "State Cities in Financial Bind," *Middletown Times Herald Record*, March 23, 1996.

17. New York State Conference of Mayors and Other Municipal Officials, *The Eroding Tax Base: New York's Property Tax at a Crossroads* (1986), p. 8; William Glaberson, "In Era of Fiscal Damage Control, Cities Fight Idea of Tax Exempt," *New York Times*, February 21, 1996.

18. George Judson, "Anguished Plea from Bridgeport for Fiscal Relief," *New York Times*, June 8, 1991.

19. David R. Berman, "Takeover of Local Governments: An Overview and Evaluation of State Policies," *Publius*, vol. 25 (Summer 1995), pp. 55–70; Dena Kleiman, "Control Board Rulings Aren't New to Yonkers," *New York Times*, August 10, 1988.

20. There is a widespread misconception about urban problems in this respect. Research conducted at the Rockefeller Institute shows that the majority of African Americans living in metropolitan areas of the United States do not reside in the most highly distressed, crime-ridden neighborhoods. See David J. Wright, "Saving City Neighborhoods" (http://www.rockinst.org/publications/pubs_and_reports.html [February 2001]).

21. The figures are 95 percent for Hudson, 96 percent for Passaic, and 90 percent for Fairfield.

22. Bureau of the Census, *County and City Data Book: 1994* (Washington: GPO, 1994), pp. 698–99, 770–71, 782–83. These communities are East Orange (94 percent minority population), Newark (85), Jersey City (54), Trenton (63), Perth Amboy (67), Passaic (71), Paterson (77), Elizabeth (59), and Plainfield (81) in New Jersey; Bridgeport (53) in Connecticut; and Newburgh (58) and Mount Vernon (63) in New York. The comparable minority population in New York City is 53 percent overall, and the borough with the highest percentage minority population is the Bronx (81 percent). Although the region's black and Hispanic minorities are concentrated in cities, the growing suburbanization of their populations has been noted. This growth tends to occur in places that have a lot of older, less expensive housing stock. The Village of Haverstraw in intermediate-ring Rockland County is an example. According to the 1990 census, 51 percent of Haverstraw's population was Hispanic; by 1996, village leaders estimated that the total had risen to 70 percent. See Mirta Ojito, "Immigrants' New Road Leads to Suburbia," *New York Times*, September 30, 1996.

23. Richard Perez-Pena, "New York Foreign-Born Population Increases," *New York Times,* March 9, 1996, paraphrasing Andrew A. Beveridge, Professor of Sociology, Queens College.

24. Myron Orfield as quoted in Patrick Mazza, "A Tale of Two Cities: Modeling Metropolitan Reform for the Nation," October 16, 1995 (www.tnews.com/text/two_cities.html [February 2001])

25. Stewart Kampel, Peter Marks, and John Rather, "Assessing Effects of Impending Cuts in Government Services," *New York Times*, January 8, 1995.

26. According to the U.S. Census, 721 special districts within counties in the states of New York, New Jersey, and Connecticut were not coterminous with towns or townships; another 44 crossed county lines. About two-fifths (41.9 percent) of the special districts in the three states were noncoterminous.

27. Bureau of the Census, *Census of Governments, 1992* (GPO, 1994), table 16: "Special District Governments by Debt Size and State."

28. Donald Axelrod, *Shadow Government: The Hidden World of Public Authorities and How They Control $1 Trillion of Your Money* (John Wiley and Sons, 1992), pp. 13–14.

29. The state comptroller of New York offers an enumeration of special districts that is independent of the census. The comptroller reported that the state had 1,297 "special purpose units" in 1992, over a third (449) located in counties in the tri-state region. Most of these were not in the Census Bureau's count. The state comptroller also counts 6,443 town special districts, 1,322 (20.5 percent) of them in the tri-state region. They were created to provide fire protection, lighting, sewerage, drainage, water, or sanitation services to parts of towns and charge, via their tax bill, only those who benefit from these services. Finally, this state official separately enumerates 848 fire districts, about a third of which (289) are in the region's counties. These are supported by special levies on the property tax, not fees for service, and are therefore not included in the count of special districts by the Census Bureau.

30. Axelrod, *Shadow Governments,* p. 13.

31. Robert Jay Dilger, *Neighborhood Politics: Residential Community Associations in American Governance* (New York University Press, 1992), p. 5. See also Edward J. Blakely and Mary Gail Snyder, "Fortress Communities: The Walling and Gating of American Suburbs," *Landlines*, vol. 5, no. 7 (1995), p. 1. (*Landlines* is the newsletter of the Lincoln Institute of Land Policy.) This point is discussed further in chapter 4.

32. Twenty-seven percent of the state's 285 special taxing districts extant in March 1988 were created in the 1980s. (Memo prepared by Sandra Norman-Eady, senior attorney for the Office of Legislative Research, Connecticut General Assembly, October 20,1993. Files of the authors.)

33. Interview with Susan Wallerstein, former council member, Town of Norwalk, January 26, 1996.

34. New York Laws of 1937, chap. 170; New Jersey Laws of 1937, chap.148. Congressional approval was given on August 19, 1937.

35. There are a number of multistate agencies established by interstate compact in which New York is associated with Connecticut, New Jersey, or other states to regulate rivers and water basins; these transcend the tri-state region.

36. Interstate compact quoted in Interstate Sanitation Commission, *Organization and Regulations* (New York, undated).

37. Joan Aaron, *The Quest for Regional Cooperation* (University of California Press, 1969), pp. 94–95.

38. See Michael N. Danielson and Jameson W. Doig, *New York: The Politics of Urban Regional Development* (University of California Press, 1982).

39. Mark Solof, "History of Metropolitan Planning Organization—Part 4" (www.njtpa.com/hist_mpo4.htm [December 2000]), p. 3.

40. Robert D. Yaro, "Growing and Governing Smart: A Case Study of the New York Region," in Bruce Katz, ed., *Reflections on Regionalism* (Brookings, 2000), p. 60.

41. Robert W. Bailey, "The City of Greater New York," in Sara F. Liebschutz, ed., *New York Politics and Government* (University of Nebraska Press, 1998), p. 165.

42. Gerald Benjamin, "The Political Relationship," in Gerald Benjamin and Charles Brecher, *The Two New Yorks* (New York: Russell Sage Foundation, 1988), pp. 120–21.

43. Wallace S. Sayre and Herbert Kaufman, *Governing New York City* (Russell Sage Foundation, 1961), p. xxxv.

44. This subject is discussed in Richard P. Nathan and Thomas L. Gais, *Implementing the Personal Responsibility Act of 1996: A First Look* (Albany, N.Y.: Rockefeller Institute, 1999), pp. 35–39, on "second-order devolution."

45. The system of Board of Cooperative Educational Services (BOCES) was established in New York State in 1948 to enhance educational opportunities for children outside big cities through regional collaboration.

Chapter 2. The Values of Regionalism

1. D. W. Meinig, "The Colonial Period, 1609–1775," in John Henry Thompson, ed., *The Geography of New York State* (Syracuse University Press, 1977), p. 129.

2. Office of the Special Master, *Final Report re: State of New Jersey* v. *State of New York*, no. 120 (October Term, 1996), pp. 35ff.

3. In 1798 New York State gave Robert Livingston a monopoly over steamboat operation on the state's navigable waters, including the entire Hudson River and New York Harbor. Livingston's support for Robert Fulton led to the construction of the Clermont, first put into service in 1807. This monopoly was enormously disadvantageous to New Jersey, and a "legislative jousting contest" ensued. (Special Master, *Final Report*, p. 38). In 1824 in the case of *Gibbons* v. *Ogden* (9 Wheaton 1 [1824]), the U.S. Supreme Court ruled that New York's regulation of commerce in the harbor burdened interstate commerce in violation of the Constitution. Perhaps this is part of the reason why, when New Jersey sought to bring its boundary claims before the Court four years later, New York leaders questioned the Court's jurisdiction and refused to appear. Although perhaps less obvious today, the issues of federalism raised by this posture were enormous. At a time when national power was only just being asserted, Chief Justice John Marshall feared that a serious questioning of central authority from the North, added to massive decentralizing pressures from the southern states, would tear the nation apart. While the New Jersey–New York dispute was before the court, Marshall wrote to Joseph Storey: "The Union has been prolonged thus far by miracles. I fear they cannot continue." (John Marshall to Joseph Storey, September 22, 1832, cited in Reverend William D. Driscoll, "Benjamin Butler: Lawyer and Regency Politician," Ph.D. dissertation, Fordham University, 1965, p. 226). See also Maurice G. Baxter, *The Steamboat Monopoly: Gibbons* v. *Ogden* (Knopf, 1972).

4. See also Charles Z. Lincoln, ed., *Messages from the Governors*, vol. 3 (Albany, N.Y.: J. P. Lyons, 1909), pp. 356–63.

5. In the mid-1980's Governors Cuomo and Kean agreed to share sales tax revenues generated on Ellis Island. The legislature of New Jersey agreed but that of New York did not, rejecting this collaborative compromise much as it had the proposed compromises of the early nineteenth century. Then the prospect of Supreme Court intervention encouraged negotiation between the states. More recently, Supreme Court action resulted from the failure of interstate negotiations. Linda Greenhouse, "Supreme Court Will Resolve Ellis I. Dispute," *New York Times*, May 17, 1994.

6. Thomas. M. Pitkin, *Keepers of the Gate* (New York University Press, 1975), p. 6.

7. "Islands Make New York New York," *New York Times*, February 15, 1994; Neil A Lewis, "With Immigration Law In Effect, Battles Go On," *New York Times*, April 2, 1997.

8. Linda Greenhouse, "High Court Gives New Jersey Most of Ellis Island," *New York Times* May 27, 1998.

9. Ibid.

10. Neal R. Peirce with Curtis Johnson and John Stuart Hall, *Citistates: How America Can Prosper in a Competitive World* (Washington: Seven Locks Press, 1993), p. 32.

11. Citistates Group LLC, "What's a Citistate?" (www.citistates.com/whatis.htm [January 2001]).

12. Neal R. Peirce and others, *Citistates*, p. 32. Emphasis added.

13. Peter F. Drucker, *Managing in a Time of Great Change* (New York: Truman Tally Books/Dutton, 1995), p. 32.

14. Ibid., p. 35.

15. Bureau of the Census, *1997 Census of Governments*, vol. 1: *Governmental Organization* (GPO, August 1999), pub. GC97(11)-1, p. vii.

16. Kathryn A. Foster, "The Fish Stores of Government and Other Musings on Specialization," *Intersight*, vol. 1, no. 3 (1995), pp. 47–54.

17. David Rusk, *Cities without Suburbs* (Washington: Woodrow Wilson Center, 1993).

18. David Rusk, *Inside Game/Outside Game* (Brookings, 1999).

19. Carl Calabrese, remarks delivered at the Chautauqua Conference on Regional Governance, June 1–4, 1997.

20. For a good summary, see H. V. Savitch and Ronald K. Vogel, *Regional Politics: America in a Post-City Age* (Thousand Oaks, Calif.: Sage Publications, 1996), chap. 1.

21. Margaret Weir, "Poverty, Social Rights and the Politics of Place," in Stephan Liebfried and Paul Pierson, eds., *European Social Policy: Between Fragmentation and Integration* (Brookings, 1995), pp. 330–31.

22. Kenneth T. Jackson, *Crabgrass Frontier: The Suburbanization of the United States* (Oxford University Press, 1985), pp. 304–05.

23. Richard Briffault, "Our Localism: Part I—The Structure of Local Government Law," *Columbia Law Review*, vol. 90, no. 1 (1990), pp. 1–115 (quotation p. 114); "Our Localism: Part II—Localism and Legal Theory," *Columbia Law Review*, vol. 90, no. 2 (1990), pp. 346–454 (quotation p. 348).

24. Rusk, *Cities without Suburbs*, p. 85.

25. Rusk, *Inside Game*, pp. 10–11.

26. Nancy Burns, *The Formation of American Local Governments* (Oxford University Press, 1994), p. 117. Burns's focus is on the creation of special districts to serve the economic and social goals of private developers or small groups of citizens.

27. Anthony Downs, "Debate on the Theories of David Rusk," *The Regionalist*, vol. 2 (Fall 1997), pp. 22–23. This is a theme in all of Downs's writing on the subject. See also Anthony Downs, *Urban Decline: The Future of American Cities*; *Neighborhoods and Urban Development* (Brookings, 1981), and *New Visions for Metropolitan America* (Brookings, 1994).

28. Weir, "Poverty," p. 352.

29. David B. Walker, "Regionalism in Connecticut and the Country: Dormant or Resurgent?" *The Regionalist*, vol. 1 (Fall 1995), p. 62.

30. C. James Owen and York Wilburn, *Governing Metropolitan Indianapolis: The Politics of Unigov* (University of California Press, 1985).

31. Indiana House of Representatives, HB 1013, 1997, sponsored by William Crawford, an African American legislator representing parts of Marion County.

32. Howard Husock, "Let's Break Up the Big Cities," *City Journal*, vol. 8 (Winter 1998), p. 77.

33. Even before they gained control in cities, minorities resisted metropolitan areawide mergers. In Indianapolis and Jacksonville, the African American community maintained that consolidation was designed to block them from gaining control of city government.

34. Myron Orfield, *Metropolitics: A Regional Agenda for Community and Stability* (Brookings, 1997).

35. Ibid., pp. 12–13.

36. See Rusk, *Inside Game/Outside Game,* chap. 11.

37. Anita Summers, remarks delivered at the Chautauqua Conference on Regional Governance, June 1–4, 1997.

38. Ibid.

39. John Kincaid, "The End of Mainframe Consolidation," *The Regionalist,* vol. 2 (Spring 1997), p. 57.

40. Ibid., p. 58.

41. Roger Parks, "Observations on the Research Agenda," *The Regionalist,* vol. 2 (Spring 1997), p. 62.

42. Ted Hershberg, "Regional Cooperation: Strategies and Incentives for Global Competitiveness and Urban Reform," *National Civic Review,* vol. 85 (Spring-Summer 1996), p. 25.

43. William Barnes and Larry C. Ledebur, *The New Regional Economies: The U. S. Common Market and the Global Economy* (Thousand Oaks, Calif.: Sage Publications, 1998).

44. There is another view, one that carries some weight with functional regionalists. Public choice theorists argue that competition between local governments within regions helps to keep officials responsive and costs down. Proponents of this position argue that a government offering locational incentives, especially ones that involve one-time costs or that will phase out after a period of time, may attract businesses ready to move and thus gain a benefit for the community that far outweighs the cost over the long term.

45. David Rusk quoted in Orfield, *Metropolitics,* p. xii.

46. Quoted in Charles V. Bagli, "Hudson Battle Heats Up over Standard and Poor's," *New York Times,* April 19, 1997, p. 23.

47. Dick Netzer, "An Evaluation of Interjurisdictional Competition through Economic Development Incentives," in Daphne A. Kenyon and John Kincaid, eds., *Competition among States and Local Governments* (Washington: Urban Institute, 1991), pp. 221–45.

48. Joe Mattey, "On the Efficiency Effects of Tax Competition for Firms," *The Region,* vol. 10 (June 1996), pp. 50–51.

49. David Crockett, remarks delivered at the Chautauqua Conference on Regional Governance, June 1–4, 1997.

50. River Valley Partners, Inc., *Chattanooga, Tennessee: Community Visioning/Vision 2000* (1998). Files of the authors.

51. "Cuyahoga River Fire," in David D. VanTassel and John J. Grabowski, eds., *The Encyclopedia of Cleveland History* (Indiana University Press, 1987), p. 324.

52. Bruce Adams, "Citizen Leadership for the 21st Century: Cleveland, the Partnership City," Academy of Leadership, University of Maryland, College Park, 1997, typescript, p. 4.

53. James Austin and Jaan Elias, *The Cleveland Turnaround (D): Challenges for the Future,* case no. 796-154, (Harvard Business School, 1996).

54. David C. Sweet, Kathryn W. Hexter, and David Black, eds., *The New American City Looks to Its Regional Future* (Ohio University Press, 1999), p. 7.

55. Richard Shatten, "Organizing Civic Leadership Systems to Gain Economic Advantage," in Center for Regional Economic Issues, *Cleveland's Path to Regional Economic Advantage* (Weatherhead School for Management, Case Western Reserve University, 2000), pp. 34–39.

Chapter 3. One Grand and Glorious City

1. David Nasaw, *The Chief: The Life of William Randolph Hearst* (Houghton Mifflin, 2000), p. 124. The internal quotes are from the *New York Daily Tribune,* January 1898.

2. In the late nineteenth century, the term "Greater New York" came into use to describe the idea of a city that went beyond Manhattan, to include what is now the Bronx, Brooklyn, Queens, and Staten Island. More recently, the term has been used to loosely describe the tri-state region. See "Greater New York," in Kenneth T. Jackson, ed., *The Encyclopedia of New York City* (Yale University Press, 1995), p. 502.

3. Bird S. Coler, *Municipal Government* (New York: Appleton and Co., 1900), p. 165.

4. Coler, *Municipal Government*, p. 3.

5. Peter Rose, *A History of Long Island* (New York: Lewis Publishing Co., 1903).

6. The rationale behind borrowing for capital purposes is that the costs of improvements shouldn't be borne all at once by current taxpayers but rather shifted into the future, to be paid by those who actually benefit from the facility. For general-purpose governments, shifting costs into the future also makes borrowing a plus politically: it allows leaders to produce visible results with fewer immediate costs and thus lower taxes.

7. "Comprehensive Outline of the Work of the Greater New York Commission," reprinted in John Ford, *The Life and Public Services of Andrew Haswell Green* (Garden City, N.Y.: Doubleday, Page and Co., 1913), p. 290.

8. Gerald Benjamin, "Origins of the Borough System," draft report for the New York City Charter Revision Commission (November 27, 1988), p. 11.

9. Richard L. McCormick, *From Realignment to Reform: Political Change in New York State, 1893–1910* (Cornell University Press, 1981), chap. 3.

10. Reverend Charles Parkhurst accused Tammany Hall and the New York City police of being at the center of "organized crime," a term he coined. In 1894 a state appropriation for a special committee to look into Parkhurst's charges was vetoed by Democratic Governor Roswell P. Flower. An investigation financed by the state's chamber of commerce and chaired by Republican state senator Clarence Lexow of Nyack proceeded nevertheless and produced a five-volume report documenting widespread corruption in city government.

11. In fact, the consolidated city was passed over the suspensive "home rule" veto of New York City's Mayor Strong. (See subsequent discussion in text.)

12. DeAlva Stanwood Alexander, *Four Famous New Yorkers* (New York: Henry Holt and Company, 1923), p. 243.

13. Ibid., pp. 291–92. Alexander's somewhat arcane language refers to Platt manipulating Black's hope of renomination in order to get the governor to sign the consolidation bill.

14. Benjamin, *Origins*, p. 20, citing Barry Jerome Kaplan, "A Study in the Politics of Metropolitanization: The Greater New York City Charter of 1897," Ph.D. dissertation, University of Buffalo, 1975, p. 315.

15. Ibid., p. 27.

16. "City Charter Criticized: Andrew H. Green Says the Borough System Is Bad," *New York Times*, March 23, 1902.

17. David Hammack, *Power and Society: Greater New York at the Turn of the Century* (New York: Russell Sage Foundation, 1982), p. 225.

18. Figure 3-1 shows the cities and towns that anteceded Greater New York, but it does not include incorporated villages. The villages of Brooklyn and Williamsburgh were subsumed earlier in the cities that took these names. Similarly, the village of Astoria became part of Long Island City when it was created. In Richmond incorporated villages that were displaced at consolidation were Edgewater, New Brighton, Port Richmond, Tompkinsville, and Tottenville; in Queens the incorporated villages were Arverne, College Point, Far Rockaway, Hempstead, Richmond Hill, Jamaica, and Whitestone. Eastern Queens became Nassau County as a result of consolidation, and the dozens of villages created there in the first half of the twentieth century suggest what might have happened in the more heavily settled part of Queens had consolidation not occurred.

19. New York State Assembly, Special Committee Appointed to Investigate the Public Offices and Departments of the City of New York and of the Counties Therein Included (Mazet Committee), *Final Report*, document no. 26 (January 15, 1900), p. 11.

20. The Citizens Union was organized in 1897 to work against the Democratic machine (Tammany Hall) and for reform of New York City government. It was, at first, the electoral vehicle for "fusion" efforts that included reformers in both major parties. Early in its history it ceased to contest elections and turned instead to encouraging "a municipal democracy that values its citizens, that tackles key issues, and that operates fairly, transparently, and economically." See "About Citizens Union" (www.citizensunion.org/cutoday.html [February 2001]).

21. See generally, Coler, *Municipal Government*.

22. Ibid., pp. 12–13.

23. The term *submayor* is borrowed from Frank J. Goodnow, "The Charter of the City of New York," *Political Science Quarterly*, vol. 17, no. 1 (March 1902), p. 16.

24. Benjamin, "Origins," p. 53.

25. *Morris* v. *Board of Estimate,* 489 U.S. 688 (1989).

26. Borough boards are created in chapter 6, section 85 of the city charter. Composed of the borough president, the city council members from the borough, and the chairs of all the community boards in the borough, they are empowered to hold public hearings and to advocate for borough interests in the city's central governing institutions and administrative agencies.

27. Benjamin, "Origins," p. 58.

28. Alison Mitchell, "Borough Presidents Seek Stronger Role in City," *New York Times*, February 24, 1993.

29. Clifford J. Levy, "Borough Development Units Are Turned Down by Pataki," *New York Times*, November 6, 1996.

30. Pam Belluck, "A New Star in the Constellation of Arts Giants," *New York Times*, May 21, 1996.

31. Jonathan P. Hicks, "New York City's Presidents without (Much) Portfolio," *New York Times*, March 12, 1996.

32. Ibid.

33. Mathew Purdy and Maria Newman, "Students Lag in Districts Where Patronage Thrives," *New York Times*, May 13, 1996.

34. Ibid., and Mathew Purdy, "Web of Patronage in Schools Grips Those Who Can Undo It," *New York Times*, May 14, 1996.

35. Diane Ravitch, *The Great School Wars, New York City, 1805–1973: A History of the Public Schools as Battlefield of Social Change* (Basic Books, 1974), p. 83.

36. Mayor's Advisory Panel on Decentralization of the New York City Schools, *Reconnection for Learning* (Praeger, 1968).

37. Ravitch, *Great School Wars*, p. 386.

38. New York Legislature, Assembly Bill A10410-A and Senate Bill S6082, and S5839, 1996.

39. This outcome was accepted by Mayor Giuliani because of his confidence in and relationship with the sitting chancellor, Rudy Crew. James Dao, "Albany in Schools Accord to Give Chancellor Power and Weaken Local Boards," *New York Times,* December 18, 1996; Joseph Berger, "Scandals at the School Boards Led to Loss of Their Powers," *New York Times,* December 18, 1996; Pam Belluck, "School Measure Aids Bureaucrats," *New York Times*, December 19, 1996; Matthew Purdy, "Rare Alliance Gave Crew Tighter Control of Schools," *New York Times,* December 23, 1996.

40. Editorial, "The Real Schoolwork Begins," *New York Times*, December 19, 1996.

41. See, for example, the remarks of Ed Miller and Robert Berne in Joseph Berger, "Albany in Accord to Raise Chancellor's Hiring Power," *New York Times*, December 18, 1996, and Peter Applebome, "Who's Minding the Schools," *New York Times*, Dec. 22, 1996, sec. 4.

42. Louis H. Massotti, "The Possibilities for Urban Revitalization," in John P. Blair and David Nachmias, *Fiscal Retrenchment and Urban Policy* (Thousand Oaks, Calif.: Sage Publications, 1979), p. 62.

43. Jonathan Barnett, *The Fractured Metropolis* (Harper Collins, 1995), p. 76.

44. Tony Hiss, "The 'Sacred Sites' That Make a Neighborhood Work," *New York Times*, March 21, 1995.

45. Kenneth A. Scherzer, "Neighborhoods," in Kenneth T. Jackson, ed., *The Encyclopedia of New York City* (Yale University Press, 1995), p. 804.

46. Samuel P. Hayes, "City Fathers and Reform: The Politics of Reform in Municipal Government, in Frank Otto Gatell, Paul Goodman, and Allen Weinstein, eds., *The Growth of American Politics since the Civil War* (Oxford University Press, 1972), p. 194.

47. Robert K. Merton, "The Functions of the Political Machine," in Frank J. Munger and Douglas Price, eds., *Readings in Political Parties and Pressure Groups* (Crowell, 1964), pp. 215–26.

48. The political machines did their electoral job well. New York City's population was about the same in 1937 as it was in 1993, but a half-century ago, old-fashioned party politics prevailed. The 1937 mayoral race was not very motivating for Democratic borough organizations: the party was divided and Fiorello LaGuardia (a friend of FDR) was heavily favored for reelection. Still 2,183,607 people voted in the city's mayoral election. By contrast, in 1993 millions were spent on media in the close, hot rematch between David Dinkins and Rudy Giuliani; yet only 1,821,894 New Yorkers appeared at the polls, one-sixth fewer than had voted half a century earlier.

49. John Mudd, *Neighborhood Services* (Yale University Press, 1984), pp. 20–21.

50. "Home Town in the Great City," *The Searchlight*, vol. 37 (1947).

51. David Rodgers, "Community Control," in Jewell Bellush and Dick Netzer, eds., *Urban Politics: New York Style* (Armonk, N.Y.: M. E. Sharpe, 1990), p. 164.

52. Mudd, *Neighborhood Services*, p. 152.

53. Robert F. Pecorella, *Community Reform in a Post-Reform City* (Armonk, N.Y.: M.E. Sharpe, 1994), pp. 192–94.

54. Robert F. Pecorella, "Community Governance," in Gerald Benjamin and Frank J. Mauro, eds., *Restructuring New York City Government: The Reemergence of Municipal Reform* (New York: Academy of Political Science, 1989), pp. 103, 105.

55. Vernice D. Miller, "Planning, Power and Politics: A Case Study of the Land Use and Siting History of the North River Water Pollution Control Plant," *Fordham Urban Law Journal*, vol. 21 (1994), pp. 707–22.

56. Richard J. Rodgers, "New York City's Fair Share Criteria and the Courts: An Attempt to Equitably Redistribute the Benefits and Burdens Associated with Municipal Facilities," *New York Law School Journal of Human Rights*, vol. 12 (1994), pp. 193–242.

57. See Barbara Weisberg, "One City's Approach to NIMBY: How New York City Developed a Fair Share Siting Process," and Joseph B. Rose, "A Critical Assessment of New York City's Fair Share Criteria," *Journal of the American Planning Association*, vol. 59 (1993), pp. 93–100.

58. The time required just for formal review of a project is substantial. Under the current regulations the City Planning Commission has six months to certify a project for review. For subsequent reviews the community board is given sixty days; the borough president thirty days; the planning commission, another thirty days; the mayor, five days;

and the city council, ten days. See David W. Dunlap, "Council's Land-Use Procedures Emerging?" *New York Times*, January 3, 1993.

59. Ibid.

60. Miller, "Planning," pp. 707–22.

Chapter 4. Creating Real Local Government in New York City

1. Robert A. Dahl, "The City in the Future of Democracy," *American Political Science Review*, vol. 61 (1967), p. 968.

2. Port Authority of New York and New Jersey, *Proceedings of the Regional Roundtables: Prospects and Strategies for the Twenty-First Century* (September 24 and December 15, 1993, and January 12, 1994), p. 170.

3. Mailer is quoted in John Tierney, "Brooklyn Could Have Been a Contender," *New York Times Magazine*, December 28, 1997.

4. Paul E. Kerson, "New York Gained Empire, But Lost Democracy," *New York Times*, December 31, 1997.

5. According to legend, Staten Island was kept in New York when Captain Christopher Bishop sailed around it in twenty-four hours. In 1683 the island became New York's County of Richmond. Its status as part of New York State was confirmed in the 1832 agreement with New Jersey, discussed in detail in chapter 2. See Charles W. Lenz and William T. Davis, *Staten Island and Its People* (New York: Staten Island Edison, 1924).

6. There has been some effort since the early 1960s to carve a new county, Peconic, from the five East End towns of Suffolk County on Long Island. Like Staten Islanders, East Enders, with 38 percent of Suffolk's land area but only 8 percent of its population, feel trapped in the wrong metropolitan ring. They want to separate from Suffolk because they feel more rural—or at least more exurban—than suburban. See Tom Twomey, "Should Suffolk Let Peconic County Go?" *Newsday*, November 5, 1995. In 1994, with funding from the five towns and the state legislature, the East End Economic and Environmental Institute completed a study indicating that the creation of Peconic County was feasible and would benefit local residents. Bills introduced in the state legislature in 1995 by State Senator Ken LaValle (S.3740A) and Assemblymembers Fred Thiele and Patricia Acampora (A. 6382A) call for a permissive (advisory, not binding) referendum in the five East End towns on their separation from Suffolk and the creation of Peconic County.

7. *Morris* v. *Board of Estimate*, 489 U.S. 688 (1989). For an explanation of the role of the Board of Estimate, see chapter 3. See also Richard Briffault, "Voting Rights, Home Rule, and Metropolitan Governance: The Secession of Staten Island as a Case Study in the Dilemmas of Local Self-Determination," *Columbia Law Review*, vol. 92 (1992), p. 775, at 782 ff; Joseph P. Viteritti, "Municipal Home Rule and the Conditions of Justifiable Secession," *Fordham Urban Law Journal*, vol. 23 (1995), pp. 1–68.

8. New York Laws of 1989, chap. 773; amended by New York Laws of 1990, chap. 15.

9. Briffault, "Voting Rights," p. 786.

10. New York Constitution, art. 9, sec. 2(b)2. For a summary discussion of home rule in New York, see Gerald Benjamin, "The Political Relationship," in Gerald Benjamin and Charles Brecher, eds., *The Two New Yorks* (New York: Russell Sage Foundation, 1988), pp. 114–19.

11. *City of New York* v. *State of New York*, 158 A.D. 2d 169, 173 (1990), quoted in Viteritti, "Municipal Home Rule," p. 18.

12. *City of New York* v. *State of New York*, 86 N.Y. 2d. 286 (1995), cited in Viteritti, "Municipal Home Rule," p. 17. Interestingly, Judge Levine did not include cities and villages in his list of the state's local agents. These entities in New York are created as a re-

sult of local initiative. Cities are still separately chartered; villages are created under general law but were formerly separately chartered as well. Because it functions sometimes as a city or a county or a school district, New York City is, as usual, a special case.

13. Jim Yardley, "Not Just a New Year: A 100th Birthday for a Unified City," *New York Times*, January 1, 1998.

14. Tierney, "Brooklyn."

15. See the New York City Office of the Comptroller website (www.comptroller.nyc.gov).

16. City of New York, Office of the Comptroller, Bureau of Management, "Audit Report on the Internal Controls and Operating Practices of the Grand Central Partnership Business Improvement District" (June 1997), quoted in Edward T. Rogowsky and Jill Simone Gross, "To Bid or Not to Bid: Economic Development in New York City," *Metropolitics*, vol. 1, no. 4 (1998) (www.sipa.columbia.edu/CURP/resources/metro/v01n0402.html [February 2001]).

17. New York City Local Law 2 of 1982, cited in Council of the City of New York, Committee on Finance, *Cities within Cities* (1995), p. 6.

18. Council of the City of New York, Committee on Finance, *Managing the Micropolis: Proposals to Strengthen BID Performance and Accountability,* staff report (November 1997), p. 17.

19. Jerry Mitchell, *Business Improvement Districts and Innovative Service Delivery* (New York: Price Waterhouse Coopers Endowment for the Business of Government, November 1999), p. 15.

20. Robert J. Dilger, *Neighborhood Politics: Residential Community Associations in American Governance* (New York University Press, 1992), p. 5.

21. Council of the City of New York, *Managing the Micropolis*, pp. 17, 20.

22. Bruce Lambert, "A Report Criticizes Improvement Zones in New York City," *New York Times*, November 8, 1995.

23. Tom Gallagher, "Trespasser on Main Street (You!)," *The Nation*, December 8, 1995, pp. 787–88.

24. Thomas J. Lueck, "The Mayor's Reach," *New York Times*, April 5, 1988. A few months later, the city's Department of Business Services announced that it would not renew its contract with the Grand Central Partnership, effectively denying this BID the capacity to collect the fees upon which it relied for its operations. Deputy Mayor for Operations Joseph J. Lhota said that this BID "stuck out like a sore thumb" for its failure to comply with regulations and its noncooperation with the city. A special object of city enmity was Daniel Biederman, the district's president. Biederman also served as head of two other BIDs and ignored a city directive that he not head more than one such agency at a time. Only after Biederman resigned as chief executive of the Grand Central Partnership and its chairman was replaced by a Giuliani ally did the mayor relent and agree to renegotiate the BID's contract with the city. Thomas J. Lueck, "Business Improvement District at Grand Central Is Dissolved," *New York Times*, July 30, 1998; Charles V. Bagli, "Business Group Fails to Mollify Giuliani," *New York Times*, September 24, 1998.

25. Dan Barry and Thomas J. Lueck, "Control Sought on Districts for Businesses," *New York Times,* April 2, 1998.

26. Editorial, "The Mayor vs. the BID's," *The New York Times,* April 3, 1998.

27. For a brief history of charter revision in New York City, see Joseph P. Viteritti, "The Tradition of Municipal Reform: Charter Revision in Historical Context," in Frank J. Mauro and Gerald Benjamin, eds., *Restructuring the New York City Government* (New York: Academy of Political Science, 1989), pp. 16–30.

28. New York State Municipal Home Rule Law, art. 4, sec. 36. 2 and 36.4.

29. Ibid., sec. 36.3.

30. Some examples are Kingsbridge in the Bronx; Astoria, Flushing and Jamaica in Queens; Bushwick, Flatbush, and New Lots in Brooklyn; and Castleton on Staten Island.

31. New York City Charter, sec. 52.1c.

32. For a discussion of major American cities with elected neighborhood-based units of local government, see Jeffrey M. Berry, Kent E. Portney, and Ken Thomson, *The Rebirth of Urban Democracy* (Brookings, 1993).

33. Richard Perez-Pena, "Democratic Party Loves Vallone, But He's Mostly Unknown Upstate," *New York Times*, May 25, 1998.

34. James Dao, "Immigrant Diversity Slows Traditional Political Climb," *New York Times*, December 28, 1999.

35. See Joseph P. Viteritti, *Community Government, the City Council and the Reform Agenda: The Case for Full Coterminality* (Robert F. Wagner Graduate School of Public Service, New York University, May 1991).

Chapter 5. The Limits of Metropolitanism

1. John Bollens and Henry Schmandt, *The Metropolis*, 2d ed. (Harper and Row, 1965), p. 6, quoting Bureau of the Census, *Tenth Census of the United States: Social Statistics of Cities* (1886), part 1, pp. 531–32.

2. William H. Frey and Alden Speare Jr., *Regional and Metropolitan Growth and Decline in the United States* (New York: Russell Sage Foundation, 1988), p. 28.

3. For a history and analysis of the legal development of American cities, see Gerald E. Frug, *City Making* (Princeton University Press, 1999), pp. 15–70.

4. See Peter J. Galie, *The New York Constitution: A Reference Guide* (Westport, Conn.: Greenwood Press, 1991); for historical background, see Peter J. Galie, *Ordered Liberty: A Constitutional History of New York* (Fordham University Press, 1996).

5. See the discussion of Staten Island secession in chapter 4.

6. Anthony J. Blackburn, *Housing New York City, 1993* (New York: Department of Housing Preservation and Development, 1995), pp. 142–43. See also Richard Perez-Pena, "Fears of New Rent Laws, Beyond Manhattan," *New York Times*, June 1, 1997; Frank Padavan, "A Republican for Rent Regulation," *New York Times*, June 12, 1997; James Dao and Richard Perez-Pena, "Rent War Redux: As Dust Settles, A Tortuous Inside Story Emerges," *New York Times*, June 29, 1997.

7. James C. Musselwhite Jr., "A Comparative View," in Gerald Benjamin and Charles Brecher, *The Two New Yorks* (New York: Russell Sage Foundation, 1988), pp. 44–45.

8. Charles R. Morris, *The Cost of Good Intentions: New York City and the Liberal Experiment* (W.W. Norton, 1980), p. 12.

9. Ibid., p. 194.

10. Steven Greenhouse, "Layoffs Rupture Tie between Giuliani and Labor Leader," *New York Times*, April 25, 1998.

11. Citizens Budget Commission, *Budget 2000 Project: Restructuring Government Services* (New York, 1996), p. 44.

12. Cited in New York State, Office of the Deputy State Comptroller for the City of New York, "The New York City Region in the 1990's: A Look at Economic Performance Compared to the Nation's Largest Cities," Technical Memorandum 2-98 (Office of the Deputy State Comptroller for the City of New York, October 1997), p. 10.

13. Quoted in Howard Husock, "Let's Break Up the Big Cities," *City Journal*, vol. 8 (Winter 1998), p. 82.

14. Ibid., pp. 82–83. See several studies cited there.

15. Paul E. Peterson, *City Limits* (University of Chicago Press, 1981), chap. 4.

16. Wayne Barrett, "Train Runs Over Rudy," *Village Voice*, May 19–25, 1999. State senate Republicans, perhaps assuming that the action would be blocked by the assembly's Democrats, advanced the idea of repealing this tax to assist their candidate, Tom Morahan, in a close race for a senate seat in a special election in Rockland County. Sixteen assembly Democrats based in the suburbs of New York City, led by Richard Brodsky of Westchester, supported repeal. In a surprising move, Assembly Speaker Sheldon Silver—a Democrat based in New York City's lower east side but no friend of Mayor Giuliani (who was reporting surpluses in the city budget and advancing tax cuts)—produced a majority in his city-Democrat-dominated house for the repeal, in support of the Democratic senate candidate, Ken Zabrowski. Governor George Pataki, a Republican from Northern Westchester County and also no great friend of Giuliani, signed the bill. The city lost an estimated $360 million in revenue. The Republicans retained the state senate seat, avoiding a further narrowing of their slim majority in that house.

17. Cynthia Green and Paul D. Moore, "Public Finance," in Gerald Benjamin and Charles Brecher, *The Two New Yorks* (New York: Russell Sage Foundation, 1988), chap. 8.

18. Charles Brecher, *Budget 2000 Project: Tax Policy* (New York: Citizens Budget Commission, 1995), p. 1.

19. Galie, *Ordered Liberty*, p. 219.

20. See chapters 6 and 7 on transportation in the region.

21. Clifford J. Levy, "Cap on Borrowing Jeopardizes Plans in New York City," *New York Times,* November 29, 1996; Richard Perez-Pena, "Accord in Albany on the City's Debt Limit," *New York Times*, February 12, 1997.

22. Citizens Budget Commission, *Budget 2000 Project: Capital Investment and Debt Service* (New York, 1996), p. 50. Additionally, the cost of debt incurred for the newly created Water Finance Authority in 1995 was $379 million.

23. Office of the State Comptroller, *How Debt Finances New York City's Capital Program*, Report 12-2000 (Albany and New York City, March 2000).

24. See "Westchester Is Ashiver over Annexation: Bill to Allay Fears Approved in Albany," *New York Times*, January 28, 1925; Editorial, "More Scared Than Endangered," *New York Times*, January 29, 1925; Editorial, "Constitutional Amendments," *New York Times*, March 30, 1927. See also State of New York, Home Rule Commission, *Second Report,* legislative document no. 72 (Albany, N.Y., 1925), p. 43.

25. Editorial, "Constitutional Amendments."

26. New York State Constitution, art. 9, sec. 1.d.

27. David Rusk, *Cities without Suburbs*, 2d ed. (Johns Hopkins University Press, 1995).

28. Regional Plan Association, *The Second Regional Plan* (New York, 1968); Robert D. Yaro and Tony Hiss, *A Region at Risk: The Third Regional Plan* (Washington: Island Press, 1996).

29. See Edgar M. Hoover and Raymond Vernon, *Anatomy of a Metropolis* (Doubleday, 1962).

30. Task Force on the Future of New York City, *New York: World City* (Cambridge, Mass.: Oelgeschlager, Gunn and Hain, 1980), p. 54.

31. Bruce Berg and Paul Kantor, "New York: The Politics of Conflict and Avoidance," in H. V. Savitch and Ronald K. Vogel, eds., *Regional Politics: America in a Post-City Age* (Thousand Oaks, Calif.: Sage Publications, 1996), pp. 29–30. For Berg and Cantor the central business district is New York County, and the inner ring counties are the remaining four boroughs of New York City and Hudson County, New Jersey.

32. Philip J. Schwarz, *The Jarring Interests* (SUNY Press, 1979), and Peter S. Onuf, *The Origins of the Federal Republic* (University of Pennsylvania Press, 1983).

33. Letter from Vaux to Green, January 20, 1894. Calvert Vaux Papers, New York Public Library. We greatly appreciate having this letter brought to our attention by Steve Levine of the Graduate Center of the City University of New York.

34. Wendell and Schwann, "Interstate Areas," in Advisory Commission on Intergovernmental Relations, *Substate Regionalism and the Federal System*, vol. 1 (Government Printing Office, 1979), p. 279. See also Advisory Commission on Intergovernmental Relations, *Multi-State Regionalism* (GPO, 1972).

35. National Academy of Public Administration, *Building Stronger Communities and Regions: Can the Federal Government Help?* (Washington, 1998), p. 16.

36. Evelyn Nieves, "'Downstate': A Nice Place Not to Visit," *New York Times*, April 28, 1996.

37. Benjamin and Brecher, *The Two New Yorks*, p. 118.

38. Clyde Haberman, "Time Again For Old Idea: 51st State?" *New York Times*, December 17, 1996.

39. Iver Peterson, "South Jersey: Nice Shore, but Definite Attitude," *New York Times*, June 27, 1994. See also Iver Peterson, "Down Here vs. Up There," *New York Times*, January 14, 2000.

40. "Save the Whalers Effort is Extended for Two Weeks," *New York Times*, May 4, 1996.

41. Daniel Elazar, *American Federalism: A View from the States*, 3d ed. (Harper and Row, 1984), pp. 94, 107 (map).

42. Ibid., chap. 5.

43. Tom Redburn, "New Flare-Up in Region's Border Wars Kills an Oft-Ignored Truce," *New York Times*, October 16, 1994. See also the following reports in the *New York Times*: Thomas J. Lueck, "Rejecting New York City's Bid, Bank to Move to Connecticut," September 22, 1994; Thomas J. Lueck, "New York City Is Vengeful in the Face of a 'Raid' by Connecticut," October 11, 1994; "Legislators Approve Swiss Bank Move," October 13, 1994; Steven Lee Meyers, "Giuliani Says Connecticut Broke Truce," October 14, 1994. For other examples of interstate rivalries in the tri-state region, see chapter 2.

44. Ian Fisher, "House GOP Strikes Deal to Save New York Forest from Development," *New York Times,* July 27, 1996.

Chapter 6. Across State Lines: The Port Authority

1. Anita A. Summers, "Regionalizing: We're All Doing It," delivered at a meeting of the Wharton Regionalization Project, 1996, p. 4.

2. "Traffic Volume Sets Record at Port Authority Crossings, and E-ZPass Helps Keep Cars and Trucks Moving," April 15, 1998 (www.ettm.com/news/pa_record.html [February 2001]).

3. Andrew C. Revkin, "Giuliani Proposes Rail Tunnel to Carry Freight Past Hudson," *New York Times*, January 15, 1997.

4. See his autobiography, *They Built Better Than They Knew* (New York: Messner, 1946).

5. Erwin Wilkie Bard, *The Port of New York Authority* (New York: AMS Press, 1968), pp. 60–61.

6. In 1921 a bill was passed allowing New York City to build the Narrows Tunnel, a freight and passenger tunnel between Staten Island and Brooklyn. Construction began, and this project proceeded until 1925, when financing ceased. See Bard, *Authority*, pp. 50–53.

7. In recognition of his role in helping to create the agency, Smith was among the first appointees to the Port Authority's board in 1921. He won back the New York governorship in 1922 and served until 1928, when he was defeated for president of the United States by Herbert Hoover.

8. The city Board of Estimate sought to represent New York on the board, or to have two of its members be named to the board. See Bard, *Authority*, pp. 29–32. See also Louis L. J. Gambaccini, "The Port Authority of New York and New Jersey," in V.V. Ramanadham, ed., *Public Enterprise* (London: Frank Cass and Co, 1986), p. 134. Mr. Gambaccini served as assistant executive director of the Port Authority.

9. New York Laws of 1921, chap. 154.

10. Ibid., art.16. See also Gambaccini, "Port Authority," p. 140.

11. Wallace Sayre and Herbert Kaufman, *Governing New York City* (New York: Russell Sage, 1961), p. 321.

12. The Holland Tunnel, opened in 1927, was begun before the Port Authority was created in 1921 and ultimately came under the authority's control.

13. New York Laws of 1946, chap. 370.

14. Jameson W. Doig, "Regional Conflict in the New York Metropolis: The Legend of Robert Moses and the Power of the Port Authority," *Urban Studies,* vol. 27, no. 2 (1990), p. 214.

15. New York Laws of 1921, chap. 154.

16. Doig, "Regional Conflict," pp. 108–13.

17. Michael N. Danielson and Jameson W. Doig, *New York: The Politics of Urban Regional Development* (University of California Press, 1982), p. 330.

18. Thomas J. Lueck, "Port Authority Offers Its Vision of New York Harbor," *New York Times,* January 14, 1999.

19. Steven Lee Meyers, "City Dumps to Ask Fees of Two Agencies," *New York Times*, Feb. 25, 1996; Jonathan P. Hicks, "Mayor Sharply Attacks Port Authority," *New York Times*, August 24, 1995.

20. Rothschild Inc., *The Port Authority of New York: A Preliminary Report* (May 1996). Files of the authors.

21. Mark Green, *Follow the Money: How the Port Authority of New York and New Jersey Has Favored New Jersey over New York* (New York: Office of the Public Advocate, 1996). In his accompanying press release, Green said: "Analysis of 46 Port facilities shows New Jersey got $856 a year per capita and NY $485, even though Jersey facilities lost $588 million compared to $669 million profit from New York State facilities."

22. Steven Lee Meyers, "Mayor Urges Breakup of Port Authority," *New York Times*, June 1, 1996.

23. See, for example, New Jersey Senate, Independent Authorities Committee, *Public Hearing before the Senate Committee on Independent Authorities on the Port Authority of New York and New Jersey, April 11, 1986* (Trenton, N.J.: Office of Legislative Services, 1986).

24. Meyers, "Mayor Urges Breakup," p. 23.

25. Jonathan P. Hicks, "Giuliani Fires Blast at Port Authority," *New York Times*, August 24, 1995.

26. Clifford J. Levy, "The PATH War," *New York Times*, August 27, 1995.

27. Alan Finder and Jacque Steinberg, "In Eye of Economic Storm, the Port Authority Battens Down," *New York Times*, November, 22, 1991.

28. *United States Trust Company* v. *New Jersey,* 431 U.S. 1, 7 (1976), citing Laws of New Jersey of 1931, chap. 5, and Laws of New York of 1931, chap. 48. This 10 percent level was reached in 1946.

29. Ibid., p. 6, footnote 7.

30. Personal communication from Stephen L. Carlson, March 2, 1998.

31. As noted, the Port Authority aggregated revenues and expenditures for fiscal and political reasons. But after it assumed responsibility for the PATH lines, the agency changed its bookkeeping practices to allow it to prove that it incurred annual losses.

32. Danielson and Doig, *New York*, pp. 245–46.

33. *United States Trust Company* v. *New Jersey*.

34. Danielson and Doig, *New York*, pp. 245–50; Ralph Blumenthal, "Port Authority Admits Aiding Hilton in Bid," *New York Times*, November 8, 1977.

35. New York Laws of 1978, chap. 651.

36. Ralph Blumenthal, "Goldmark Is Tackling More Than a Scandal," *New York Times*, November 27, 1977, sec. 4.

37. A state legislative study estimated in 1982 that the World Trade Center might be sold for between $1.2 and $1.5 billion. New York State was paying $10 a square foot for space in the building; the market rate was $35 a square foot. The study estimated further that a sale would produce $400 million to $500 million in cash, generate $65 million in additional property tax revenues, and free the Port Authority of $8.4 million in annual expenses. New York State Assembly, Committee on Corporations, Authorities and Commissions, *Agency out of Control* (Albany, N.Y.: 1982).

38. Geographical equity is an issue within Greater New York as it is in the Port Authority region. Manhattan residents regularly complain about "redistribution" of their tax money to the outer boroughs, while people in the outer boroughs argue that their needs are neglected. See John Tierney, "We Want to Be Alone," *New York Times Magazine*, July 14, 1996, p. 12.

39. Edward I. Koch, *Politics* (New York: Simon and Schuster, 1984), p. 173.

40. Edward A. Gargan, "Governors Bar Sale of Trade Center," *New York Times*, June 20, 1984.

41. David Bird, "Use of Trade Center Rentals for Transit Urged," *New York Times*, May 30, 1982; Editorial, "Yes, Trade on the Trade Center," *New York Times*, June 19, 1982.

42. Mario M. Cuomo, *Public Papers of the Governor, 1983* (Albany, N.Y., 1983), pp. 1112, 1606.

43. Ibid., pp. 1629.

44. Josh Barbanel, "Cuomo Issues Call for 'Partnership' to Spark Growth," *New York Times*, Jan. 6, 1983. See also the following articles in the *New York Times*: Joseph P. Sullivan, "Kean to Seek More Influence over Port Authority Policies," Jan 10, 1984; Edward A. Gargan, "Governors Bar Sale of Trade Center," June 20, 1984 ; Edward A. Gargan, "The Put-Off Port Authority," April 22, 1984.

45. Mario Cuomo, *Public Papers of the Governor, 1987* (Albany, N.Y., 1987), p. 857.

46. Robert D. McFadden, "Cuomo Calls for Review of Port Authority Plans," *New York Times*, May 18, 1992.

47. *Hess* v. *PATH*, 809 F. Supp. 172 (1992); *Hess et al.* v. *PATH,* 8 F.3d 811 (1993).

48. *Hess et al.* v. *PATH Corp.*, 513 U.S. 30, 56, 61 (1994).

49. Ibid.

50. Finder and Steinberg, "In the Eye of Economic Storm."

51. Ibid.

52. "To identify and meet the critical transportation infrastructure needs of the bistate region's businesses, residents and visitors: providing the highest quality, most efficient transportation and port commerce facilities and services that move people and goods within the region, providing access to the rest of the nation and the world, and strengthening the economic competitiveness of the New York–New Jersey metropolitan region." Quoted in Joe Mysack and Judith Schiffer, *Perpetual Motion* (Los Angeles: General Publishing Group, 1997), p. 272.

53. Neil MacFarquar, "Javits Center President Reportedly Tops Pataki's List to Take Over Port Authority," *New York Times*, January 25, 1997.

54. Mitchell Pacelle and Charles Gasparino, "Trade Towers: To Sell or Not—New York Landmark Sparks Open Feuding among Top Politicians," *Wall Street Journal*, February 11, 1998. Again the interests of the city and the Port Authority diverged. New York City receives $23.4 million in yearly payments in lieu of taxes from the World Trade Center. A sale that put the property back on the tax rolls would produce $103 million in annual revenue. But a ninety-nine year lease to a private buyer with the tax exemption intact would give the Port Authority a much higher return: estimated value at sale in 1997, $565 to $755 million; value of long-term lease, $897 million to $1.07 billion.

55. James Dao, "Jitters for Port Authority's Bondholders," *New York Times*, March 30, 1997.

56. Port Authority of New York and New Jersey, *Proceedings of the Regional Roundtable* (1994), p. 10.

57. Ibid.

Chapter 7. Single-State Agencies: The MTA and NJT

1. New York Laws of 1954, chap. 801; New Jersey Laws of 1954, chap. 44.

2. Metropolitan Regional Transit Commission, *Rapid Transit for the New York–New Jersey Metropolitan Area* (New York, January 1958). In the state of New York, the counties were New York, Orange, and Rockland; in New Jersey, they were Bergen, Essex, Hudson, Mercer, Middlesex, Monmouth, Morris, Passaic, Somerset, and Union. Interestingly, the proposed district included New York *County* but not all of Greater New York City.

3. This account is summarized from Jameson Doig, *Metropolitan Transportation Politics and the New York Region* (Columbia University Press, 1966).

4. Under one governance arrangement proposed for the agency, New York County was given fourteen votes and the two other counties in New York State one vote each. The more populous New Jersey counties got two votes each; the rest received one. A coalition composed of the counties of New York and Rockland in New York State and Bergen in New Jersey—where the strongest support for creating the new agency was located—would constitute a majority of the board. See William Miller, *Metropolitan Rapid Transit Financing: A Report to the Metropolitan Rapid Transit Survey of New York and New Jersey* (1957).

5. Editorial, "As the MTA Takes Over," *New York Times*, February 16, 1968, cited in Michael N. Danielson and Jameson W. Doig, *New York: The Politics of Urban Regional Development* (University of California Press, 1982), p. 233; Robert Connery and Gerald Benjamin, *Rockefeller of New York* (Cornell University Press, 1979), p. 279.

6. MTA (www.mta.nyc.ny.us [January 2001]). The New Haven line is operated by Metro-North, an MTA subsidiary, in conjunction with the Connecticut Department of Transportation. Two commuter lines terminating in Rockland County, New York, are operated jointly by New Jersey Transit and the MTA. See John Fink, "Railroads," in Kenneth T. Jackson, ed., *The Encyclopedia of New York City* (Yale University Press, 1995), p. 984.

7. New Jersey Transit (www.njtransit.state.nj.us.[January 2001]). New Jersey Transit operates an Atlantic City rail line, taken over from Amtrak in 1995 with expanded service. The Delaware River Port Authority (DRPA) operates the only rapid transit line in southern New Jersey, the Port Authority Transit Corporation (PATCO).

8. David Jones, *Urban Transit Policy: An Economic and Political History* (Englewood Cliffs, N.J.: Prentice-Hall, 1985), p. 10.

9. Annmarie Hauck Walsh, *The Public's Business* (MIT Press, 1978), p. 390. Footnote 24 is an excellent brief summary of the organizational history of mass transit in New York City. We rely on it here.

10. Wallace S. Sayre and Herbert Kaufman, *Governing New York City* (New York: Russell Sage Foundation, 1960), p. 323.

11. Peter Derrick, "Subways," in *The Encyclopedia of New York City*, p. 1139.

12. Sayre and Kaufman, *Governing New York City*, p. 322.

13. Walsh, *The Public's Business*, p. 215. Near the end of Moses's tenure, Mayor John Lindsay did challenge him regarding board appointments.

14. For a history of the development of the board, see Danielson and Doig, *New York*, p. 35, note 78. Initially the agency board had nine members. Three were to be appointed "only on the written recommendation of the mayor of the city of New York," but all were appointed by the governor.

15. Robert Kiley, former chairman of the agency, quoted in Richard Perez-Pena, "Fares' Divergent Tracks," *New York Times*, November 11, 1995.

16. Robert Caro, *The Powerbroker: Robert Moses and the Fall of New York* (Knopf, 1974), pp. 1132–44.

17. New Jersey State Senate, Committee on Transportation, *Hearings on the New Jersey Public Transportation Act of 1979*, Senate Bill 3137 (Trenton, N.J., March 28, 1979), Pp. 20.

18. Guy T. Baehr, "NJ Transit Hailed as Success on Its 15th Birthday: Desperation of Early Years is Remembered," *Newark Star-Ledger*, July 15, 1994.

19. George M. Smerk, *The Federal Role in Urban Mass Transportation* (Indiana University Press, 1985), pp. 59–63

20. L. Greg Ovchecka, "New Jersey Transit Gets on the Right Track," *Business Journal of New Jersey*, vol. 2, January 10, 1985.

21. New Jersey Department of Transportation, *Long Range Plan: Surface Transportation Element* (Trenton, N.J., 1981), p. 30.

22. See Smerk, *The Federal Role*, pp. 59, 70.

23. For a summary of federal legislation in the 1960s and 1970s, see Jones, *Urban Transit Policy*, p. 7.

24. Richard Briffault, Elliott D. Sclar, and Walter Hook, *Fairness and the Fare* (Columbia Law School, 1998), p. 8.

25. Guy T. Baehr, "Picking Up Steam," *Newark Star-Ledger*, October 10, 1994.

26. Guy T. Baehr, "NJ Transit Looks to Cut Service But Raise Fares," *Newark Star-Ledger*, April 19, 1992; Ron Morisco, "New Jersey Transit Grilled on Budget, Railyard," *Newark Star-Ledger*, April 28, 1992; Ron Morisco, "GOP Vows $34 Million Cut in NJ Transit Budget 'Waste,' *Newark Star-Ledger*, June 4, 1992; Ron Morisco, "NJ Transit to 'Analyze' GOP Budget Cut Plan," *Newark Star-Ledger*, June 5, 1992; Guy T. Baehr, "NJ Transit Clears 'Tight' Budget to Hold Line on Service and Fares," *Newark Star-Ledger*, July 17, 1992.

27. James T. Prior, "Assembly Speaker Chuck Haytaian," *New Jersey Business Journal*, August 1992, p. 48.

28. Freylinghausen and DeLibero quotes from the *Newark Star-Ledger*, April 19, 1992.

29. For a good summary of the MTA's early years, see Danielson and Doig, *New York*, pp. 226–43.

30. An excellent summary of the evolution of the financial condition of the subway system may be found in a report by Jack Bigel, *Financing New York's Public Transit System* (New York: Program Planners, Inc., 1980). Writing in 1980, Bigel reported that the last year the NYCTA had a surplus was 1961.

31. There were seven subway and bus fare increases by the TBTA between 1980 and 1995. There were five commuter rail fare increases during this period. See Briffault and others, *Fairness and the Fare*, pp. 5–6.

32. Metropolitan Transportation Authority, "Message of Chairman Robert Kiley," *Annual Report, 1983*, p. 3.

33. Mario Cuomo, *Public Papers of the Governor* (Albany, N.Y., 1985), p. 1154.

34. Under contract with the MTA, Connecticut pays 65 percent of the commuter rail deficit attributable to operating the New Haven Line ($40 million in 1998) and 54 percent of losses at Grand Central Terminal ($5.3 million in 1998). Connecticut litigated without success in the mid-1990s to reduce its obligations to the MTA. The state raised fares for Connecticut riders on the New Haven Line four times between 1996 and 1999 to cut these deficits. See Thomas J. Lueck, "Connecticut May Seek Metro-North Fare Rise," *New York Times*, February 24, 1999.

Localities in New York State pay for the maintenance of commuter railroad stations within their boundaries: $109 million in 1996. This was an issue in Nassau and Westchester in 1998; see, for example, Westchester County, Office of the County Executive and Board of Legislators; *1998 Joint Legislative Program* (1998). New York City pays, too, for policing the subways and for reduced fares for schoolchildren, although it unilaterally cut its contribution in 1995–96 to $45 million, a third of the total estimated cost. See Briffault and others, *Fairness and the Fare*, pp. 9–10.

35. These taxes include sales and compensatory use taxes; a temporary regional mass transit business tax surcharge on utility services; a temporary regional mass transit business tax surcharge; a temporary regional tax surcharge on banks; a temporary regional surcharge on utilities; and certain mortgage recording taxes.

36. Metropolitan Transportation Authority, "Discussion of Service Benefits and Contributions for the Twelve Counties of the New York Metropolitan Region" (1983), typescript on deposit in the New York Public Library, *ZT-1551 No. 14.

37. New York Laws of 1986, chap. 930.

38. Mario Cuomo, *Public Papers of the Governor* (Albany, N.Y.: 1988), p. 159.

39. For example, see the description of the settlement of the 1980 transit strike in New York City in Ed Koch, *Mayor* (Simon and Schuster, 1984), chap. 14.

40. New York Laws of 1981, chap. 314, sec. 1269. B.3.

41. Perez-Pena, "Fares' Divergent Tracks."

42. *N.Y. Urban League, et al.* v. *MTA et al.*, 905 F. Supp. 1266 (1995), Memorandum of Law on Behalf of Defendants Metropolitan Transportation Authority and E. Virgil Conway in Opposition to Motion for a Preliminary Injunction (files of the authors).

43. *N.Y. Urban League, et al.* v. *MTA et al.*, 1266.

44. Quoted in Briffault and others, *Fairness and the Fare*, p. 28.

45. *N.Y. Urban League, et al.* v. *the State of New York, et al.*, 71 F.3d 1031 (1995).

46. Briffault and others, *Fairness and the Fare*, p. 28.

47. Commuters gained too, however. They received a 9 percent discount on their monthly rail fare if they bought a Metrocard built into their monthly pass. This, of course, reduced the redress of the subsidy imbalance achieved for subway riders by the introduction of the Metrocard.

48. Elizabeth Kolbert, "In Transfers, Pataki Finds a Free Ride," *New York Times*, June 23, 1997.

49. State Transportation Campaign, *Mobilizing the Region*, no. 153 (December 8, 1997).

50. Different executive directors have displayed varying degrees of independence from gubernatorial direction. Richard Ravitch, appointed by Governor Hugh Carey in 1980, achieved legislative passage of the first massive capital plan in 1981 by working directly

with legislative leaders during a time when they were at war with the governor. "In order to get things done, you need the governor, the Legislature, the mayor and the county executives," Ravitch noted, " . . . and it's easier to do that if you are not the agent of only one of those players." See James Lardner, "Painting the Elephant," *The New Yorker*, June 25, 1984, p. 71.

51. New York State Department of Transportation, *Management Study: MTA* (Albany, N.Y., April 1976), available from the New York Public Library, JLF 77694.

52. Walsh, *The Public's Business*, p. 190.

53. Robert D. Yaro and Tony Hiss, *A Region at Risk: The Third Regional Plan* (New York: Regional Plan Association, 1996), p. 164.

54. Ibid., p. 155. Emphasis added.

55. Ibid., pp. 212–16.

56. Metropolitan Transportation Authority, *Annual Report, 1995* (New York, 1995), p. 12.

57. Metropolitan Transportation Authority, *Annual Report* (New York, various years).

58. Briffault and others, *Fairness and the Fare*, p. 74.

59. NJT reported in 1988 that completion of this system was planned for 1999. As of this writing, funds were in place to build light rail from Bayonne to Hoboken but not for the remaining section to Ridgefield Park.

60. DeLibero's performance helped her survive the transition to the Republican Whitman administration. She announced her resignation late in 1998 to head the Houston Transit System.

61. This trust fund was first established in 1984 with revenues from the gas tax, motor vehicle registration fees, and contributions from highway authorities to meet capital needs for transportation. It has since been reauthorized three times, most recently under Governor Whitman on July 20, 2000. Press release, "Governor Signs Transportation Trust Fund Bill Providing $3.75 Billion for Road and Transit Projects through 2004" (www.state.nj.us/transportation/press/2000releases/f000720.htm).

62. Jane Gross, "E-ZPass Living Up to Name," *New York Times*, March 25, 1997.

63. Melody Peterson, "E-ZPass Deal in New Jersey Is Not So Easy," *New York Times*, March 23, 1997; Larry M. Greenberg, "Financing for New Jersey E-ZPass Expects Violators to Help Pay the Bill," *Wall Street Journal*, March 16, 1998.

64. For more background and information on the E-Zpass system, see www.ettm.com.

65. For example, see Council of State Governments, *Book of the States*, vol. 33 (Lexington, Ky., 2000).

66. Yaro and Hiss, *A Region at Risk*.

Chapter 8. The Persistence of Suburban Localism

1. New Jersey Laws of 1977, chap. 435, sec. 2; Consolidated Laws of New Jersey, 40:43-66.35.

2. Consolidation Study Commission, *Thinking as One Town* (Princeton, N.J.: July 1996), p. 3. This is the commission's final report, retrievable at www.princetonol.com/gov/final.htm.

3. Consolidated Laws of New Jersey. 40:43.66-35 through 66-77.

4. W.C. Dowling," Town Talk: Save Princeton Borough," letter to the editor, January 11, 1996 (www.princetonol.com/towntalk/consolidate/000.htm [August 1998]).

5. Marvin Reed, interview by Gerald Benjamin, July 17, 1995; Ben Jenson, "The War of the Princetons," *New York Times*, October 20, 1966. Melody Petersen, "Two Princetons Consider a Merger, Once Again," *New York Times*, November 5, 1996.

6. This was outside the tri-state region: Vineland Borough was joined with Landis Township. See New Jersey Department of Community Affairs, "Local Government Shared Services and Municipal Consolidation: A Report and an Agenda" (www.state.nj.us/dca/lgshar5.htm [February 2001]).

7. Ibid.

8. New York State, Village Law, art. 19.

9. See, for example, Temporary State Commission to Study the Catskills, *The Future of the Catskills* (Stamford, N.Y.: 1975), p. 57.

10. Andrea Ball, "The Village People," *Huguenot Herald*, p. 1.

11. This account of the abolition of county government in Connecticut relies upon Roseline Levenson, *County Government in Connecticut: Its History and Demise* (University of Connecticut Institute of Public Service, reprinted 1981).

12. E. J. Haller and David Monk, "New Reforms, Old Reforms and the Consolidation of Rural Schools," *Educational Administration Quarterly*, vol. 24 (November 1988), p. 473.

13. Ina Aronow, "Weighing the Pros and Cons of Merging School Districts," *New York Times*, May 8, 1994.

14. The *Census of Governments* reported 481 school districts in New Jersey and 3 in Connecticut operating as separate governments in 1952; the numbers for 1972 were 527 and 14. In New Jersey voters can choose by local referendum to convert school services from dependency on general-purpose government (type 1) to independent status (type 2) at referendum. They have been inclined to do so. Between 1967 and 1992, the number of dependent districts dropped from 58 to 27.

15. In Connecticut 149 school systems (all but the 17 regional districts) are administered by elected governing bodies but are fiscally dependent on cities or towns and are therefore not counted by the census as separate governments.

16. New Jersey Quality of Education Commission, *All Our Children*, ERIC Document 356543 (1993).

17. Christine Todd Whitman, *State of the State of New Jersey, 1998* (www.state.nj.us/governor/news/p8011b.htm). See also Jennifer Preston, "Whitman Restates Pledge on Taxes and Insurance," *New York Times*, January 14, 1998. Interestingly, Whitman was pursuing a strategy similar to that used to create Greater New York a century earlier: she was seeking popular approval in the larger jurisdiction, where it might be obtained, not in each affected smaller jurisdiction, where it would surely be denied.

18. Ernest C. Reock Jr., *A Plan for School District Consolidation in New Jersey*, Occasional Paper No. 4 (Center for Governmental Services, Rutgers University, July 1995); Public Affairs Research Institute (PARI) of New Jersey, Inc., *Reducing the Number of New Jersey School Districts: Regionalization and Consolidation Options* (April 1996), pp. 10–11.

19. The Commission on Educational Excellence for Connecticut, *Final Report* (Hartford, Conn.: State Education Department, 1994), pp. 19, 44; Robert A. Frahm, "The Failure of Connecticut's Reform Plan: Lessons for the Nation," *Phi Delta Kappa*, vol. 76 (October 1994), p. 156–59.

20. "The Administrative Transformation of American Education: School District Consolidation," *Administrative Science Quarterly*, vol. 32 (1987), pp. 352–66. See also L. Harmon Zeigler and others., "How School Control Was Wrested from the People," *Phi Delta Kappa*, vol. 58 (1976), pp. 58, 534–39.

21. Harlan Hoyt Horner, ed., *Education in New York: 1784–1954* (University of the State of New York; State Education Department, 1954), pp. 156–60. The unit rule for consolidation was changed at the initiative of the State Education Department in 1989. It reasoned (contrary to its earlier thinking, and erroneously) that citizen resistance to

consolidation would be reduced if each community was allowed to vote separately on the question.

22. New York State Education Department, "District Organization" (August 1995 [typescript]).

23. Thomas Sobol, "School District Consolidation and Shared Services," memorandum to the Board of Regents, December 10, 1992, cited in Mary Anne Raywid and Thomas A. Shaheen, "In Search of Cost Effective Schools," *Theory into Practice* (Spring 1994), p. 67. Emphasis added.

24. Long Island Regional Planning Board and Center for Regional Policy Studies (SUNY Stony Brook), *Financing Government on Long Island* (Stony Brook, N.Y.: New York State Temporary Commission for Tax Relief on Long Island, 1992), cited in Raywid and Shaheen, "In Search of Cost Effective Schools," p. 68.

25. Raywind and Shaheen, "In Search of Cost Effective Schools," p. 69, citing *Rockland Journal News*, "Back to School," August 26, 1992.

26. Suzanne Spear, interview with Gerald Benjamin, January 29, 1996.

27. This point is also made by Haller and Monk, "New Reforms, Old Reforms."

28. This is discussed in greater detail in chapter 10.

29. For a number of essays advancing this view, see *Source Book on School District Size, Cost and Quality* (North Central Regional Educational Laboratory of the Hubert Humphrey Institute of Public Affairs, University of Minnesota, 1992). For an interesting case study, see Alan Peshkin, *The Imperfect Union: School Consolidation and Community Conflict* (University of Chicago Press, 1982). Michael Kirst is quoted in Sarah Kershaw, "A Town That Once Saw Benefits in Size of School District Has Second Thoughts," *New York Times*, February 7, 1996.

30. H. J. Walberg and W. J. Fowler, "Expenditure and Size Efficiencies of Public School Districts," *Educational Researcher*, vol. 16 (1987), pp. 5–13.

31. See the several studies summarized in Raywid and Shaheen, "In Search of Cost Effective Schools," pp. 68–69.

32. Gary Orfield and others, *The Growth of Segregation in American Schools,* ERIC Document ED366 689 (Harvard Project on School Desegregation and the National School Boards Association, 1993), p. 18. Many measures were used in this study; most ranked the New York, New Jersey, and Connecticut school systems among the ten most segregated in the country. For example, New York ranked third, New Jersey fourth, and Connecticut tenth in the percentage of black students attending schools with student bodies composed of at least 90 percent or more minority group persons (p. 8). In both 1980 and 1991–92, New York was the most segregated state in the nation for Hispanic students. See also New York State Special Commission on Educational Structure Policies and Practices, *Putting Children First*, vol. 1 (Albany, N.Y., 1993), p. 35. In Connecticut 80 percent of minority students go to school in 18 of 166 school districts; 140 other districts are more than 90 percent white. See G. Tirozzi and T. Jones, "Current School Funding Policy Issues in Connecticut," presented at the Annual Meeting of the American Educational Research Association, New Orleans, 1994, ERIC Document ED 375 486. Efforts at voluntary regional desegregation initiated by Governor Lowell Weicker largely failed. As a consequence of patterns of segregation, de facto segregation is the basis of state constitutional lawsuits seeking to fundamentally alter educational finance practices in the tri-state region's states.

33. Kimberly J. McLarin, "Schools Brace for Impact of State Budget," *New York Times,* January 26, 1995.

34. Chris Ctania and Jack O'Shea, "White Parents Picket Rooney," *Suburbanite*, October 28, 1998, p. 1.

35. Joseph Berger, "Despite Protests, O'Rourke to Proceed with Privatizing Plans," *New York Times*, December 21, 1995.

36. Applied Data Services, *Regionalization Study*, executive summary and vol. 2 (Trenton: New Jersey Department of Education, 1995); Harry Galinsky, "Alternatives to Regionalization in Eastern Bergen County, New Jersey," report to the Commissioner of Education, 1995; Jane Rimbach, "Englewood School Merger Rejected," *Bergen Record,* February 7, 1997 (see especially the chronology of this dispute, published in the *Record* with this article); Robert Hanley, "Board Tells Englewood School to Form Own Integration Plan," *New York Times*, October 8, 1998. See also the excellent clipping files on this subject in the Englewood Public Library.

37. PARI, *New Jersey School Districts* , p. 5.

38. Whitman, *State of the State 1998;* Robert Hanley, "Englewood Mayor Seeks Better Education and Desegregated School," *New York Times*, January 14, 1998.

39. David B. Walker, "Regionalism in Connecticut and the County: Dormant or Resurgent?" *The Regionalist,* vol. 1 (Fall 1995), p. 64.

40. Westchester 2000, *Governments at the Crossroads: Re-Engineering Westchester County for the Twenty-First Century—A Taxpayer's Report to Taxpayers* (December 1993), sec. 4. Several alternative plans for school district consolidation were proposed in this document.

41. This and the following quotes are from Raymond Hernandez, "Report Proposes Combining County Services and Localities," *New York Times,* April 7, 1994; Ina Aronow, "It's Time to Change, a Planning Study Says," *New York Times*, April 10, 1994.

Chapter 9. Two Approaches: Bottoms Up and Top Down

1. Westchester County is a large inner-ring suburban county (population 882,000) north of New York City. Bordered by Connecticut to the east and the Hudson River to the west, and abutting the Bronx in New York City to the south and Putnam County to the north, Westchester contains six cities, seventeen towns, twenty-two villages, and forty school districts, of wide-ranging sizes.

2. All quotes from Linda Puglisi in this section are from *Proceedings of the New York State Government Finance Officers' Annual Meeting* (Albany, N.Y., March 24, 1995), pp. 154–74.

3. Edward G. Michelian Institute, *Town of Mount Pleasant and Village of Pleasantville Police Study: Financial and Legal Options for Cost Savings* (Pace University, Dyson College, 1992).

4. Ibid., p. 26.

5. Somerset Alliance for the Future, *A Focus on Sharing Services: Summary of Findings and Conclusion* (Somerville, N.J., 1994), quoted in Patria De Lancer, "Shared Services: The Answer to Economic Pressures," in Ralph Caprio and Marc Holzer, eds., *Outsourcing and Shared Services among New Jersey Municipalities* (Rutgers-Newark Graduate Department of Public Administration, 1995), p. 42.

6. Bill Varner, "The Price of Protection," *Standard Star* (Gannett Westchester Suburban Newspapers), April 18, 1996.

7. Ralph Caprio and Marc Holzer, eds., *Outsourcing and Shared Services among New Jersey Municipalities* (Rutgers-Newark Graduate Department of Public Administration, 1995), p. 4.

8. Ibid., p. 82.

9. The findings suggested by our two cases and by the Rutgers survey in New Jersey were generally confirmed by information gathered by reporters for a five-part series on intergovernmental collaboration and consolidation published by the Gannett newspapers in suburban Westchester and Rockland counties in 1995. Escalating service costs force local

jurisdictions to consider service delivery mergers with neighbors. Public policy experts—and some politicians—argue that these kinds of actions would result in reduced costs without reduced services. But opposition is substantial among local government employees, who fear a loss of jobs, and those who are concerned about a decline in service level and quality. Often, too, the defense of the status quo is cast in terms of preserving the community itself. Mayor Eugene Bifano of the Village of Briarcliff Manor opposed the merger of his community's fire department with that of neighboring Ossining because, he said, "We would lose our identity."

10. As noted earlier, this exercise involved adapting previously collected information to our purposes. The reports compiled are from three states; they were written at different times and employed different selection criteria. Although the reports included many examples from the tri-state metropolitan region, they covered activities statewide in the three states. We did not attempt to separately classify experience within the tri-state region.

11. One recent example illustrates this difficulty. In New Jersey, Mercer County Executive Robert D. Prunetti suggested that the county's thirteen municipalities voluntarily contract for solid waste services "a la carte," paying a basic fee of $35 a ton to cover overhead. (As is explored later in chapter 9, this is similar to the arrangement for the delivery of shared education services developed by BOCES in New York, with mandatory charges to cover administrative costs and voluntary "buy-ins" for services.) Mercer County has already borrowed and spent $110 million for planning, permits, fees, and upgrading of existing facilities—and still exports all its waste.

By mid-1996 eight localities, producers of 85 percent of the county's trash, agreed provisionally to twenty-year contracts under Prunetti's plan. But both the borough and township of Princeton continued to resist. Marvin Reed of the borough made an economic argument. The tipping fee, he said, would rise over twenty years from $47 a ton to $120 a ton under the plan advanced by the county improvement authority. Township mayor Michele Tuck-Ponder expressed concerns about the project's size and environmental impact and argued that "we stand to have to pay a lot of money for something that we will not use, we never intended to use, and about which we were never consulted." Andy Newman, "Garbage Ruling Leaves the Counties in a $1.7 Billion Hole," *New York Times*, July 21, 1996.

12. Westchester 2000, *Sharing Survey* (White Plains, N.Y., January 23, 1995), pp. 12–13.

13. Jacques Steinberg, "Bridge over a Chasm of Tension," *New York Times*, June 17, 1995.

14. Rockefeller Institute of Government, Urban Studies Group. "Working Paper on Majority-Black Residential Areas" (Albany, N.Y., March 1997 [typescript]).

15. John Nolan, "The Erosion of Home Rule through the Emergence of State Interests in Land Use Control," *Pace Environmental Law Review*, vol. 11 (Spring 1993), pp. 497–562. Solid waste disposal is an example of a functional area in which state law and regulation were used to override local land-use controls. In chapter 10 we discuss in detail how the tri-state region's states—in response to the environmental movement, encouraged by federal incentives, and under federal pressure—substantially succeeded in shifting responsibility for solid-waste disposal upward from the very local level.

16. Ronald Sullivan, "Jersey Zoning Rules Upset," *New York Times,* March 21, 1975.

17. For background on the development of this case and the social research that supported it, see Norman Williams and Anya Yates, "The Background of Mount Laurel I," *Vermont Law Review,* vol. 20 (Spring 1996), pp. 687–97. Quoted in James E. McGuire, "The Judiciary's Role in Implementing the Mount Laurel Doctrine: Deference or Activism," *Vermont Law Review,* vol. 20 (Spring 1996), p. 1279.

18. Ronald Sullivan, "Jersey's Zoning Laws Are Upset," *New York Times*, March 25, 1975; Donald Janson, "Mt. Laurel's Poor Hail Zoning Ruling," *New York Times*, March 29, 1975.

19. Janson, "Mt. Laurel's Poor."

20. *Southern Burlington County NAACP* v. *Township of Mount Laurel*, 92 N.J. 158 (1983).

21. Barbara G. Salmore and Stephen A. Salmore, *New Jersey Politics and Government: Suburban Politics Comes of Age* (University of Nebraska Press, 1993), p. 296.

22. Salmore and Salmore, *New Jersey Politics*, pp. 199–200. A later court decision exempted "fully developed communities" from any "fair-share" housing obligation. Some speculated that there was a link between the timing of the state supreme court's acceptance of the 1985 legislation and legislative consideration of Judge Wilentz's reappointment.

23. John M. Payne, "Norman Williams, Exclusionary Zoning and the *Mount Laurel* Doctrine: Making the Theory Fit the Facts," *Vermont Law Review*, vol. 20 (Spring 1996), p. 667.

24. Ibid., pp. 676–77.

25. David M. Herszenhorn, "To Meet Goal for Housing, Suburb Seeks to Pay City," *New York Times,* August 4, 1998.

26. Ibid.

27. Salmore and Salmore, *New Jersey Politics*, pp. 295–97.

28. Payne, "Norman Williams," pp. 673–74.

29. David W. Chen, "Slouching toward Mount Laurel," *New York Times*, March 31, 1996, sec. 13, p. 1.

30. Salmore and Salmore, *New Jersey Politics*, p. 292.

31. Williams and Yates, "The Background of Mount Laurel I," p. 694; Salmore and Salmore, *New Jersey Politics*, p. 300.

32. *Berenson* v. *Town of New Castle*, 38 N.Y. 2d 102, 341 NE 2d 236, 378 N.Y.S. 2d 62-72 (1975).

33. Patricia E. Salkin, "Regional Planning in New York State: A State Rich in National Models, Yet Weak in Overall State Planning Coordination," *Pace Law Review*, vol. 13 (Fall 1993), pp. 505–55.

34. Melinda Westbrook, "Connecticut's New Affordable Housing Appeals Procedure: Assaulting the Presumptive Validity of Land Use Decision," *Connecticut Bar Journal,* vol. 66 (1992), pp. 180–81.

35. Ibid., p. 175, quoting Representative William Cibe's remarks in the 1989 legislative session.

36. Terry Tondro, remarks delivered at "State and Regional Planning: An Idea Whose Time Has Come," conference held at St. John's University Law School, Queens, New York, February 19, 1999.

37. Edward J. Lyons and Michael W. Lyons, "Connecticut Crosses the Line: The Affordable Housing Appeals Act," *Connecticut Bar Journal*, vol. 65 (1991), pp. 289; Eleanor Charles, "Comprehensive Land Use Bill Faces Tough Fight," *New York Times*, September 23, 1996. The General Assembly Task Force on the State Plan of Conservation and Development, chaired by Mary Mushinsky, a Democrat of Wallingford, introduced a bill in 1993 and again in 1994 that would have required each region to adopt land-use regulations consistent with a state plan, and each town or city to follow suit.

38. Josh Barbanel, "Court Halts Projects Planned for Pine Barrens," *New York Times*, March 12, 1992.

39. A detailed statutory history is provided by Judge Vito Titone in *Long Island Pine Barrens Society* v. *Planning Board, Town of Brookhaven*, 80 N.Y. 2d 500 (1992).

40. New York Laws of 1987, chap. 628.

41. A state law passed in 1990 required environmental impact statements to discuss the "effects of any proposed action on, and its consistency with, the comprehensive management plan." New York Laws of 1990, chap. 219.

42. *Long Island Pine Barrens Society* v. *Planning Board, Town of Brookhaven*, 581 NYS 2d. 803, 810 (NY App. Div., 1992).

43. A bill submitted by Assemblywoman Erlene Hill, a Democrat from Hempstead, seeking to bar the requirement of a comprehensive study prior to development in the Pine Barrens, found no additional sponsorship or support in either house. John Rather, "Builders Rally to Free Up Pine Barrens," *New York Times*, May 17, 1992.

44. New York Laws of 1990, chap. 814. John Rather, "Developers' Nightmare, Environmentalists' Hero," *New York Times*, November 22, 1992.

45. Sarah Lyall, "Court Clears Way for Building on Pine Barrens of Long Island," *New York Times*, November 21, 1992.

46. Michael R. Jung, "The Pine Barrens: A New Model for Land Use Control for New York," *Buffalo Environmental Law Journal*, vol. 3 (1995), p. 54, citing *Long Island Pine Barrens Society Inc.* v. *Planning Board, Town of Brookhaven*, 606 N.E. 2d 1373, 1381 (N.Y. 1992). Claiming aquifer protection to be in the public interest, Connecticut courts have also supported state action to supersede local land-use decisions that appear to threaten underground water reserves. The courts' only demand is that state government actions be "reasonable." Interestingly, local governments have also successfully invoked aquifer protection to defend their own land-use decisions. Thomas W. Fahey Jr. and Richard T. Roznoy, "Aquifer Protection in Connecticut: Environmental Land Use Restrictions Run Deep," *Connecticut Bar Journal*, vol. 68 (April 1994), pp. 98–128.

47. Matthew Crosson, "LI Can Shape Its Future at the 1994 Summit," *Newsday*, September 19, 1994.

48. Stephen Kass and Michael Gerrard, "Pine Barrens: The Fruitful Compromise," *New York Law Journal*, August 27, 1993.

49. Robert D. Yaro and Tony Hiss, *A Region At Risk: The Third Regional Plan* (New York: Regional Plan Association, 1995), pp. 95–96.

50. Herbert M. Balin, "The Long Island Pine Barrens Protection Act: A Model of Compromise between Home Rule and State Intervention in Land Use Control," *New York State Bar Journal*, vol. 66 (September/October, 1994), pp. 42–45.

51. Ibid.

52. This section draws upon Gerald Benjamin's experience as the chief elected official in Ulster County, New York, while these decisions were being made.

53. "The Development of 9-1-1" (www.nena.org/pressroom_publications/9-1-1_facts.htm [January 2001]).

54. The possibility for greater efficiency is compromised, however, by the increased number of 911 calls for nonemergency purposes. There were 13.6 million emergency calls to police agencies in 1995, 98 percent of them false alarms. The growing number of nonemergency 911 calls led to a proposal by President Clinton in 1996 for the creation of a 311 option for nonemergencies. This idea is opposed by many professionals in the field. See Gordon Witkin and Monika Guttman, "911. . .Please Hold," *U.S. News and World Report*, June 17, 1996; Simon Hakim and Erwin Blackstone, "Crying Wolf with Public Safety," *American City and County*, vol. 111 (August 1996), p. 54; "Clinton: New Emergency Number," *FCC Report*, vol. 15 (July 31, 1996), p. 15; and Marlys R. Davis, "King County, Washington—Regional 3-1-1 Feasibility Study," *NENA News* (December 1997) (www.nena.org/PressRoom_Publications/nenanews_archives/12-97_archives.htm [February 2001]).

55. New York Laws of 1989, chap. 756, New York County Law, sec. 303–08. An amendment to the statute in 1996 allowed money from this fund to be dedicated to oper-

ating expenses. New York Laws of 1996, chap. 309, sec. 243). Under the original statute, the potential of additional personnel costs arising from the installation of emergency-911 had an important effect on the politics and decisionmaking surrounding its adoption.

56. Nationwide in the mid-1990s, the number of 911 calls averaged two for each local resident. See Robert Cobb, "'Nine-One-One': Three Little Words, Three Big Issues," *American City and County* (June 1996), p. 48.

57. The surcharge was authorized by Ulster County Local Law No. 3 of 1990.

58. In 1999 Helen Delaney was still serving as the chair of the Ulster County 911 Advisory Committee.

59. University of the State of New York, *Education in New York State, 1784–1954* (Albany, N.Y.: State Education Department, 1954), p. 160.

60. New York State Education Department, *46th Annual Report* (Albany, N.Y., 1949), p. 14.

61. New York Laws 1948, chap. 861.

62. These original BOCES governance and administrative arrangements later proved to be quite troublesome. From the first the selection process for the governing boards distanced the agencies from the communities they served. And the dual sources of pay for the district superintendents obscured their compensation levels. Reforms made in the mid-1990s, in response to the Murphy case (see subsequent text), shortened the terms of board members from five to three years and capped superintendent salaries to partially deal with these problems.

63. Originally, five-member boards were provided for by law; currently, board size ranges between five and fifteen. There is a requirement for residency and for geographical distribution of members.

64. Later, for functions for which even larger scale operations made sense, the BOCES supervisory districts themselves came to be combined, with a single BOCES serving a much larger region. Computer and library services based in the Ulster BOCES, for example, are provided through the entire Mid-Hudson Valley.

65. New York State School Boards Association and New York State Bar Association, *School Law: 25th Edition* (Albany, N.Y., 1996), pp. 77–88.

66. The law also permits, as an alternative method of calculating aid, the use of the ratio between the full value of real property in each district and its value in the entire supervisory district.

67. This allocation of administrative costs is a source of discontent in a number of supervisory districts. Reforms of the mid-1990s increased component district oversight of BOCES administrative budgets: school boards in a majority of districts served by a BOCES must now approve the annual administrative budget. If they do not, the BOCES is operated on a contingency administrative budget no greater than that for the previous year.

68. New York State Education Department, *Report to the Governor and the Legislature on the Financial and Statistical Outcomes of Boards of Cooperative Educational Services* (January 1996), pp. 33–35.

69. See the following articles in the *New York Times*: Josh Barbanel, "Educator's $960,000 Payment Prompts Outrage," December 9, 1992; Sam Howe Verhovek, "Embarrassed Republicans Take Look at School Funds," December 19, 1992; James Dao, "Abrams Sues to Void Retirement Deal for School Official," January 26, 1993.

70. Winifred Sanchez Eisen, "BOCES: The Education Service Agencies of New York State," in New York State Special Commission on Education Structure, Policies and Practices, *Putting Children First* (Albany, N.Y., 1993), ERIC Document 518 464 5060; see also New York State Temporary Commission for Tax Relief on Long Island, "School Operations: An Analysis of BOCES," in *Financing Government on Long Island*, chap. 12.

71. Peter F. Drucker, *Managing in a Time of Great Change* (New York: Truman Tally Books/Dutton, 1995), p. 32.

72. Jeffrey Bowen and Nancy Penska, "Cost Saving Strategies and Shared Services among School Districts in New York State," *ESR Spectrum*, vol. 11 (Fall 1993), pp. 16–25.

73. Gary Enos, "Competition or Else," *Governing*, vol. 9 (November 1996), pp. 40–41.

74. Susan Wallerstein, "The Application of a Cost-Effectiveness Model to Connecticut's Regional Educational Service Centers" (August 1996 [typescript]), pp. 18, 25.

Chapter 10. The Case of Solid Waste

1. Phil Patton, *Open Road* (Simon and Schuster, 1986), p. 70. Citing Robert Caro, Patton notes that in the 1930s Robert Moses intentionally built parkways in the region with bridges too low for buses to "keep out the unautoed and presumably unwashed." See also John Robinson, *Highways and Our Environment* (McGraw-Hill, 1971).

2. "22.5 Million Lost in Garbage Fraud," *New York Times*, August 24, 1994; Jeff Bailey, "In a Tussle over Trash, Two Haulers Could Win Ruling Costly to Towns," *Wall Street Journal*, February 28, 1994.

3. The text of this local law is bound with the Supreme Court decision in *C & A Carbone Inc.* v. *Town of Clarkstown, New York,* 114 S. Ct. 1677 (1994).

4. This was an application of the "dormant" commerce clause, an interpretation of the constitutional provision that "prohibits 'protectionist' local action (e.g., ordinances, taxes or licensing requirements) which discriminates against a unified national economy." See David L. Snyder, "So You Want to Be a Market Participant . . . ," address given at the state meeting of the New York State Bar Association, Section on Municipal Law, September 1996 (files of the author). Citing *Philadelphia* v. *New Jersey,* 437 U.S. 617 (1978), Associate Justice Kennedy also remarked that the offending law "hoards a local resource . . . for the benefit of local businesses" (*C & A Carbone Inc.* v. *Town of Clarkstown*).

5. For citations to state laws, see Jeffrey L. Oberhaus, "Note: The Dormant Commerce Clause Dumps New Jersey's Solid Waste 'Flow Control' Regulations," *Rutgers Law Journal*, vol. 29 (Winter 1998), pp. 439–74.

6. State of New Jersey, County and Municipal Government Study Commission, *Solid Waste Management in New Jersey: Today and Tomorrow* (Trenton, N.J.: New Jersey First Inc., 1987), p. 1.

7. New Jersey Laws of 1975, chap. 326. Additionally, the Hackensack Meadowlands Development Commission was designated a planning district for solid-waste purposes.

8. State of New Jersey, *Solid Waste*, p. 49.

9. Ibid.

10. Barry G. Rabe, "Environmental Regulation in New Jersey: Innovations and Limitations," *Publius,* vol. 21 (Winter, 1991), pp. 83–103.

11. *DEP* v. *Middlesex County Board of Chosen Freeholders,* 206 N.J. Super. 206 (1985).

12. Carl E. Van Horn, *Breaking the Environmental Gridlock* (New Brunswick, N.J.: Eagleton Institute, 1988), p. 102.

13. *Atlantic Coast Demolition and Recycling Inc., et al.* v. *Board of Chosen Freeholders of Atlantic County, et al.*, 931 F. Supp. 341, 346 (D. N.J. 1996).

14. *Atlantic Coast Demolition* v. *Atlantic County*, 347, 349.

15. Andy Newman, "Garbage Ruling Leaves Counties in a $1.7 Billion Hole," *New York Times,* July 26, 1996.

16. Charles Atkins, telephone interview with Gerald Benjamin, January 1997.

17. This account relies on an undated written summary entitled "Solid Waste Management in Connecticut during the Past 25 Years," prepared in April 1995 by Charles L. Atkins, Supervising Sanitary Engineer, State of Connecticut Department of Environmental Protection.

18. Cited in ibid., p. 3. See also Connecticut Resources Recovery Authority, *Comprehensive Annual Financial Report, FY 1995* (Hartford, Conn., 1996), p. 3.

19. Diane Henry, "New Garbage Law Perplexes Officials," *New York Times,* June 4, 1978. The failure to bring on line the Bridgeport waste-to-fuel plant, described later, made this requirement especially limiting.

20. Connecticut Department of Environmental Protection, *Waste Shed Assessment* (Hartford, Conn., June 30, 1981).

21. Connecticut Public Act 89-384.

22. Connecticut Department of Environmental Protection, *State of Connecticut Adopted Solid Waste Management Plan* (Hartford, Conn., February 1991), p. 13.

23. Ibid., p. 4, quoting Connecticut Public Act 87-544 and Regulations of Connecticut State Agencies (RCSAs) 22a-241b-1 through 22a-241b-2, cited therein. The department was also charged with designating categories of recyclables. At first recyclables were required by law to be banned from landfills and burn facilities as of January 1, 1991, the implementation date of mandatory recycling in the state, but this provision was repealed before its effective date.

24. John S. Rosenberg, "Waste as Fuel and Materials Source Not Yet a Winner," *New York Times,* September 7, 1980; John S. Rosenberg, "Garbage Processor Pledges Continue," *New York Times,* November 9, 1980.

25. Connecticut Resources Recovery Authority, *1997 Annual Report* (Hartford, Conn., 1998 [unnumbered pages]).

26. As of June 30, 1997, the CRRA had borrowed $932.5 million; $674.7 million of this debt was still outstanding. The projected agency operating budget for 1999 was $156.7 million.

27. Connecticut Public Act 89-386, cited in Connecticut Department of Environmental Protection, *Adopted Solid Waste Management Plan,* p. 27. At the same time, a statutory cap was placed on statewide burn capacity.

28. Connecticut Office of Policy and Management, *Conservation and Development Plans for Connecticut* (Hartford, Conn.: 1995), p. 85.

29. Some limited cooperation between jurisdictions with complementary facilities and needs occurred, but it was the exception, not the rule—perhaps owing to public hostility to "importing" garbage. Matters were further complicated because responsibilities for planning, oversight, and regulation of the solid waste system were shared by two different state agencies in New Jersey: the Department of Environmental Protection and the Public Utility Commission.

30. Complexity was added, of course, by the operation of two agencies statewide—the CDEP and the CRRA—and because private operators with interests to protect ran the CRRA burn facilities.

31. Senate Committee on Environment and Public Works, Subcommittee on Superfund, Waste Control and Risk Assessment, *Hearing on Flow Control and Interstate Transportation of Solid Waste,* 104 Cong. 1 sess. (March 1, 1995), p. 71.

32. Jeff Bailey, "Moody's Links Trash Disposal to Debt Quality," *Wall Street Journal,* June 2, 1995; *Moody's Credit Report* (May 1995), pp. 2–3; "New Jersey Solid Waste Bond Ratings at a Crossroads," *Moody's Credit Perspectives* (June 1996), p. 10.

33. Michael J. Cahill and Joseph D. McCann, "Garbage and the Mob: Licensing Waste Collection after *Carbone,*" *Journal of Urban Technology*, vol. 1 (Summer 1994), p. 52.

34. George Bevington, President, New York State Association for Solid Waste Management, letter to Gerald Benjamin, July 23, 1996; Jennifer Preston, "New Jersey's Landfills Want the Right Stuff," *New York Times*, December 6, 1998.

35. Jeff Bailey, "Waste Company Takes 32% Price Cut in Contract with Bergen County, N.J.," *Wall Street Journal,* January 4, 1995, and "Moody's Assigns Lower Credit Ratings to Five Big Trash Projects in New Jersey," *Wall Street Journal*, February 21, 1995.

36. Settlements were reached that required localities to meet their obligations but allowed them earlier termination of their agreements with two years' notice to the agency. See Morgan Stanley Dean Witter, Bond Offering Document: *Connecticut Resource Recovery Authority* (March 6, 1998), p. 31.

37. Senate Committee, *Hearing on Flow Control,* p. 66.

38. Connecticut Resources Recovery Authority, *Comprehensive Annual Financial Report, FY1995* (Hartford, Conn., 1996), p. ii.

39. *Atlantic Coast Demolition* v. *Atlantic County*, 349.

40. Brett Schundler, "This Proposal Is Just Garbage," *Wall Street Journal,* May 16, 1995.

41. Senate, *Hearing on Flow Control*, p. 104.

42. *Atlantic Coast Demolition* v. *Atlantic County*, 356.

43. John Tierney, "Recycling," *New York Times Magazine,* June 30, 1996; Vivian S. Toy, "Giuliani Attacks Recycling Goals as a Suit Is Filed," *New York Times,* July 3, 1996, and "Giuliani Says Recycling Law Already Met," *New York Times,* July 4, 1996.

44. Senate Committee on Environmental and Public Works, *Hearing on Transportation and Flow Control of Solid Waste,* 105 Cong. 1 sess., March 18, 1997, testimony of Tony Ciofolo of the National Solid Waste Management Association (www.penweb.org/waste/importation/nswma_testimony.txt [January 2001]).

45. David Hosansky, "Backers May Push Garbage Bill in Session after Election," *Congressional Quarterly Weekly Reports* (October 15, 1994), p. 2949.

46. The words are those of Senator Robert C. Smith (R-N.H.), quoted in Allan Freedman, "Senate Panel OK's Bill Allowing Limits on 'Imported' Trash," *Congressional Quarterly Weekly Reports* (March 18, 1995), p. 810.

47. *Congressional Record*, 104 Cong. 2 sess., January 30, 1996, p. H937. Remarks of Ms. Blanche L. Lincoln (D-Ark.).

48. Senate Committee, *Hearing on Transportation and Flow Control*, pp. 1–2.

49. David L Snyder, personal communication (letter) to Gerald Benjamin, 1996.

50. *SSC Corp.* v. *Town of Smithtown,* 66 F.3d. 502 (2d Cir. 1995), cert. denied, 116 S. Ct. 911 (1966); *USA Recycling* v. *Town of Babylon,* 66 F.3d. 1272 (2d Cir. 1995), cert. denied 116 S. Ct. 1419 (1996); *Sal Tinnerello and Sons Inc.* v. *Town of Stonington*, 143 F.3d 46 (1998), cert. denied S. Ct. 278 (1998).

51. Jennifer Preston, "New Jersey's Landfills Want Right Stuff," *New York Times,* December 6, 1998.

52. Senate Committee, *Hearing on Transportation and Flow Control,* testimony of Tony Ciofolo of the National Solid Waste Management Association, p. 17.

53. Jan Barry, "Bailout of Trash Debt on the Agenda," *Bergen Record,* July 14, 1998; Bret Schundler, "The Last Thing New Jersey Needs Is a New Trash Tax," *Bergen Record,* August 27, 1998.

54. Tri-State Regional Planning Commission, *Solid Waste Problems, Proposals and Progress in the Tri-State Region: A Reconnaissance* (New York, 1971), p. 3.

55. The landmark federal legislation was the Resource Conservation and Recovery Act (RCRA) of 1976. For a history of the development of federal legislation on solid waste, see U.S. Senate, Committee on Environment and Public Works, *A Legislative History of the Solid Waste Disposal Act,* 102 Cong. 1 sess. Y4.P 96/10:S. Prt. 102-35, vol. 1 and 2.

56. Senate Committee, *Hearing on Transportation and Flow Control,* p. 3.

57. Ibid., p. 12.

58. Barnaby J. Feder, "Waste Hauling Companies Announce $13 Billion Merger," *New York Times,* March 12, 1998; Jeff Bailey, "USA Waste Is on a Mission to Expand in Trash Business," *Wall Street Journal,* May 15, 1998; and James P. Miller, "U.S., Three States Ask Federal Court to Block Waste Management's Planned Acquisition," *Wall Street Journal,* November 18, 1988.

59. Douglas Martin and Dan Barry, "Giuliani Ignites Border Tension on Trash Plan," *New York Times,* December 3, 1998.

60. Eric Lipton, "Powerful Friends Help Trash Industry Protect Its Interests," and (with Justin Blum) "Gilmore Orders Moratorium on Construction, Expansion of Landfills," *Washington Post,* November 14, 1998.

61. James Gilmore, *State of the State of Virginia* (Richmond, Va., January 13, 1999).

62. Terry Prestin, "New York Trash Imports Have Virginia in a Tizzy," *New York Times,* January 13, 1999.

Chapter 11. Lessons for the Future

1. This subject is discussed in Richard P. Nathan and Thomas L. Gais, *Implementing the Personal Responsibility Act of 1996: A First Look* (Albany, N.Y.: Rockefeller Institute, 1999), pp. 35–39 on "second-order devolution."

2. Charles V. Bagli, "Port Authority Struggles to Keep Two Shippers," *New York Times*, February 14, 1999.

3. Editorial, "More Sacred Than Endangered," *New York Times*, January 29, 1925.

4. See Westchester 2000, *Governments at the Crossroads: Reengineering Westchester County for the 21st Century* (White Plains, N.Y., 1993). Westchester 2000, a planning and reform group, counted a total of 500 separate jurisdictions operating in the county as of December 1993.

5. Citizens Budget Commission, *Budget 2000 Project: Restructuring Government Services* (New York, 1996).

6. For a comprehensive review, see Richard Briffault, "A Government for Our Time? Business Improvement Districts and Urban Governance," *Columbia Law Review*, vol. 99 (March 1999), pp. 365–477.

7. Portland's Metro does this for solid waste disposal and several other functions. For a description of Portland's directly elected metropolitan government that serves three counties, see www.metro-region.org/glance/glance.html.

8. For example, see State Commission on the Capital Region, *Growing Together within the Capital Region* (Albany, N.Y.: Rockefeller Institute of Government, 1996). Unfortunately, this study did not have a big or lasting impact. Perhaps in this situation the lessons of this chapter would have helped in selecting feasible targets of opportunity for increasing the willingness of local governments in this six-county region to work together collaboratively.

9. Woodrow Wilson, *Constitutional Government in the United States* (Columbia University Press, 1908), p. 173.

10. National Academy of Public Administration, *Building Stronger Communities: Can the Federal Government Help?* (Washington, 1998), p. v.

Index